# The Male Escort's Handbook

# The Male Escort's Handbook
Your Guide to Getting Rich the Hard Way

Aaron Lawrence

The Male Escort's Handbook: Your Guide to Getting Rich the Hard Way. Copyright © 2000 by Aaron Lawrence. All rights reserved. No part of this book may be used or reproduced in any manner without written permission from the author except for brief quotations for review purposes.

Published by:   Late Night Press
                P.O. Box 4001
                Warren, NJ 07059

Author Website:  http://www.aaronlawrence.com
Author E-mail:  njescort@aol.com

Cover model:  Jeffrey Kracht
Cover photos:  David J. Martin
Cover design:  Andy Sanitate

ISBN 0-9667691-1-2
Library of Congress Catalog Card Number 00-105437

*For all men available by the hour.*

### About the Author

Aaron Lawrence has worked as an escort since May 1995, and is the author of *Suburban Hustler: Stories of a Hi-Tech Callboy*. When not entertaining clients, he writes an online sex advice column and produces a line of amateur adult videos. Aaron has posed for *Freshmen* and *Inches* magazines and appeared in *The Dream Team*, the 1999 GayVN Winner for Best Gay Video. He is the webmaster of www.aaronlawrence.com, the most popular escort homepage on the Internet. Aaron lives in suburban New Jersey with his lover and their three-legged, half-tailed cat.

# Contents

| | |
|---|---|
| Preface | xi |
| Who Am I, and Why Am I Writing This Book? | 1 |
| The Escort Quiz | 5 |
| Making the Big Decision | 13 |
| The Real Story | 19 |
| Agencies and Brothels | 28 |
| The Independent Route | 40 |
| Print Advertising | 50 |
| Online Advertising | 57 |
| Handling Potential Clients | 75 |
| Sorting the Other Calls | 89 |
| Meeting Clients | 100 |
| Types of Clients | 117 |
| The Hard Way | 135 |
| Problem Clients | 150 |
| Protecting Yourself | 157 |
| Sexually Transmitted Diseases | 162 |
| Maintaining Your Health | 181 |
| Legal Issues | 192 |
| Managing Your Money | 205 |
| Branching Out | 216 |
| A Few Other Issues | 230 |
| Professional Advice | 240 |
| Afterword | 257 |
| Online Advertising Opportunities | 259 |
| Resources for Escorts | 262 |
| Related Reading | 266 |
| Checking Your Partner for STDs | 270 |

# Acknowledgements

I would like to thank everyone who helped make this book possible. Dozens of people contributed in some fashion, and it would be impossible to name them all. In particular I want to thank the men of the Escortmale listserv. In spite of my constant questioning, they never once complained as they volunteered their vast array of insights into the nature of male escorting. I also want to thank Jordi for his lesson about working as an openly HIV-positive escort, Big Moe for his help on the legal section, Greg and Zoe for looking over the section on taxes, Dr. Stephen E. Goldstone for verifying the accuracy of the chapters on STDs and health, David for his help with the section about deaf clients, and Vena Blanchard from the International Professional Surrogates Association for her examination of the information on surrogate partners. I also want to thank the many friends who helped me proofread this manuscript, among which Jack Phillips stands out for his tireless devotion and long hours. The rest of you know who you are, and how important you are to me. Finally, a special note of appreciation goes to my husband, Jeff, for his patience and support throughout the writing process.

*Sex and money are the two building blocks of life.
Fortunately if you have one, you can always get the other.*

--Anonymous

## Preface

Prostitution is the age-old art of trading sex for money. It is considered fashionable by some and degrading by others. Everyone has an opinion on the subject.

I am no exception, and in fact have more interest in the subject than most. You see, for the past four years I have worked as a male prostitute, or "escort" as those of us in the business call it. Starting in 1995 by hustling in Internet chat rooms, I taught myself the tricks of the trade with little help from others. Since then, I have entertained men who have paid me hundreds of thousands of dollars for my time, experience, and body. I have been flown to dozens of cities around the world ranging from Buffalo to Rome. I have bought a house, invested heavily in my retirement, and have even paid taxes on my income in the process. In short, I have taken prostitution as most people see it and transformed it into a viable career.

To be honest, it wasn't easy. I had to teach myself about pricing, advertising, interacting with clients, and what to do when things go wrong. Only briefly was I lucky enough to have a mentor in the business. I distinctly remember wishing someone would write a how-to book on the subject.

Imagine my surprise when I discovered that someone had written one. John Preston's 1994 book, *Hustling: A Gentleman's Guide to the Fine Art of Homosexual Prostitution*, was exactly what I had been searching for. I bought it immediately and took it home and read the entire book in one sitting. I was ecstatic that I had finally verified that I was taking the right steps towards my goal of being a successful escort.

Once my initial excitement wore off, I remember wanting to read more about becoming a male escort. Preston's book was written too early to address how escorts can use the Internet. I also wished the book provided more assistance for those with drive and ambition, rather than providing tips on how to mooch beer and cigarettes from your clients. I believed, and still feel today, that such tips only degrade the profession as a whole.

In time my friends began urging me to write my own how-to book about the subject. It was an appealing idea to me; I certainly like to write, and God knows I sometimes act like I know everything. After pondering the topic for a year or so, the idea of the book began to grow on me. Eventually the urge to write grew so large that I had to take time off work, sit in front of my computer, and write it out of my system.

Just as my first book, *Suburban Hustler*, was the result of wanting to satisfy people's curiosity about my career, *The Male Escort's Handbook* is a product of people approaching me who want to enter the business. So many would-be escorts have asked me for advice during the past four years that it would be impossible to teach them all. So when I wrote this book, I endeavored to provide as many angles on the industry as possible. Whether a potential escort sees himself as a hot daddy, a muscle boy, or a barely legal twink, I wanted this book to contain everything he needs to know to begin in the profession.

Experienced escorts should find the book useful as well. Throughout the writing process, I strove to balance the fundamentals with advanced lessons. Additionally, underlying each chapter is a consistent theme of escorting as a professional endeavor for those who want to make serious money. Apply your ambition to the information inside this book, and the money will come pouring in.

My own long-term goal is to make millions from my career in the sex industry then retire in style. Whether your goal is earn a little spending money, pay for college, buy a house, or retire early, I hope you find *The Male Escort's Handbook* to be an invaluable resource.

Oh, I almost forgot. Before you begin reading this book, I have a standing rule you need to know. If my advice helps someone earn an extra thousand dollars, he owes me and my lover dinner. I expect to hear from you when the time comes. And mind you, I've developed a taste for lobster.

Aaron Lawrence

## Chapter One
## Who Am I, and Why Am I Writing This Book?

I knew I loved escorting half an hour after I shot my first load with a client. That was when he put the cash in my hand: one hundred dollars in the form of five crisp twenties. The feeling was like magic. I had actually been paid for sex. Me! The bookworm who had bad acne in high school. The kid with few friends and even less self-esteem had actually been paid for sex. My escorting experience was beyond anything I ever thought possible.

I'm afraid that I am getting ahead of myself. If you want to understand how I came to write this book, you need to understand where I came from. Let me back up two decades to my boringly normal childhood.

I say my childhood was normal because that is what it was. My father did not die when I was young, and I did not come from a dysfunctional family. Instead, my siblings and I grew up in the upscale New Jersey suburbs west of New York City, where we were sheltered and protected from the evils of the world. My parents are educated and responsible members of the community. My mother worked as a teacher, and my father was an electrical engineer. I may have inherited my love of sex from them, because I have four siblings.

As I survived my teenage years, I began to come out as being gay. It was an easy experience for me. Having never been particularly accepted, I was not unhappy to find I was different from my peers. I knew there were other gay people in New Jersey, because as early as 1986 I was communicating with them using my computer. Most were men in their thirties or forties, but some were a bit younger. Unfortunately, no one was close to my age.

I lost my virginity when I was 15 to one of the men I met online. He was 22 and liked guys younger than himself. The fact that I looked about 13 drove him wild. I remember not finding him particularly attractive. He was overweight and was greasy-looking. I did think I was in love with him, so I returned to his bed five more times before he dumped me. I cannot help but wonder if I would be an escort today if I had never met him. Our relationship taught me you did not have to be attracted to your partner to have sex.

High school graduation found me with an acceptance letter to Iowa State University, so in the fall of 1989 I moved away to college. I finally developed a sense of self-esteem through gay student activism, and met Jeff, the man who is still my lover today. More often than not though, I found life in Iowa to be boring and uneventful. I missed the gay community in New Jersey and its numerous opportunities for sex.

During college, I visited New Jersey perhaps four times each year. I always felt ignored and alone when I did, as my younger brothers took up all of my parents' attention. On one such visit, I found myself horny on a Saturday afternoon. Looking for a bit of action, I walked around New York City's Times Square in search of male strippers. I sat down in an aisle seat of one adult theater and watched the dancers do their stuff.

The show itself was rather boring. The strippers were not particularly interested in their work, although they were quite friendly. They kept approaching me to ask if I was interested in a "private show." I eventually told an attractive Italian dancer that I was, so he began to lead me downstairs. He asked $100 for the show, but I had only $40. He looked me up and down, accepted, and led me into a sleazy back room. That was where I learned what a private show really is! He dropped to his knees, pulled down my pants, and began giving me oral sex. I received an unexpected education that day, along with my first experience with a prostitute.

Six months later, I found myself selling sex for the first time. I met an attractive gentleman over the Internet who offered me $100 for an hour of sex. I accepted, and we drove to a sleazy motel together. The place was a complete dump, but I didn't care. I was enamored with the idea that I was actually being paid for sex. It never occurred to me that this might become my career.

Two years later, I graduated with my master's degree only to discover I couldn't find a job. I started having anonymous sex in bookstores to cheer myself up, but only briefly. Someone put the idea in my head that I should try escorting as a part-time job, so I went online and gave it a try. To my surprise, my whole life suddenly clicked into place. I loved my new hobby (I didn't think of it as a career yet) and was amazed at the amount of money I could earn. Though I was 40 pounds overweight, cyberhustling in the chat rooms of America Online generated more than $1,000 per week.

After several months of hustling the Internet, I quit escorting at Jeff's request. I found a "normal" job after months of searching and became desperately unhappy. The work was demeaning, and the pay was low, so I resigned after six months and returned to escorting. Jeff grudgingly gave his approval, and my life was changed forever.

Since that time I have worked as a career sex worker. Most of my work involves "vanilla" types of sex, but on rare occasions I have found myself dabbling in bondage, sadomasochism (SM), and other fetishes. I have had three-ways and foursomes, and have been the center of groups too numerous to count. My work has required sex in houses, hotels, cars, outdoors, garages, pools, and even a boiler room of a local hospital. I have entertained over a thousand appointments for more than 600 clients. I was even awarded "1999 Escort of the Year" by the Male 4 Male Escort Review (http://www.male4malescorts.com).

In addition to my escorting, I have undertaken a wide variety of projects. I launched a successful porn career and appeared in three professional videos. I founded my own amateur video business and produced six videos. I posed for *Freshmen* and *Inches* magazines, spoke publicly about my career as an escort, created an online sex-advice column, built one of the largest escort home pages on the Internet, and wrote my first book, *Suburban Hustler*. It is in this spirit that I elected to write this book. I enjoy new challenges; writing a how-to book on male escorting is certainly an unusual project.

In case you are wondering, I have not written this chapter to boast about my accomplishments. I am proud of my life, but there are many escorts in the country who have developed their businesses to similar levels. Rather, I have written about myself to give you an idea of what may be possible for you in the industry.

Are you curious to learn more? Turn the page and begin reading about what it takes to get ahead in this dynamic, rewarding, and unique profession.

Chapter Two
## The Escort Quiz

*His picture was one I would definitely not call attractive. He had an unflattering expression on his face, and looked as if he had not shaved in days. His hair was an unkempt mop and certainly needed a trim. His oversized red shirt looked ridiculous, and only partially managed to hide his considerable stomach oozing out of his pants. In spite of this, he was writing to ask if I would be willing give him any of my clients. "As a matter of fact," he added, "you can even keep the money. I just want them to top me." Needless to say I choked at the thought, and respectfully declined his suggestion.*

If you have ever opened up your local community's gay bar guide, you have probably seen the listings for escorts in the back. The guides in most major cities feature dozens of advertisements for escorts ranging from boyish and slender types to super-muscular bodybuilders. You may have looked at these ads and thought you could do as well as the best of them. Or you may have wondered how you could compete against someone with twice as much physical definition as yourself.

Fortunately for all of us, the diversity of client tastes makes many personal traits irrelevant when considering your ability to escort. The fact that some clients desire one type of person balances out that other clients have a preference for another. The vast number of clients that have no preference at all makes these characteristics even less important. Circumcision is a perfect example of this. There are many people who prefer circumcised dicks, and many who prefer them uncircumcised. Still other people have no preference at all and view the trait as being irrelevant when they are shopping for an escort. No matter what type of dick you have, there will be clients who will want to see you.

Likewise, your hair color is irrelevant when considering your ability to escort. There are successful prostitutes with every natural hair color. Some even have no hair – buzzed and skinhead haircuts are popular among certain clienteles. Even a bit of gray hair is not a major problem as long as the escort is attractive and runs his business well. You may have difficulty finding clients if your hair is pink or blue, but even then you will find the occasional client who is into alternative looks.

Eye color is an even more irrelevant trait. No matter what color your eyes are, there are clients who will find them attractive. Similarly, your height is not an issue. You cannot be too tall or too short to be an escort. Many clients have no preference either way. Escorts can also be successful regardless of whether they have a beard, moustache, a goatee, or are clean-shaven. Your overall appearance is far more important than a single characteristic.

Contrary to what you see in porn movies, the amount of chest hair you have is unimportant as well. There is a strong public pressure towards smooth and shaved bodies, but there are plenty of escorts who do extremely well with chest hair. Porn stars shave their chests because it makes them appear younger and more defined. As long as you are not striving for a boyish or gymnast appearance, you will do fine with chest hair.

The physical appearance of your race and ethnicity is not a factor either. Many clients do not consider a person's race when selecting an escort. Body type, age, and any of a dozen other traits are far more significant to these clients. Additionally, there are many men who are specifically attracted to members of one ethnic group or another. No matter what your background is, there will always be clients who have a preference for your race and ethnicity.

In regard to masculinity and femininity, there is clearly a preference among clients for male escorts to exhibit masculine characteristics. Fortunately there is a surprisingly large subset of clients who prefer feminine-acting males. Effeminacy can even be taken to extremes in the case of transsexual, transgendered, and cross-dressing escorts. If you fall into this category, there is certainly a market for your services.

How dominant or submissive you are can also be incorporated into your work, as there are plenty of clients who prefer each style. You will be able to find clients who are a good match for you as long as you explain your preference in advance. That is true for almost any characteristic when it comes to escorting.

Obviously, you do not have to fit a strict mold to be a successful male prostitute. Male escorts are as diverse as men's sexual tastes. Having said that, there are still a number of traits that most escorts have in common. You do not need to have all of them to escort on occasion, but you will need most to do this for a living.

Curious to learn if you have what it takes? Here is a quiz along with a brief explanation of how each point is important. Count the number of times you answer "yes" as you respond to following questions:

*1 – Do you look like you are age 35 or younger?* There is clearly a beauty standard in our society favoring youth. It is not critical to be young, but looking like you are under 35 is a definite advantage. Fortunately for those of you who are outside of this range, taking good care of yourself in other ways can keep you competitive well into your late thirties, and in some cases into your forties or longer.

In regard to being too young to escort, I most definitely do not recommend, encourage, or support the idea of escorting under the age of 18. Do not ever doubt that there is some demand for this – there is, although I will not discuss how or where young escorts ply their trade. Most legitimate clients are not willing to play with anyone under 18 because of the strict penalties involved. Clients who ignore these laws and specifically search for minors are potentially dangerous. Combine this danger with an underage escort's lack of worldly experience and inability to recognize dangerous situations, and you have a potentially lethal combination.

*2 – Are you in good physical condition?* Many escorts, such as muscle boys and bodybuilders, use their bodies as their main selling point. Yet just as many clients prefer someone who is more slender or toned, or even a man with an average body. There is a fair amount of flexibility when it comes to being in shape.

When considering your body type, there is one notable exception to the rule that escorts must be in shape. "Bears," or "cubs" as their younger counterparts are known, have a "manly man" image. A bit like the stereotypical Canadian lumberjack, they frequently have a beard, a hairy body, and a bit of a stomach. Although the demand for bears is not so great as the desire for some other types of men, one could easily attract business in the escort industry.

*3 – Is your face attractive?* Like having a good body, an attractive face is extremely useful for the aspiring escort. Precisely what is attractive will depend on the look you are going for and will also be determined by your clients. No two people have exactly the same taste, after all. As long as you have at least an average face, you should do fine as an escort.

Keep in mind that what is attractive for one type of escort may be unsuitable for others. For example, I look ridiculous in leather because I have an innocent and boyish look. Someone with a more mature and weathered face may look far more impressive, attractive, and believable as a master.

*4 – Do you have an average or large dick?* When it comes to an escort's endowment, bigger is better. At least from an advertising perspective. Many clients prefer big-dicked men, which gives an advantage to those fortunate enough to have been born that way.

Although it may surprise you, dick size is not nearly as important as many believe. It clearly is an advantage, but even escorts with medium-sized ones find clients with little difficulty. Only those with small dicks will lose business with any regularity. Fortunately this is not an insurmountable problem. Many clients find dick size to be unimportant, especially if they are looking for a bottom during anal sex. There are even clients who seek out escorts with small dicks to learn how to bottom.

*5 – Do you have a college education, or are you working on one?* A college education is exceedingly useful for an escort. Many clients prefer escorts with a college education, particularly if they will be traveling together. The escort's education may provide additional benefits as well, such as knowledge of human psychology or sexuality.

There are many specific skills that are clearly useful to an escort. For example, knowing how to design websites will give an escort an advantage when it comes to building an online presence. Massage skills will be useful for sex workers who prefer giving erotic massages to having sex with clients. Perhaps most importantly, business skills are extremely handy for anyone working as an independent escort. Escorting is a business like any other, and your services need to be marketed as such.

*6 – Are you comfortable having sex with numerous types of men?* Escorts must be willing to have sex with a wide variety of clients. Virtually all of these are men; women hire escorts on only the most rare occasions. Some of these men are attractive, but many others are not. This includes men who are unattractive because of age, weight, appearance, hygiene, and more. Being willing to perform sexually with all types of clients is part of what makes an escort rise to the top. This does not mean there is not a point where you should apologize and leave; it simply should not happen very often.

Your willingness to have sex with men who are married or have lovers is similarly important. Married men make up a high percentage of an escort's clients, and it would be virtually impossible to run a business without them. If your ethics find this behavior reprehensible, then escorting may not be for you.

If you are unsure of how well you can handle having sex with so many different types of men, try this test. Walk through a crowded store and begin surveying the men present. If you escort for any length of time, men resembling almost everyone in the store will hire you. If the idea of having sex with those men makes you feel ill, you may want to choose another career.

*7 – Are you sexually flexible in bed?* To succeed as an escort, one must be willing to provide a variety of sexual services. Deep kissing, cuddling, and giving and receiving oral sex are critical. Being able to both bottom (receive) and top (give) during anal sex is important as well. It is possible to succeed as an escort as just a top or a bottom, but it will limit your number of clients.

Some escorts take flexibility in bed to greater extremes, offering a variety of fetish services including watersports (sex with urine), role playing, and SM (sadomasochism). These escorts will attract clients who enjoy those activities but lose some others who only enjoy more "vanilla" forms of sex.

*8 – Are you gay or bisexual, and comfortable with your sexual orientation?* Your sexual orientation is a serious issue when it comes to the qualifications to be an escort. Men who are comfortable being gay tend to do best in the industry, with openly bisexual escorts following not far behind. Escorts who identify as predominantly or completely straight tend to do poorly in the industry and generally prosper only from the strength of their looks and advertising. The reason is because clients overwhelmingly want someone who will affirm their appreciation for having sex with other men through sex, intimacy, and companionship. It is impossible for a straight male escort to be completely comfortable providing these services.

*9 – Do you avoid the use of drugs?* Being drug-free is extremely beneficial for an escort and is critical if you want to rise to the top levels of the industry. Escorting is an effective way to make money, but it does have its risks. Most clients are not willing to work with an escort they know may be under the influence of drugs. Those clients who seek out escorts who "party" are at a much greater risk of becoming physically dangerous.

Prostitution is work you should want to do, and not something necessary to support a drug habit. Joey Stefano, porn superstar and six-figure male prostitute, is the classic example of how dangerous an out-of-control lifestyle in the profession can be. After years of struggling with depression and heroin addiction, he died of an overdose. Every year others in the porn and escort industries turn up dead as well. If you are prostituting yourself to fund a drug habit, it may be you one day.

*10 – Do you live in or near a medium or large-sized city?* Living in or near a major city is extremely useful for the aspiring male escort. It is not impossible to escort in rural areas, but it will severely limit your business. Access to populated areas is one of the keys to being successful in this industry.

*11 – Do you have ready access to a computer and the Internet?* Access to technology has revolutionized the prostitution industry by making it easier than ever for clients and escorts to connect. You can still run a successful business using traditional print advertisements, but the use of online advertising can attract large amounts of new business. The more access you have to computer technologies, the stronger your business will be.

*Scoring* - If you want to be an escort, you should be able to answer "yes" to at least eight of these questions. These are all important factors for an escort, and having most of them in your favor is necessary to succeed. Indeed, if you plan on becoming rich in the profession, you should be able to answer affirmatively to almost all of the questions.

If you answered "yes" to fewer than eight of the above questions, it does not mean you need to give up the idea of becoming an escort. It just means your business will be limited, and you will experience difficulty building and maintaining a clientele. If you are interested in escorting for extra money or the thrill of it, you may want to enter the profession anyway. Or, perhaps you just need to continue thinking about the questions until you can honestly change some of your answers or decide you are comfortable with a career in another field.

Always remember that these are the basics to enter the profession. Your success as an escort will ultimately be determined by how well you meet the needs of your clients. We will come back to this point later in the book. In the meantime, it is time to consider whether you want to make the jump into the escort industry.

### Chapter Three
### Making the Big Decision

*Parents usually have a difficult time accepting that a child work in the sex industry. Knowing this fact, most escorts make a concerted effort to keep their work secret. Keeping this in mind, I was understandably startled one day to learn that an escort I knew not only lived with his mother, but she knew what he did for a living. "Really?" I asked him in surprise, "Does it bother her what you do?"*

*"Not at all," came his reply "She used to work in the business too."*

The decision to escort is not one to be taken lightly. Escorting can open and close doors in your life faster and easier than you may realize. If you are going to escort, it is a good idea to consider both the good and bad points that await you.

**The Upsides**

The good news is that many wonderful things may happen to you as a result of your work in the sex industry. Here are just a few of the benefits of escorting:

*Sex* – You will be having a great deal of sex as an escort. You will have many great sexual experiences and will frequently learn new techniques and skills from your partners. Sometimes attractive men will hire you. Even those clients who do not excite you may surprise you with their sexual energy. As your erotic skills increase, so will your ability to apply them to your personal life. You will also have the opportunity, if you wish, to experience a wide variety of sexual fetishes, such as bondage, group sex, foot worship, and much more.

*Money* – Skilled escorts earn a great deal of money. Whether you are escorting part-time or as a career, the money will almost certainly be greater than any other comparable job you could have. You will constantly have large amounts of cash that will allow you to live a higher standard of living than you are accustomed to, or at the very least will allow you to get out of debt or pay for college.

*Gifts* – Some of your clients will buy you gifts. In my own work, clients have presented me with clothing, jewelry, sex toys, bottles of wine, gourmet food, investment advice, and books. I have heard of clients who have offered escorts everything from free dentistry to inside stock tips. You never know what you may receive.

*People* – You will meet many interesting people as an escort. I have heard clients talk about everything from repairing pipe organs to selling cookware to piloting a Boeing 747 airplane. Many of the clients you will meet will be pleasant and enjoyable people as well. Sometimes you will even "click" personally, creating a friendship that will last long after they cease hiring you.

*Status* – Escorting is considered exciting and trendy among certain circles. People who previously ignored you will suddenly start hitting on you. You will constantly have people wanting to ask you about your work and will never be short of stories to tell at parties.

*Opportunities* – You never know what may happen during your escort career. Some escorts find true love through their work, either in a client or another escort. Other escorts are sometimes offered great jobs outside the industry from their contacts and leave escorting to follow their dreams.

*Self-esteem* – Many people find escorting to be an empowering experience. If you have doubts about your attractiveness, they will quickly vanish as people pay thousands of dollars for your time. Running your own business is an exciting prospect, and watching it grow can be as rewarding as advancing in any traditional career.

*Flexibility* – Unless you work for an agency or brothel, you will act as your own boss. You have f8ull control over your hours and can even cancel appointments if you do not feel like working. Career escorts can sleep late, work full time as an escort, and still be able to pursue their own hobbies and interests.

*Travel* – As you develop your clientele, a few of your clients may start to invite you with them as they travel. In the past four years, clients have flown me to Las Vegas, Toronto, Amsterdam, Acapulco, and more than a dozen other cities around the world. Other escorts I know have been to even more exotic locations such as France, Norway, and Russia.

*Modeling / Porn* – Someone may approach you with an offer to appear in adult magazines and videos. Although doing so is not for everyone, you may find it stimulating and a great way to gain publicity and to expand your business.

## The Downsides

Of course, escorting is not always an ideal field in which to work. There are plenty of drawbacks, some of which can leave lifelong marks. How to avoid these problems is addressed in later chapters, but for now it is important to be aware of the pitfalls that await you.

*Medical risks* – There are numerous medical risks associated with escorting. AIDS/HIV is the most obvious one, but there are plenty of others. Escorts can easily contract hepatitis, syphilis, gonorrhea, and a host of other sexually transmitted diseases (STDs). Rimming (oral-anal contact) can expose an escort to parasitic infections. Anal warts, caused by another STD, are also linked to increased rates of anal cancer.

*Social risks* – Not everyone will be as keen on prostitution as you are. Relationships with your family and friends may be strained or severed if they learn that you are escorting. Few escorts find their parents are capable of fully accepting what they do. This can cause scars that can last for a lifetime.

*Legal risks* – With the exception of a few straight brothels in rural Nevada, prostitution is illegal in the United States. Even in countries where it is legal, the police often arrest escorts on charges such as loitering, living off immoral earnings, and running a business without a permit. If you are arrested, you will have a police record for the rest of your life. Your name may appear in the newspaper, you may go to trial, and you may go to jail. Some states and cities post pictures on the Internet of those arrested for prostitution-related offenses. You may even be required to register as a sex offender with your local police department.

*Crime* – Escorts are often unwilling to go to the police if something happens to them because of the illegal nature of prostitution. As a result, escorts are highly vulnerable to crime. I have friends in the industry who have been attacked, raped, and robbed. In extreme cases, I have even heard of escorts being tortured and killed.

*Drugs* – Escorts who are not into the drug scene will be exposed to it. In the past few years, I have seen clients use poppers, marijuana, cocaine, ecstasy, and crack. Some of this can be avoided through screening your clients, but some drug users are bound to slip through.

*Degradation* – You will sometimes come home from a day on the job feeling used and degraded by your clients. There are hordes of strange people out there, some of whom delight in physically and emotionally degrading escorts. Other clients are physically and mentally distasteful and will leave you feeling dirty and unclean.

*Loneliness* – Escorting can be lonely work. Your busy times will be evenings and weekends, the same times that your friends with day jobs are usually free. Your work with clients will be intimate and close, but requires you maintain a certain level of distance and professionalism, even when you are creating the illusion than no such distance exists.

*Boredom* – An escort's work can be boring. Sometimes your business will be quiet for days on end for no apparent reason. Even when you are entertaining a client, it may be dull and monotonous. Escorts in suburban and rural areas will also spend many long hours driving back and forth to their destinations.

*Tax risks* – The police are not the only ones interested in escorts. Many escorts either partially or completely underreport their income. Although the IRS rarely catches them, those escorts who aggressively hide their income can be inviting targets.

*Relationship problems* – It is extremely difficult to maintain a romantic relationship while you are escorting. Your work will likely make him insecure, and his jealousies will flare up when he is angry or hurt. Sex within the relationship may become a much lower priority as well, much to your boyfriend's distress. For single escorts, building new romantic relationships can be almost impossible at times.

*Lack of benefits* – Escorts are self-employed, meaning there are no employment benefits in most countries. If you cannot work for any reason, you will earn absolutely nothing. You may also have to pay for your own insurance as well. The same applies to your retirement savings. You will need to make your own investments if you want to live well when you retire.

As you can see, escorting is neither the ideal paradise nor the nightmarish existence some make it out to be. Still, for many people the benefits outweigh the risks. You should consider your goals and whether you believe escorting is a viable way for you to reach them. If it still seems like a good idea, then you should take a closer look at exactly what your life may be like as an escort.

Chapter Four
**The Real Story**

*Visiting Amsterdam was a culture shock for me. Coming from a country where prostitution is illegal, seeing women working in the windows of the red light district was a fascinating concept. I found visiting the local brothels to be equally fascinating. I spent hours talking to one boy in particular about his life in the brothel. What I was not expecting was that he found my life as intriguing as I found his. Having worked only for brothels and agencies, he had never worked as an independent escort before.*

*We enjoyed learning about each others' different worlds. I liked the idea of constantly having peers to talk to, but thought that the constant regimen of working in a brothel would be too stifling for my taste. Similarly, he envied the freedom I had as an independent escort, but was frightened at the prospect of not having someone else's management to fall back on. Although we decided in the end that we preferred doing things our own way, I suspect that we both would have been glad to trade lives, if only for a little while.*

You have looked yourself in the mirror, grudgingly given yourself a passing grade, and made the decision to give escorting a try. You are excited at the thought of the money you will be making. Before you run out and announce your grand opening, take a few moments to learn a bit more about the industry you want to join.

For starters, there are five different types of escorts. The first type is independent escorts, meaning those who find their own clients and either work out of their homes or visit clients elsewhere. The second type includes those escorts who work for a brothel. Clients hire brothel escorts by coming to a central location where the escorts are located. The third type of escort is those who work for escort agencies, the modern-day equivalent of a "pimp." Like a brothel, an agency has a number of escorts working for it. In this case, escorts are sent out to meet a client elsewhere, rather than entertaining on the premises. There is some overlap between brothels and agencies, but in general the two are very different businesses.

The fourth and fifth types of escorts are hustlers and dancers. Hustlers are male hookers and primarily find their clients on the streets or in bars. Dancers are strippers who perform in clubs and theaters but also prostitute themselves with interested clients who proposition them. This book does not specifically focus on the business strategies of either of these types, although much of the information will be highly relevant to them as well.

**The Independent Escort's Business**

Although we have already established in chapter two that there is no such thing as a typical escort, let us put that aside for a moment and consider how most independent escorts run their businesses. If you take the independent route, your business will bear a strong resemblance to what is described here.

For starters, most independent escorts are part-time sex workers. They have a central focus in their lives outside of male prostitution. This is often college or a full-time career but does not have to be. Many escorts work to pay their bills while they pursue less lucrative careers such as acting or modeling. Others spend their days doing volunteer work or political activism. It is not unheard of for even Olympic hopefuls to escort while in training.

All independent escorts, whether full-time or part-time, place ads and wait for potential clients to contact them.

Advertisements can be placed in local gay publications, national magazines, in Internet newsgroups, and on a number of websites. Several less-common methods of advertising exist as well. For example, the United Kingdom is famous for escort advertisements posted on call boxes (telephone booths). New York City has a phone line specifically designed for escorts and clients to meet each other. Cyberhustlers find their clients through direct contact in Internet chat rooms. Although this is more akin to hustling than escorting, it is still considered a form of escorting because the initial contact is not made face-to-face.

Precisely what information an ad contains will vary based on the type and size of the advertisement. In general an ad contains a rough physical description of the escort along with his phone number or e-mail address. Ads may also contain descriptive words about what services he provides, such as "top," "oral," "affectionate," "master," or "muscle worship." Abbreviations like FF (fistfucking), WS (watersports), and SM (sadomasochism) are also common, particularly among those escorts offering fetish services. You will learn how to design your own ad in chapters seven and eight.

Regardless of the type of ad an escort runs, once it is published he will start receiving inquiries from clients. These are usually requests for additional information, although sometimes the client will immediately set-up an appointment. The typical escort will receive at least five inquiries for every one that actually turns into a client.

Once it has been established that the client wants to arrange an appointment, the next step is to determine when and where to meet, and for how long. The client will usually take the initiative in this area, often suggesting an "outcall," which is a visit outside of the escort's residence. An outcall is typically in the client's home or a hotel room. (An "incall" refers to an appointment in the escort's home.) Sometimes the client will be unable to suggest a meeting place, in which case the escort should be ready to suggest a location. If the meeting is in a hotel or motel, it is customary for the client to pay for the room. The client and escort then set the time and length of the appointment.

Once the escort has met the new client, they will typically spend several minutes talking and getting to know each other. As the client and escort become more familiar, they will begin fooling around and having sex. The specifics of sex are covered in chapter thirteen, but for now it is enough to know that the escort spends the majority of his appointments having sex. When the sex is over they cuddle and talk for a while, clean themselves off, get dressed, take care of the money issue, and say goodbye.

If the escort successfully met his client's needs during the meeting, he may have a new addition to his regular clientele. Repeat appointments are similar to new ones, except the sex usually begins faster. The meetings themselves tend to be more relaxed, since the escort and client are comfortable with each other.

After an appointment, the escort completes the encounter by updating whatever records he keeps. He also fills out any financial books that he uses for his business. He then returns to waiting for his next inquiry, and the cycle continues. Periodically, the escort should review the effectiveness of his advertisements, either adding, deleting, or changing them based on how well they have performed.

The life of a cyberhustler varies only slightly from this process. Instead of placing advertisements and waiting for the phone to ring, he spends his time in Internet chat rooms searching for clients. Cyberhustling is traditionally more of a beginner's approach and can produce clients in short periods of time. It is also useful for filling in last-minute gaps in an escort's schedule. Many people use both regular advertising and cyberhustling as a way of attracting even more business.

## The Agency Escort's Business

The business of an escort agency employee is similar to that of an independent escort, but is considerably easier. Unlike the independent escort who is expected to find potential clients and handle client inquiries, escorts who work for agencies have much less work to do. The agencies coordinate and pay for advertising, as well as handle client inquiries through a central office. In exchange for being spared the hassle and expense of running a business, the escort pays 30-50% of the fee to his employer.

A typical agency escort has set shifts he is expected to work. Precisely how these shifts are assigned varies, but in general the escort is expected to be on call at certain times. During his shift, he is free to go wherever he would like, as long as he is reachable by phone or pager. When the central office has an appointment for him, he will be contacted and told where to meet his client.

Once the escort arrives at the assigned appointment, he usually calls the agency to check in. At that time, the "meter" begins running. The escort then puts the client at ease and has sex within the pre-allotted time. At the end of the session, the escort calls the agency to let them know he has finished. The agency tallies the total bill, and the escort collects the fee. Frequently he will find that the agency already has another appointment set for him. At some point along the way, usually at the end of the day, the escort visits one of the employees of the agency and turns over the agency's share of the money.

Escort agencies are covered in more detail in chapter five.

## The Brothel Escort's Business

Although gay brothels are nonexistent in the United States, they can be found in a number of countries including the United Kingdom, Holland, Israel, and Thailand. The typical brothel employee usually has scheduled work shifts, although he is almost always welcome to show up and work whenever he would like. Some brothels have the boys congregate in a central room where clients may examine them through a one-way mirror, but others are more like small bars where the boys are free to walk around and strike up conversations with clients as they would like.

In either case, once the client indicates his intent to hire one of the boys, the escort takes the client into a bedroom where the two can talk and have sex in private. Once their time is up, the client pays the escort. The escort then prepares the room for the next visitor, pays the management its share of the fee, and returns to the main room to await his next client.

Brothels frequently double as escort agencies, in which case the escort may be sent out to meet his client elsewhere. In this case, his work is conducted exactly like an employee of an escort agency.

As a group, brothel employees tend to be much younger than any other type of escort, with the possible exception of street hustlers. It is almost impossible to escort in a brothel beyond your late twenties.

**The Escort's Hidden Services**

Whether you realize it or not, escorts routinely provide a number of additional services to their clients. These are based on needs that clients often do not realize they even have. If you want to succeed as an escort, you will need to learn how to provide those services on at least a minimal level.

For example, because an escort works with sex for a living, clients will expect you to be a clearinghouse for all types of sexual information. From sexual positions for beginners to where the prostate gland is located, you will be asked for advice on a regular basis. This is especially true when it comes to safe sex. Your clients will routinely be unsure of what is or is not safe, and you will be expected to provide them with answers.

Another service you will be expected to provide is the ability to listen. During your meetings, clients will confide in you their deepest sexual secrets. These discussions are difficult for many clients but are less threatening with a "safe" person like a caring escort. Additionally, your clients will sometimes discuss problems in their lives and ask for your advice. The ability to listen to your clients will earn you a great deal of respect and will vastly increase your clients' enjoyment of your sessions.

As an escort, clients will often count on you to serve as their outlet in the gay world. A high percentage of your clients will be married or deeply closeted. Being able to make your clients feel comfortable with their sexuality may even be their greatest need. For many clients, an escort is the only person with whom they are comfortable discussing their sexuality. Being able to make your appointments a safe haven for them is a must.

This is doubly true if you expect to entertain clients in your home. Clients who keep their sexuality hidden may never have seen a gay adult magazine or pornographic movie. Talking to clients who are examining them can yield a great deal of information about their needs and desires, which in turn will make you better able to meet them. Your home may become one of the few places in your clients' lives that they can be themselves.

Similarly, your clients will often ask you to serve as their resource for exploring the outside gay world. They will ask for a variety of referrals on everything from pornography to the local gay bars. You should be able to answer their questions, or at least be able to refer them to a resource that can.

Although most clients do not realize it, one of the most basic qualities they are looking for is professionalism. Escorts who behave professionally always discuss their fees upfront, arrive on time, call if they will be late, appear as advertised, and show up sober and ready to work. These business practices may seem like common sense, but in the escort industry they are far from standard. Any escort-review website will reveal dozens of horror stories about unprofessional escorts.

Another service offered by escorts is discretion. Escorts have an ethical obligation to keep their meetings with clients confidential. Whether leaving a message on a client's answering machine or talking with other escorts, it is important to respect your client's right to privacy. This right to privacy is not so high as a discussion with a doctor or lawyer but nevertheless should be kept confidential whenever possible.

**The Good and Bad News About Your Sex Life**

The good news is that many people consider escorts to be sex symbols. The same people who may ignore your "civilian" self will find your escort identity irresistible. If you escort for any length of time, you will meet people who will proposition you for free sex. You will probably pass on most offers, but some will be from attractive men who interest you. Have fun if you would like. It is one of the fringe benefits of escorting.

Unfortunately, most everything else on this topic is bad news. In my experience, escorts routinely have less sex in their personal lives than non-escorts. That is because the more sex you have at work, the less you will want at home. After a busy day, sex with your lover or a hot trick may be the last thing on your mind. This will definitely not make your lover happy.

Your work life may also be in trouble because of the reverse of this. The more sex you have in your personal life, the more difficult it is to maintain an erection with your clients. This is a particularly important issue for escorts who depend on prostitution income for a living. Cutting down on the amount of sex in your personal life will make it easier to perform with your clients. The same can be said for avoiding masturbation. The more you jack-off, the less you will be able to perform when you are with a client.

Incidentally, some of you may not have this problem at all. When porn star Drew Andrews danced at the Nob Hill Adult Theatre in San Francisco, he performed four jack-off shows per day for an entire week. According to popular legend, he was said to have truthfully boasted that not only did he cum during every single show but he also came with all of the numerous clients he entertained during the week. "Cumming makes me horny," he is rumored to have said. Unless you have his stamina, you will be forced to develop a balance between your personal and professional sex lives.

If your newfound insight into the escorting business has not scared you off, then it is time to make your second big decision. Do you want to work for an escort agency or brothel, or do you want to go independent and run the business yourself? Don't be nervous, because once you turn the page you will find an entire chapter dedicated to helping you determine how agencies and brothels fit into your business.

## Chapter Five
## Agencies and Brothels

*Not too long ago, a friend of mine made an unusual career change; he retired from his executive-level position, bought a Dutch brothel, and moved to Amsterdam to manage it. A slightly-plump friendly gentleman in his early sixties, he found the brothel to be the perfect addition to his life. He not only had the opportunity to have sex with dozens of attractive young men, he was able to befriend them well as a father figure to them.*

*As my friend tells the story, some months after he began his new career, a man in his fifties came into the brothel with an attractive young escort from London. The man hired one of the boys in the brothel, and quickly disappeared into a back room Seeing the young escort sitting by himself, my friend suggested that he hire someone for fun.*

*The escort thought about the suggestion for a moment, then said that he didn't care for the young men in the brothel. To my friend's surprise, the young escort continued by saying that he would be happy to pay for an hour of my friend's time.*

Ask any feminist what she thinks of brothels and chances are that you will receive a scathing review describing how they degrade women into the realm of subhuman sex objects. Even pro-sex work feminists concede that many brothels treat women as slaves. Although not all operate like this, they are correct when discussing the many brothels in Eastern Europe or the Asian "massage parlors" in many American cities. Women working in those establishments have often been kidnapped or smuggled across international lines, beaten, raped, and threatened with violence to themselves or their families should they attempt to escape and return home.

Fortunately, this is most definitely not the case with male brothels and escort agencies. For a variety of social and economic reasons, working conditions for men in brothels are much better than for women. Although there are still pitfalls to navigate, working for an employer is usually a safe and lucrative job option. The key is to find the right agency or brothel for you.

**The Pros and Cons of an Employer**

There are a number of advantages to working for an agency or brothel, starting with how easy it is to obtain a job. Organized prostitution businesses have an extremely high turnover and are always recruiting new escorts. Even those brothels that limit the number of escorts they employ are often looking to recruit new talent. You will almost certainly be able to find a job with an agency or brothel as long as you are in good physical condition.

Even more handy is the ability to avoid the hassle of running your own business. This is especially useful for escorts whose lives do not allow them the freedom to run a business. If you work for an agency or brothel, you do not have to worry about advertising. You also do not have to worry about answering phone calls, arranging meetings with clients, and handling the business finances. In the case of clients who pay by credit card, you do not even have to worry about collecting the money because your employer does that for you. All you have to do is show up on time, put the client at ease, and have sex with him. That is how easy it can be.

Working for a brothel or agency also has the advantage of solving your pricing and negotiating troubles. Although many female brothels allow the women to set their own rates, all male brothels that I have heard of have a set price for their escorts. In the case of agencies, having an established clientele allows the employer to set these prices slightly higher than many independent escorts in the area. Some agencies even have special techniques to encourage clients to pay more (more on that in a few pages).

There is also the issue of client records. Escort agencies frequently keep written records that can inform you about a client's needs and preferences before you ever meet him in person. Although brothels rarely keep written records on clients, they often have an extensive "oral history" instead. Often you can learn about a client by asking the other employees if they recognize him. Both types of client information also help avoid unstable or potentially dangerous clients.

Brothels, and to a lesser extent escort agencies, also give you an opportunity to befriend other escorts. Constantly being in contact with other escorts is useful on a social level because it decreases the feelings of isolation and loneliness in the business. Having peers in the business also provides you with a chance to learn from them.

Although rare in most countries, another advantage of working for someone else is the possibility of fringe benefits. At least one brothel in Amsterdam (where prostitution is legal and taxed) provides its employees with free medical screenings for STDs on a monthly basis. The employees are also offered the option of having taxes taken out of their wage each time they work, so at the end of the year the escort will not owe any tax on their escorting income.

All brothels and some agencies also have a place to conduct incalls, saving time and energy traveling to visit clients. Working on an incall basis also provides greater protection. If a client becomes violent during a session, there are plenty of people nearby to come to your rescue.

Of course, not everything about agencies and brothels is ideal. The most obvious disadvantage is that you give up a big chunk of your money. Agencies typically take 30-50%, and brothels take more like 40-60%. Typically they charge clients a bit more to offset this. Tips help as well, but the result is that you still make less than most independent escorts.

If you work for an agency, you are also not able to screen your clients in advance. This means you may show up to find clients drunk, high, or otherwise mentally unbalanced. You may even be sent to meet with clients who want services you cannot provide, such as topping you when you are not a bottom. This may happen by accident or may be done on purpose by an uncaring call screener at the agency. There are even reports of agencies knowingly sending an escort to meet with entire groups of clients without warning the escort in advance.

Escorts working for agencies and brothels can be subject to sexual harassment by the management as well. This is especially true of less reputable employers or those businesses that function in countries where organized forms of prostitution are illegal. Similarly, escorts who work for less established agencies may find themselves cheated out of money. When this happens, there is not much you can do about it.

There is also a loss of freedom when working for an agency or brothel. Many establishments have set ways of doing business, such as strict time controls or limited situations under which an escort is allowed to leave an appointment. Often you do not have control over your schedule, and if you irritate the management they may assign you to work less profitable shifts. Furthermore, agencies typically require you to make an extra trip to drop off their share of the money at the end of each shift.

Finally, working for an agency or brothel is often boring. Not every day is a busy one, and often hours will pass by without a single client. Agency escorts who have cellular phones or pagers have the advantage here, in that they do not have to sit in until they are sent on a call.

**Making the Decision**

Depending on where you live, the decision whether to work for an agency, brothel, or as an independent may be made for you. For example, in Amsterdam the vast number of male brothels and agencies have put out of business all but the hardiest independent escorts and street hustlers. In the United States, years of active law enforcement have shut down all the gay brothels. Escorts in the United Kingdom are spoiled for choice. Cities like London have a selection of all three options.

Your situation in life will also suggest how you should operate your escort business. Agencies and brothels are both ideal for the part-time escort who does not have the time, inclination, or ability to operate a more structured business. Full-time students and hustlers who want to get off the street are also ideal candidates to be employed by someone else. On the other hand, unemployed college graduates, people with less demanding day jobs, and those with greater levels of ambition may be better-suited for the independent route.

Overall, brothels provide the greatest support to the escort, followed closely by escort agencies. Independent escorts have a greater earning potential but must work harder on their own to reach that level. If you carefully consider your own situation and goals, you will probably know which method is right for you.

**Selecting an Employer**

The next step in working for an agency or brothel is to find the one that is right for you. Unless you have a friend or acquaintance who can fill you in about the situation in your area, you should find a local gay publication. They are usually distributed in bars and other meeting places. Take a look in the escort section, and make a list of every agency or brothel in your area. A quick scan of the help-wanted ads will often net a few possibilities as well. If you are in the United States, you should look in *Unzipped* magazine, since not all agencies advertise locally. If you are on the Internet, you will also want to do a search looking for agencies that primarily advertise on the Web. You can also look in your local telephone book under "escorts," although you are more likely to find straight than gay escort agencies.

Once you have made your list, it is time to narrow it down. Some agencies specialize in other types of escorts, such as muscular men or boyish types. Do not necessarily be put off if they advertise escorts within a specific age range. The age range is the age that you look, not necessarily your actual age. Escort agencies hide the true ages of their employees, in the same way independent escorts often do. You should also cross out any agency that advertises both men and women. Such agencies are almost always completely straight.

There are several ways you can narrow down the remaining names on your list. Pretend you are a client and call each agency or brothel on your list to inquire about their outcall services. Judge them based on both the information that you learn as well as how polite and friendly they are on the phone. Agencies are used to having multiple inquiries for each successful "sale" they make, so they will not mind your call. A few good questions to ask are:

- Do you have anyone (describe your own physical type) working for you over the next few days?
- What are the escorts willing to do sexually?
- How much would he cost for an hour? For a night?
- How should I handle tipping the escorts? Or is that not necessary?
- How much advance notice do you need to set-up an appointment?
- How late at night can I call to set-up an appointment?
- What is your policy if an escort is not as described?
- (If an agency) Do you offer incall services?

You should also try calling them two or three times over a 24-hour period, so you can judge the responses of different employees of the agency. Cross off your list any agency that is unfriendly, unhelpful, or suggests poor working conditions. If prostitution is illegal in your area, write off any business that promises sex acts from their escorts. Those agencies are legal trouble waiting to happen.

You can narrow down your list of remaining names even further if you wish by visiting your local gay bookstore and looking up the remaining agencies and brothels in guidebooks about your area. They may have reviews on the establishments (usually brothels), in which case you can find out more about them. You can do an even more effective job of researching potential employers on the Internet by visiting sites like the Male For Male Escort Review (http://www.male4malescorts.com) and Cruisingforsex.com (http://www.cruisingforsex.com), and the If a business has a bad reputation, you should not associate yourself with it.

You can also call an independent escort in your area to ask what he knows about the agencies and brothels on your list. Not all escorts will be able to help you, but many of them will. If you call other escorts, do not ask them to find clients for you. Not only is it inappropriate to ask but such a request instantly brands you as an extremely clueless novice. Expect your conversation to end quickly if you ask for much more than advice. Independent escorts are not in the business of finding clients for other escorts. Even if they need someone for threeways, they will want to work with someone who has a good reputation and an established track record in the industry.

If you are truly ambitious (and horny), you can hire an escort from the largest of the agencies or brothels. Over the course of an hour of sex, make a point of asking him about agencies and brothels in your area. You may be amazed at how much information you will receive. You will certainly learn more than from a simple phone call.

When you have finished narrowing down your list of potential employers, you should ideally be left with at least three or four options on your list. If you have more than that, you can afford to be particularly choosy regarding which businesses to pursue. Give your selections a call, and ask if they are currently hiring. Almost without exception, they will be looking for new employees. Set up your interviews, and get ready for the next step.

An interview with an agency is not unlike applying for any other job. It is more flexible and casual because the work is unique, but all the basic rules of interviewing still apply. You should show up on time, be positive and upbeat, and dress nicely. Most of the interview will be spent answering the questions of the interviewer. He may ask everything from your name to your dick size. Depending on the country you are working in and the legal status of prostitution, he may ask for necessary tax information (such as your Social Security number). If you are concerned about your privacy, you should respectfully decline to answer prying questions until you decide to work for the agency.

Some interviewers may request to see your body. Whether or not to honor their request is completely up to you, although there is some business merit to their request. A fair compromise is to allow the interviewer to see your body but not to touch you or see you with an erection. You should also know it is completely inappropriate for the interviewer to make sexual advances on you. As with any other industry, the basic rules of sexual harassment apply here, so be prepared to tell the interviewer to "go to hell" and walk out if he asks for sex.

The only exception to this rule is if he offers you the agency's standard "escort pay" to hire you for an hour. In such a case, you may want to accept his offer. If you have even the slightest concern that the business does not seem "quite right" or you are worried the interviewer may not pay you after sex, then you should politely decline his offer. **Under no circumstances during an interview should you have sex for free.** I know of one escort in dire need of money who responded to a "help wanted" ad from an escort agency in Ireland. Not knowing this rule, he showed up and had sex with the interviewer because the employer "needed to know what the escort's skills were in bed." Only weeks later did he learn that there was in fact no escort agency – he had responded to an ad designed to obtain free sex with young men.

During the interview, you will also be free to ask the interviewer questions about the agency as well. Questions you may wish to ask are:

- How long has the business been in operation? Ideally the business should be in operation for more than five years. At the very least, the business should have been in operation for at least one year. Any less than a year and you will want to confirm that the establishment is reputable.
- What are their rates, and what percentage does the house take? Although rates will vary, an escort agency should take about 40% and a brothel no more than 50%. If the percentages are any higher than that, the establishment should be charging rates substantially above independent escorts in the area to make up for the high percentage. Does the business have different rates for appointments over an hour, as well as overnight visits? If a brothel offers outcall services, what are its outcall rates?
- Does the escort's percentage change depending on how long you work for the agency? Some employers may start by taking a higher percentage than normal but lower the amount periodically over the first year. This encourages you to stay with the business over a longer period of time.
- Where does the business advertise? Unless the business is old enough to have a regular clientele, they should be aggressively advertising.
- Does the business advertise on the Internet? At the very least, it should have a basic website. Ideally,

the brothel or agency should be updating its site regularly.
- Does the agency provide legal services if you are arrested? Agencies often do this to prevent the escort from turning on the agency in the event of an arrest.
- Are other benefits provided? This is uncommon but does occur in some countries.
- How does the employer handle the issue of the escort's income taxes, or is the money paid under the table? Does the agency file IRS 1099 forms, thereby requiring the escort to pay taxes on some or all of his income?
- If applying with an agency, are escorts welcome to drop in and spend their afternoon with the phone screeners? This is particularly useful for escorts from suburban areas who travel into cities to work. Otherwise you may find yourself in the city during your shift with no place to go.

Finally, you should try to get a feel for the atmosphere of the business. If your instincts say something is not right or if you do not trust the management, then avoid working for them. If there are any escorts on the premises, make a point of learning what they think of working there.

Once you are done with your interviews, it is a matter of considering what is left on your list. If you have eliminated everything, then you may want to consider a career as an independent escort. You should not work for a disreputable agency unless you are in extreme need of money. Even then, be careful to watch your back.

The interviews should give you a pretty good idea of which employers you would like to work for. You will know if you are offered a job, although often the rejection consists of saying "we'll call you." If they do not contact you within 48 hours, give them a call back. If they do not immediately make arrangements to have you work for them, you can be fairly certain you didn't get the job.

## "You're Hired!"

Once you have accepted an agency position, you are all set to begin. The agency will give you all the guidance and training you require. When you first arrive on the job, you will immediately receive a flurry of business. Many of these are from collectors. These are clients who are always on the lookout for new escorts to hire. They like escort agencies because of their high turnover, so when you begin working it is your turn to be hired. Enjoy them and learn what they think about the business, because they have seen many escorts come and go. Collectors can give you a considerable insight into how an escort should conduct his business.

After the initial flurry, you will notice your number of clients beginning to level out. As you develop your own clientele, the number may begin to increase. If your calls drop off for an extended period of time, talk to the agency's phone screeners or the brothel's manager. They will be able to give you a better idea of what may be causing the decline, and if it is affecting everyone at the business or just you. You may also want to inquire if clients have been complaining about you. If they are, learn from what they are saying. There is a good chance the complaints have some validity. If you believe you are a good employee and you are still working less and less, it may be time to shop around for another place of business or to consider going independent.

In either case, keep in mind that it is a bad idea for you to steal clients to see outside of the agency or brothel. While it does have the advantage of generating more money for you while costing the client less, this is a good way to get fired. It may be tempting at times, especially when the clients ask for your number, but you should still avoid it. Word does get around, and although you may get away with it at first, eventually you will be caught. Do not think your employer will not fire you. Agencies have a strong demand for "new talent," so they may be willing to let you go.

The exception to this rule of not stealing clients is if and when you make the decision to go independent. Depending on your timeline, discreetly inform your clients in the weeks or months before you go independent that you will be doing so and would like to hear from them when the time comes. Give them a way to contact you, or better yet, get a way to contact them. E-mail addresses are perfect for this. Once you have left the agency (hopefully on good terms), you will then have a list of clients to use as the basis for your new business.

**"Don't Call Us, We'll Call You"**

Of course, after your entire search, you may not be offered a job. When I first made the decision to escort, I interviewed with an agency in Jersey City. Had I done my research, I would have known that they specialized in muscular escorts, so I never even had a chance of landing a job with them. After a few days of unsuccessfully calling them for work, I realized I had failed their interview. I was upset for a day or so but quickly bounced back. I had begun finding clients on my own by cyberhustling and rapidly learned that I preferred to work as an independent.

Your experience may be similar. If you are not offered a position, consider why that may be the case. Do you need to work on your body? Did you act less than professional during your interviews? Are there any other obvious reasons why you may not have been hired? Even if you answer yes to these questions, all hope is not lost. You can go back to square one and begin your hunt for employment once again, considering more options this time. You can also work on your body or your interviewing skills until they are ready to work in the competitive environment of escorting.

Or you can do what I did when the agency blew me off – go independent! That's what the next chapter is all about

## Chapter Six
## The Independent Route

*Several years ago a client of mine flew a Canadian escort to New Jersey for the weekend. To his disappointment, the escort was not particularly friendly, and their weekend together was somewhat strained. To alleviate the tension, the client invited me to join them for one of their evenings together.*

*The three of us went out to dinner to get to know each other. Unfortunately it turned out to be a disaster. The escort ordered numerous drinks over dinner, and consumed most of a double-bottle of wine by himself after we returned to the room. Worse yet, he was becoming more obnoxious as the evening went on, and began an argument with the client. We finally began having sex together, only to hear the escort announce he was tired. He stated that he only wanted to get us off so he could go to sleep.*

*When I finally left, I felt bad that the other escort's behavior had ruined the evening for the client. I never forgot that he did that, and over the next two years I discouraged quite a bit of business away from him. I estimate his severe lack of professionalism cost him several thousand dollars in lost business. More importantly, other clients were diverted away from him towards other more responsible and friendly escorts.*

If you have decided to take the independent route of escorting, I congratulate you. It is the decision I made years ago, and I have not regretted it for a single day. I hope your experiences are as rewarding as mine have been.

Of course, before you can start making your millions, you have four pieces of business to address. You need to:

- Determine the image you are going to use.
- Price yourself in the market and set your rates.
- Choose an escort name for yourself.
- Develop an initial strategy for your business.

Once you have managed these tasks, you will have all of the advanced planning done and will be ready to begin the process of advertising. Once your advertising reaches the public, your business will be up and running.

**Choosing Your Image**

The first step in becoming an independent escort is to determine precisely what "type" you will be. Porn stars, tops, swimmers, and even "nasty slave boys" all have a market in the escort industry. Choosing the image that is right for you will help successfully guide your business through the planning stages into a thriving escorting business.

Every public part of your business will be affected by your image. This includes the way you phrase your advertisements, how you act on the phone, how you dress, how you interact with clients, and even how you have sex. From bottom boys to homeboyz, your image defines who you must be when you escort.

For most of you, choosing your image will be easy. If you love leather and enjoy the sight of a freshly paddled ass, chances are you are headed for a leather role. Similarly, if you spent your college years playing sports and are still physically active, you are a likely candidate for a jock. You may even be cute, friendly, and intelligent, in which case you would be well suited for the image of a boy-next-door type.

Of course, you may want to be a bit more creative or unusual with your image. In my own case, I identified as an intellectual boytoy right from the start, because of my education, my short height, and my extremely boyish appearance. A quick read through your local escort advertisements will reveal plenty of others. I glanced in *Unzipped* magazine and found ads with images such as an aggressive bodybuilder, international model, lifeguard, and muscle cop.

Your geography may also play a role. Consider where you live and what the area is amous for. New York is a great place to present yourself as a model, and anyone advertising as a student in Boston will certainly do well. Similarly, Florida and Southern California are famous for their beaches and will attract plenty of attention for those offering a surfer or beach boy image. The opposite may apply as well. A rugged Iowa farm boy may do well in New York City.

Of course, your city or state may not have a good reputation associated with it. (Living in New Jersey, I can certainly relate.) In this case there are plenty of other options to consider. Pick an image based on an important trait about you. Consider using past military service, how intelligent you are, or even what styles of clothing you like to wear. College boys, ex-Marines, and preppies are all popular options that bring specific images to mind.

Do not hesitate to use a more feminine image if that applies to you. Because the vast majority of escorts are masculine in nature, an escort specializing in gender-bending services could do well in some areas. If you are a cross-dresser or transsexual, by all means use that as your image. You will be placing yourself in a smaller market but one in which you will have far less competition.

## Pricing Yourself

Although your chosen image will help you attract customers, the ultimate test of your success will be whether potential clients are willing to pay your rate. Setting your fee is tricky business because of its extreme importance. If you set your rates too high, you will lose business. Set your rates too low and you will be swamped with low-paying, less desirable clients.

To complicate the issue even more, you should keep in mind that there is no correct way to design your rate structure. While most escorts have an hourly rate, an overnight rate, and a per-day rate for travel, others prefer more creative fee structures. Some escorts offer lower rates on additional hours, and others offer rates for 90-minute sessions. Some escorts charge less for incall services, and others ask more for appointments that require a significant amount of travel time. Other escorts will vary their charges depending on the type of services they are providing or whether the client is taking them out to dinner. A few escorts even offer package deals, charging less per appointment if the client pays in advance. I even know of one escort in California who charges $20 for 20 minutes. I cannot imagine he makes as much money as he would by using a more traditional rate system, but he insists he does well specializing in quickies. My own strategy has been to keep my rate structure as simple as possible, although for more distant clients I require a two-hour minimum.

Regardless of how you want to design your fee structure, the first step in setting your rate is to get a baseline price of what escorts charge in your area. You can do that in one of several ways. Take a look at the escort ads in your local gay publications or on the Internet. If you live in the United States, you may also wish to look at your state's listings in *Unzipped* magazine. Although not all ads list prices, you should be able to get a feel for what escorts routinely charge. You can even assess rates in your area more accurately if you concentrate on escorts who are similar in image and appearance to yourself. You should also keep in mind that people advertising as porn stars often have a slightly higher rate because of their increased visibility.

If your publication does not print prices or has too few to make a decent comparison, you may wish to call several escorts to inquire about their rates. Pretending to be an interested client is an excellent way to do this, although it is somewhat sneaky. You may also want to tell the escorts you are new to the business, in the hopes that they will offer you advice. Whatever you learn, be sure to listen to multiple opinions. Occasionally you may find an unfriendly and highly competitive escort who deliberately gives you false information.

The next stage of pricing yourself is to consider the economics of supply and demand. In simple terms, this means the more demand there is for your services, the more you will be able to charge. Similarly, the less of a supply of competition there is in your area, the more your services are worth. The opposite is true as well. If you have plenty of competition and are operating your business in a market with relatively few clients, your prices are going to be significantly lower.

Of course, escorting is not a passive activity. There are plenty of things you can do to increase the demand for your services while limiting the supply of competitors. Some of them can be done when you initially enter the industry, but others will take time to implement.

## **Your Rates Will Be Higher If You...**

- Run a large and highly effective advertising campaign.
- Are unusually intelligent and well-educated.
- Have an established clientele.
- Offer fetish services.
- Offer SM services.
- Escort in an area with a large number of business travelers and tourists.
- Live in an area with laws against prostitution (especially if they are enforced).
- Live near high-income suburban and urban areas.

- Are able to offer both incall and outcall services.
- Are famous, such as if you are a well-known porn star.
- Have a good reputation as an escort.
- Want to escort only on a limited basis.

Likewise, the opposites of these will lower your rates. There are also a number of factors that may reduce the demand for your services and supply of competition, thereby lowering your rates.

## Your Rates Will Be Lower If You...

- Are limited in what you are sexually willing to do, such as not kissing or bottoming.
- Provide bodywork and massage services rather than have sex.
- Are particularly choosy about clients you are willing to work for.
- Live in an area with large numbers of competing escorts, agencies, and brothels.
- Are difficult to contact by phone or e-mail or are not able to return messages and pages quickly.
- Have a limited schedule during which you are available.

When all is said and done, you will probably have a rate somewhere between $100 and $200 per hour and between $500 and $800 for overnight appointments. Bodyworkers will probably charge between $50 and $100 per hour and rarely have overnight appointments. If you set your starting rate higher than those rates, you may have a more difficult time developing a clientele. It also goes without saying that rates in other countries will vary accordingly.

You should also be aware that many escorts charge a higher fee for couples and threesomes. Precisely how you want to handle this is up to you. Some escorts double their rate, but others charge an additional 50%. Still other escorts, usually the more expensive ones, do not charge more for threeways because they feel their rates are already sufficient for their time (or because they like the sex). Whatever your rate for threesomes, you should be aware that this is only for meetings with two clients. It is not customary to charge an additional fee when the third person is another escort.

You may find yourself tempted to lower your rates if you lack confidence in the value of your time. While it is a personal decision, I urge you not to sell yourself short. The above rules of pricing should help determine a good starting rate. A skilled escort is always in demand, so do not undervalue the importance of your time. If you undercharge your rates in the beginning, you will be flooded with too much business and will be forced to raise rates later.

Conversely, you may feel the suggested rate is too low for you. In this case, you should not despair. Once you develop a clientele, you will find your rates steadily increasing. We will come back to the topic of raising your rates in chapter twenty-one.

Regardless of your initial rate, you should know one important lesson: There will always be people who will believe that your rates are too high. You cannot please everyone, so don't even think twice when a client complains about your rates. You are in business, after all, and a good businessman knows what his product is worth. If a potential client gripes about your rates, politely inform him that "you get what you pay for." You will still lose most of the complainers, but sometimes they will surprise you. The same client may call you an hour later and offer to pay your fee.

There are also two other types of pricing worth mentioning. The first is "negotiating down," a technique whereby an escort quotes a higher rate on the phone but is willing to settle for less money. Unfortunately, this approach is ultimately self-defeating and unhealthy for the entire escort industry. Clients learn that if they negotiate with escorts they can get a lower rate, which in turn encourages them to request discounts from other escorts. I do not recommend anyone adopt this system unless they are in immediate need of money. You would be better off lowering your initial asking price instead.

The second method is "negotiating up." In this style of pricing, an escort meets the client and begins to perform sexually, only to refuse to provide certain (often promised) services until the client pays more money. Dancers who find their clients in adult theaters, hustlers who work the streets, and "gay-for-pay" escorts most commonly practice this tactic. Practicing this technique can be dangerous, because on occasion victims of these tactics will become physically threatening or violent.

On occasion you will meet an escort who charges by the act. This is not standard and is extremely legally risky to practice. You should not consider adopting such a system. If there are sex acts you would be willing to do if people paid you more, charge more in the first place and then offer them as a service. If that idea does not appeal to you, then do not offer those acts as services at all.

Negotiating up also occurs when escorts demand more money from clients they consider unattractive, either in advance or once they arrive. This is highly unethical and is hurtful and insulting to clients. An escort who is unable or unwilling to provide services for a client should politely apologize and leave.

**Choosing an Escort Name**

The vast majority of escorts, even those who openly display their picture in advertisements, use an alias in their work. An alias will provide little legal protection, but it does give you some privacy from the general public. Escorting can be a dangerous profession on occasion, and the ability to hide your true name can be an invaluable tool when it comes to protecting yourself.

Choosing your escort name is not difficult. Unless you have plans to enter porn or otherwise become well-known, a last name is probably unnecessary. Just be sure to look through local print and online advertisements for escorts, crossing out names that are already being used.

Before you choose from the remaining selections, I can offer you one tip that I guarantee most escorts will not have considered. You should make a point of choosing your name based on letters early in the alphabet. Once you begin advertising on the Internet, you will find that many sites list escorts in alphabetical order. Having a name that begins with an early letter will give you a much stronger placement. This can be particularly important when the list has several hundred escorts on it.

**Planning Your Initial Strategy**

Now that you have determined your image and your pricing, you are ready to plan your initial business strategy. By this point, you should already have a number of ideas on the subject, so your strategy should be easy to formulate.

For starters, consider whether you plan on using escorting income to meet your basic living expenses. This includes full-time escorts, those using their escorting income to pay tuition, and people depending on escorting to pay important bills. If you will be subsisting on your escorting, you will need to pay much closer attention to what you are doing, keep better records, maintain higher standards of client goodwill, and treat your business with a greater level of professionalism. This is not to say those who escort for fun and spending money should not be maintaining high standards as well. Escorts dependent on their business income simply have much more at stake.

Another consideration for your strategy is whether to take incalls. Entertaining a client in your home has its own risks but also generates additional business. Incalls are ideally suited for escorts who live alone, although many escorts with supportive roommates offer them as well. Your home should have adequate parking, convenient access to mass transportation, and be located in a safe neighborhood. Similarly, you will need to address whether you will offer outcall services. Although the vast majority of escorts do, some choose to work only in the comfort of their own homes. If this is the case, you will need to make your limitation clear at every step of your advertising process.

How your clients contact you will affect how you run your advertising. If you do not have regular access to a computer, you will be almost completely limited to print advertising. Likewise, if you are living with your parents, you may not be able to set-up appointments over the phone and will be limited to online advertisements. Using either print or online advertisements are fine for new and part-time escorts, but career escorts will want to use both.

Finally, how much money you intend to make will affect your investment of capital. Multiple phone lines, a cellular phone, enhanced voicemail, a powerful computer, and high-speed Internet access are all useful in this line of work. Other "technical toys" like a digital camera, a scanner, a good web-design program, and encryption software are also handy. Even a suitable office area in your home is important. You will want to balance your business needs with your financial goals as you develop your escorting business, but in general the more you invest, the more money you will earn.

Once you have set your image, determined a competitive rate for your services, given yourself a name, and plotted a basic business strategy, you will be ready to begin the process of advertising your services. Chapter eight will reveal the secrets to escorting successfully on the Internet, and turning the page and reading chapter seven will tell you everything you need to know to advertise your escort services through print advertisements.

## Chapter Seven
**Print Advertising**

*A New York newspaper called me up to offer me a "special limited-time introductory deal" if I advertised for four weeks in the escorting section of their daily paper. It was mostly a straight publication, but the rate seemed reasonable so I thought I'd give it a try. I quickly created an ad, and it began running two days later.*

*Two weeks later I had my first and only client from the newspaper. I made $200 from the client, just enough to pay for the ad. When the sales representative called me back to encourage that I advertise longer, I explained that the ad had failed and would therefore not be advertising in their paper again. He understood and wished me luck with my business.*

*A year later the same representative called me back to offer me a "special limited-time introductory deal." This time I told him I only take out print ads in gay publications, and hung up.*

Ask anyone in the escort business what he considers to be his best asset and he'll probably refer to his looks, his mind, or how he interacts with his clients. Few escorts, if any, will say it is their advertising. Yet that is exactly what makes or breaks an escort. No matter how hot or personable you are, if no one knows you exist, you will not be in the business for long.

Print advertising for escorting almost always consists of taking out advertisements in gay publications. These include gay newspapers, bar guides, and regional or national publications. Designing an effective print advertisement to appear in one of these publications is easy. All it takes is a bit of research, a healthy dose of creativity, and half an hour of your time.

## A Brief Overview of Print Ads

There are three types of print advertisements – text ads, photo ads, and display ads. Not every publication includes each type, but most escort print ads fall into one of the three categories. These advertisements run in a variety of gay newspapers and magazines. Often they are distributed for free in gay bars, although they may be sold in stores or through the mail as well. Clients will usually respond to ads within the first few weeks after they run, although I still receive the occasional phone call from an ad I ran over two years ago.

Text ads are those that consist solely of words. Typically they charge by the word or line. They are the cheapest print advertisements to run and attract a reasonable response. Take a look at these actual ads that ran in New York City's *NEXT Magazine*.

*Stand at Attention*
*You will call me SIR! Looking for*
*Good slaves to put through their*
*Paces. Big Muscular Italian, 35 y.o.*
*Frank: (212) xxx-xxxx*

*Affectionate European Bottom*
*25 y.o, 160 lbs., 6' light hair,*
*green eyes, smooth, toned & sexy.*
*24 hrs. In/Out: (917) xxx-xxxx*

*Cutest Asian Student*
*24 y.o, 5'7", 125#, Silk Smooth Body*
*(Best Exotic Massage Offered Too!)*
*917-xxx-xxxx*

Photo ads are similar to text ads but have a picture attached to them. They cost the same as a text ad except for an additional charge for the photo. There may also be an additional charge to upgrade from a black and white picture to a color one. The advantage of photo ads is that they attract more calls from people who find you attractive, as well as prevent calls from those who do not like your look.

Display ads are different from the other types in that they are usually created by the magazine's graphic design department. They always contain at least a small amount of text and usually contain a photo as well. Display ads can be purchased in varying sizes because they are specifically created to take up a certain amount of space on the page. Their downside is that they are the priciest of the three ads to run.

The cost of each type of ad varies widely depending on the publication. Ads typically range from $15-20 per issue for a simple text ad all the way to $150-200 or more for a color display ad. They may offer volume discounts if you buy them for long enough in advance. Ambitious ad campaigns can be highly expensive to run. Depending on where you live and what type of advertisements you want to run, you can expect to pay anywhere from $1,500 to $10,000 per year.

Print ads also require several days or weeks before they run. This can cause an annoying downtime in your business.

**Creating Your Ad**

Before you create an ad, find out which gay publications list escorts in your area. These will most likely be newspapers and bar guides distributed in gay bars and bookstores but may also include straight (mainstream) newspapers. If you are in the United States, you may also want to pick up a copy of *Unzipped* magazine. It is the *People* magazine of gay porn and contains several hundred escort advertisements. Don't bother finding the sexually oriented nightlife guides that are commonly available in adult bookstores. Those are usually straight and are rarely worth the energy to investigate.

The publication(s) in which you want to advertise will vary depending a great deal on your budget and the strategy you planned in chapter six. If you are short on cash or are merely curious to see what results a print ad will net, a single publication will suffice. If you have money to invest or your strategy is to get rich from your escorting, you will certainly want to advertise more aggressively.

Once you have made your selections, consider which types of ads each publication allows. For example, *HX* magazine in New York City allows text and display ads. *Unzipped* takes a different approach, allowing all three types of ads but pricing the display ads so expensively as to make them almost unaffordable. Other publications, such as small and medium-sized gay newspapers, may allow escorts to run only text ads.

The next step is to decide if you want to run a photograph. It is completely optional, but a good photo will attract more business. Carefully read the publication's policies on what is allowed in photographs, and determine if you have a photo available that matches their criteria. If you do not have a photo, have a friend take a roll or two of pictures of you. You will want more than one snapshot to choose from, because you want to have the best photo possible in your ad.

If you are concerned about your privacy and do not want your face in the photo, you may wish to ask the publication to crop your head out of the picture. Alternately, the publication may be willing to blur your face. If you are willing to put your face in your ad, by all means do so. Clients like to see who they are hiring in advance. You will eventually be recognized by your friends and acquaintances, but your business will be much stronger for your sacrifice.

Once you have sorted out your photo situation, it is time to begin writing down everything you would ideally like to print in your escort ad. The list may include:

- A headline.
- Your escort name.
- A brief physical description of yourself.
- Your contact phone number.
- Your website address.
- Your e-mail address.
- What services you provide.
- Your rate.
- Whether you offer outcall services, incall services, or both.
- A brief description of your personality and attitude.
- Words or phrases that go along with the image (jock, bodybuilder, twink) that you selected for yourself.
- Anything else that may interest potential clients.

You should also search through the ads in a given publication to learn what abbreviations they commonly use. Using abbreviations saves space, which in turn saves you money. Just make sure you do not abbreviate so much that your ad is difficult to understand.

If you are new to escorting, it is generally a good idea to keep your print advertising fairly simple. Try running text or photo ads, periodically modifying the wording to see what response you attract. Once you have an ad with a proven record of success, then you may want to consider expanding your advertising. There is no sense in making expensive mistakes that can be easily avoided. In one of my earliest ads, I had a line stating "married / inexperienced ok." I meant that married and inexperienced men were welcome to hire me. Unfortunately, numerous callers misunderstood and thought I was married to a woman. A few even asked my wife to join in!

Other phrases can also lead to misunderstandings. If you use the phrase "24 hours," you had better expect to receive phone calls at all hours of the day or night. To some extent you will get this no matter what you write, but the late-night calls will be far worse in this case. You should never use the word "party" in your ad. That word is a euphemism for illegal drugs and will attract all sorts of problematic clients.

If you decide to run a display ad, the publication will most likely offer to create it for you. You need only supply them with the text and photograph that goes along with the ad. You can request that the publication fax you a copy of the ad for your approval, or you can trust their ability to design an acceptable ad. Most publications do a good job designing display ads, although you will probably want to check their work anyway.

Interestingly enough, some people will run more than one ad simultaneously in a single issue. Usually both ads have different names and phone numbers, with descriptions that vary only slightly. The escort then markets each alias with different rate structures. They hope by running different ads they will be able to attract more clients than they could through a single ad. I have never heard of this strategy as being particularly effective, but some escorts continue to use this technique, so perhaps there is merit in there somewhere. The only reason I can see for doing this is if you want to attract two different types of clientele, that may not feel comfortable knowing you offer another type of service. For example, if you advertise both as an "innocent college boy" and a "young SM leather master."

While on the subject of mistakes, whether you are running a text, photo, or display ad, you should always make a point of checking on your ad as soon as it becomes publicly available. You may have spelling errors, an incorrect picture, or the ad may be omitted completely. Mistakes do occur, and most publications offer credit only if the error is caught during its first run.

**Callboxes**

Although it would be inconceivable in many areas of the world, many escorts in the United Kingdom use an unusual form of print advertising. For a price, runners will tape a postcard-sized ad to public telephone booths in certain city districts. Although these ads are primarily straight in nature, a number of male and transsexual escorts have utilized this advertising technique to their advantage.

If you are interested in running an ad like this, drop by any callbox in your area where the ads are posted. Grab a few, and call a the escorts to inquire who does their posting. Be aware that this is not a risk-free form of advertising. British Telecommunications dislikes this practice and periodically shuts off the phone numbers listed in the ads. If you do utilize this service, make sure you are not listing your only phone number.

Regardless of how you advertise yourself, you are going to have a bit of downtime between completing your ad and rushing to answer your phone. This downtime is perfect for establishing your presence online. Not sure how? Well, you're in luck. The next chapter happens to be all about advertising on the Internet.

Chapter Eight
## Online Advertising

*Three years ago, a friend of mine decided he wanted to give escorting a whirl. He preferred dating older men, and liked the idea of the money. In spite of his busy schedule, I offered to help him get a start in the business. After several weeks of not finding any clients, he asked me what he was doing wrong. I read his online advertisement and laughed when I found the problem. His ad said he was available as an escort, but only between 9:00 and 11:00 on Monday mornings.*

During the past five years, tens of millions of Americans (and many more worldwide) have gone hi-tech and joined the information superhighway. Entire industries have been revolutionized by new advertising opportunities, and prostitution is no exception.

It is easy to understand why. Computers allow clients to find escorts from the safety and privacy of their own homes. There is no pressure, no embarrassment, and no legal risk to the client. They are able to shop online in a completely anonymous fashion for however long it takes before they find the right escort for them. Often escort home pages feature nude pictures, allowing visitors to masturbate and fantasize about what they could do together. People who never even considered hiring someone find themselves suddenly fixated on a particular escort.

For the escort, the Internet is an advertising opportunity that is evolving at an amazing rate. When I began escorting online in May of 1995, there were only a handful of others advertising their services online. The World Wide

Web was still somewhat confusing to many users, so most escorts settled for using the chat rooms on major services such as America Online, CompuServe, and Prodigy. Scanners were expensive, and digital cameras were just beginning to hit the market, so many online escorts did not have pictures of themselves.

Since that time, scanners have become so common that it is extremely difficult to escort online without a picture. So many escorts have pictures of themselves that most clients are not willing to hire one who does not. Another change in the online sex industry has been the rise in web advertising. There are hundreds of personal home pages of male escorts, with new ones appearing each week. There are also a number of escort-referral services, websites that provide free or low-cost ads for escorts to promote themselves. Not to be confused with escort agencies, referral services do not represent escorts or arrange appointments. Instead, they make their own money by running other ads, charging admissions to x-rated portions of their sites, or by charging escorts a small fee for their advertising services.

Whether you plan to find your clients in chat rooms, through referral services, or by running your own website, there is no doubt that thousands and thousands of dollars stand to be made on the Internet. Online advertising costs a fraction of the expense of print ads and can yield many times the investment.

Of course, with the rise in demand for escorting services has come a new generation of escorts. Many of these are younger and highly skilled with computers, but others are people still learning the basics of the Internet. If you fall into this latter category, or if parts of this chapter confuse you, do not despair. You do not need to know how to do everything described here in order to escort online successfully. The more confusing sections may become clear as you become more familiar with the Internet. If you truly do not understand a section, try showing it to a friend who is more computer-savvy than yourself. He may be able explain things more clearly than I.

## Screen Names

Remember when you created your escort name? Well, if you are going to work online, you will need to pick a handle/screen name to use as your e-mail address.

There are two types of screen/e-mail names that escorts generally use. The first is those people who prefer variations on their escort name. For example, if your escort name is "Christopher Robbins," you might create an e-mail address like ChrisRobbins@hotmail.com or Christopher-Robbins@yahoo.com. The second type consists of e-mail addresses that refer to the fact that the user escorts. Examples of this may include SanDiegoEscort@aol.com or CuteBoy4Hire@hotmail.com. Either method is acceptable and is a matter of personal preference. The former method is a good way of using name recognition if you are a porn star, and the latter type is better if you will be hustling in chat rooms.

## Profiles

The simplest way to advertise online is by creating a profile. Many online services, including America Online and Compuserve, allow their members to create profiles for themselves. A profile on one of these systems takes only a few moments to create and no effort to maintain. By placing information in the profile that clearly indicates you are an escort, you will invariably receive requests for information.

After you create your profile, double-check it to verify the information. Besides the fact that it is easy to mistype important information, some systems like America Online are notorious for adding extra spaces to web addresses in an attempt to... well, I'm not sure why they do it. They just do, and it makes it more difficult for people to reach your site.

As a side note, always be careful about what you put into your profile. "Obscene" content or overt mentions of illegal activity are grounds for having your profile removed on most systems, and some will delete your account entirely. Additionally, a few self-appointed guardians of morality on the Internet specifically look for escorts to harass. On occasion I have heard stories of these users figuring out who an escort is and then informing their family or friends what he does. Be careful never to reveal too much information in your profile, especially about where you live or go to school.

## Chat Rooms

Another way to escort online involves "cyberhustling" in Internet chat rooms. As I briefly mentioned in chapter four, cyberhustlers use the chat rooms on the Internet to find clients. This is most commonly done on America Online.

There is little finesse to the art of the cyberhustler. Most chat room escorts use screen names that make their intentions obvious, such as "Stud4Hire" or "PAEscortAvailable." A potential client sees a screen name that interests him, then checks the person's profile. If the escort has a website, he may look at that as well. Assuming the client is interested, he will send the escort an instant message (IM), a private form of communication. The two then begin their negotiations and arrangements, hopefully resulting in a sale.

## Message Boards and Newsgroups

Most Internet users are familiar with the concept of message boards. These are bulletin boards where people can post public messages on a topic, then come back later to read other people's responses. There are tens of thousands of message boards about every subject imaginable on websites and online services. Naturally, a few of them are escort related and are useful for your advertising purposes.

Many message boards are moderated, so off-topic posts are quickly deleted before they can irritate the legitimate users. These message boards often have other rules as well, such as prohibiting phone numbers, obscene language, or personal attacks against others on the board. Rules vary widely, so be sure to learn them before you post your own advertisement.

One special type of message board is called the newsgroups. These are almost always unmoderated and are open to anyone on the Internet. Unfortunately, such freedom comes at the price of heavy abuse by its users. The newsgroups have been subject to massive postings of off-topic advertisements, to the point where they clog the message board into unusability. On some adult-oriented newsgroups, there are hundreds or even thousands of unsolicited "spam" advertisements posted for every legitimate message. Sorting through these messages to find the real ones is an extreme annoyance at best.

In spite of these problems, it is possible to find some clients through advertising on the newsgroups. It is also free to advertise here, in that newsgroups have no cost other than basic Internet access. If time is a limiting factor for you, then your efforts will probably be better served advertising elsewhere. Almost all of the escort-related newsgroups have been spammed nearly to death. Still, if you have the time to post newsgroup advertisements, you may just pick up a few clients that way.

If you want to advertise on the newsgroups, it is important to keep the spam problem in mind. If people are going to read your message, they have to be able to instantly tell it is not spam. The best way to do this is to begin the subject of the message with the initials of the message board in parentheses or brackets. This allows legitimate users to do a quick search of the message board for those initials. Anything the search finds is probably a legitimate message.

Likewise, anything the search does not reveal is probably spam.

You should also keep in mind that escort newsgroups are not completely gay-oriented, so it is important to specify you are a male escort for men. You should also list the area in which you work to help the reader more quickly find what he is looking for. For example, a message topic in the alt.sex.escorts.advertisements newsgroup might read: [ASEA] Seattle Gay Male Escort Available.

There are a few more tips to keep in mind when using newsgroups. First, posting escort ads on sex-related non-escort-oriented newsgroups is usually considered off-topic and may be met by negative criticisms and replies. What is more important is that repeated off-topic postings may result in complaints to your Internet Service Provider (ISP), which in turn may result in your account being suspended. When posting on non-escort forums, be sure to do so with politeness and respect. A newsgroup specializing in pictures of nude men may be tolerant of your escort ad so long as you post a nude picture with it, but then again it may not.

Second, be aware of rules regarding posting pictures on the newsgroups. Newsgroups that specialize in digital images contain the word "binaries" in their titles. Posting pictures in non-binary newsgroups is considered a rule violation, as is posting an escort ad (even with a picture) in a binary area. Again, there is some flexibility on the issue. Alt.sex.prostitution welcomes escort ads, so they may be somewhat tolerant of your posting of a digital image with yours.

In regard to selecting newsgroups, there are thousands of topics and hundreds of sexually-oriented ones, but you will want to post only on the boards that are likely to bring you business. A few that may be helpful are:

- alt.sex.escorts.ads
- alt.sex.wanted.escorts.ads
- alt.sex.prostitution
- alt.binaries.pictures.erotic.male

- alt.binaries.pictures.erotica.teen.male

There are plenty of others, so search around and see where else you may want to advertise. Not all ISPs carry every newsgroup, so do not be surprised if your ISP claims some of these do not exist.

Beyond newsgroups, there are also several message boards on search engine websites like Yahoo. Some escorts find a small amount of business through them, but I have never found them to be particularly useful. If you have the time to search for lots of little places to advertise, you might be better off investing the time in learning how to build your own website. America Online has in the past run a popular escort advertising area. Recently the message board vanished as part of a larger restructuring of the gay and lesbian online forum. Hopefully it will return again in the near future.

Either way, you will want to remember that most people read only messages posted during the previous few weeks. You will need to repost your advertisements on a regular basis to keep them in the public eye.

**Listservs**

Listservs are message boards with a twist: To post a message, you must add yourself to a list of people interested in the topic. Once you have subscribed, you then send a message to a central e-mail address, which automatically forwards it back to everyone on the list. Some of those people will reply back to the central address, which in turn sends those messages to everyone by e-mail. Best of all, listservs do not contain spam messaging.

Active listservs can be an effective way to pick up clients on occasion. For example, a client may post a message saying he is looking for an athletic escort in London. If you are what he is looking for, you may respond on the newsgroup briefly describing yourself and your services. If he is interested, he would then privately e-mail or call you to discuss matters further.

Like message boards and newsgroups, there are thousands of listservs on a wide variety of topics. For escorts, there are a number that are relevant. To join these listservs, visit Egroups (http://www.egroups.com), and do a search for the word "escort." You will find numerous listservs about escorts. Most will not be what you are looking for (a discussion about Ford Escorts, for example), but some will be worth your consideration.

There are over a dozen different listservs for escorts, some larger or smaller in focus. There is one listserv dedicated to discussing issues affecting escorts in the Maryland area. Other listservs have been created specifically to help an escort or porn star discuss with fans and clients what is going on in his life. Many listservs are designed for escorts to be able to talk to each other in a private and safe space. I even once stumbled across a small listserv all about me!

The downside of listservs is that they can generate a sometimes annoying amount of e-mail. This is especially the case when two or more personalities on the list begin arguing and flaming (that's the online word for insulting) each other. Often these arguments result in dozens of messages from the combatants and their friends/enemies. Although flame wars are relatively rare and brief, they are annoying when they happen. If you can look past them, you should be able to benefit from being on a listserv.

**Escort-Referral Services**

Escort-referral services are those sites that provide escort referrals to clients in return for the opportunity to make money in other ways, such as by taking on additional advertising or selling adult memberships to private areas of their sites. Some escort-referral sites will show pictures of the escorts but charge clients a small fee to access the phone numbers. Others show a G-rated picture of the escort but charge a fee to access more revealing pictures. There is a great deal of creativity when it comes to how these referral services make money. Even if you have limited access to a computer, posting an advertisement on an escort-referral site is beneficial for your business. A few well-placed, low-cost ads can generate as much business or more than an expensive print ad.

If you are considering paying for an online ad, be wary. In spite of their grandiose claims, some pay-to-advertise escort websites have little web traffic. Before you pay to advertise on a site like this, always e-mail several escorts and ask them what response their ads have received. These sites are sometimes unnecessary for escorts who already advertise on other free escort-referral websites but are highly useful for escorts who do not otherwise have an Internet presence. Rentboy.com (http://www.rentboy.com) is the premier site of this nature, and features many advertisements from escorts like this. Expect to pay about $50 per month for an online advertisement.

A list of escort-referral sites can be found in appendix one.

## Escort-Review Sites

On rare occasions, an ambitious webmaster like "Hooboy" from the Male for Male Escort Review Website (http://www.male4malescorts.com) creates a site that is dedicated to reviewing male escorts. Most of these are straight in nature, but there have been a few gay ones. They are always immensely popular and can be a source of a great deal of additional business. Once your business begins to develop and you have loyal clients willing to tout your virtues, you should ask several to submit reviews of your services.

If you are not certain of the importance of a good reputation in the business, consider this review I found on Hooboy's site:

My first experience with Stephan was so good that I decided to see him on a regular basis. He is a nice guy, real cute. He is caring, passionate, and very creative. Great looks. Great butt. Great personality. This guy has some class!!

Sexually Stephan is skilled and diverse. He's affectionate, sensual, and loves to give a great massage. He's very upfront about being versatile Even more so than his considerable sex appeal and sexual skill, his professional attitude was what impressed me. He's everything a sex worker should be. He's caring, warm, friendly, professional, and does not advertise or promise anything he cannot provide. I strongly recommended him.

Vegas is a gamble, you sometimes lose and sometimes win, but when you are with Stephan, you will always hit the jackpot and come away a winner.

Now compare it with a review of this New York City escort/stripper.

I have to agree with the other negative reviews. I met Kirk at the Gaiety in NYC on a Friday night. After his performance we settled on $200 to go back to his hotel room. Once there, I had to pay upfront. As I got my money out, he noticed I had some "extra" and commented on how he should have asked for $300 or more.

For my $200, I was allowed to suck him ... for about 5 minutes. At that point, his roommate burst in and needed the room for his client. (the roommate was another dancer, Tom, whom I had the pleasure of being with a few months earlier. Tom was a very tall blonde hunk who was fantastic! Wish I had chosen him again at the time).

In any case, Kirk hurried me along ... began dressing as I was still servicing him. We were both out of the room in the next 5 minutes. $200 for 10 very unsatisfying minutes!!! I felt ripped off and very unfulfilled that night. Still love to look at Kirk onstage but will never waste another dollar on him!

The two reviews are perfect examples of the power of good and bad press. You can clearly see how an escort's business may be impacted by such reviews. Not everyone sees them, by any means. But enough people do that you will gain or lose clients based on what people say about you. Although you cannot post your own reviews on the site, you certainly can ask your clients to write about you.

When reading over reviews of your own services, the content should always be truthful and accurate. If a review says you are affectionate and versatile, clients will expect you to kiss and play top and bottom. If you are unwilling to do these when you arrive, you will have a disappointed client who may post a negative review of you. It is perfectly acceptable to write the webmaster to request corrections to your reviews. He will usually write an addendum to the review clarifying your services.

Should you find yourself the subject of a negative review, you should not write threatening letters to the webmaster, nor should you reply with obscenity-laden e-mail. Such behavior will only make your situation worse. Instead, you should write a professional, friendly letter explaining relevant facts that the client may have left out. If the entire review was false, then send a statement that the entire encounter was untrue and never occurred. Most users of these websites realize that not every review is accurate and are more than willing to consider your side of the story.

It should also be noted that you sometimes have the right not to be listed on these sites, as they do discuss the fact that you are engaging in prostitution. If you do not wish to be listed for this reason, you should send an e-mail to the webmaster asking that all reviews and content regarding you be removed. Most webmasters will be happy to remove an escort's reviews following any polite request. As with before, do not send threatening or insulting letters to the webmaster. They may result in him posting the letters rather than removing the review.

## Websites

For about $2,500-3,500, you can run a display ad in a print publication for a year. The ad will be approximately one inch tall and perhaps one and a half inches wide. For half of that cost, you can hire a company to host your own website. A website, I might add, that can be a thousand times the size and detail of your largest display ad.

The catch is that you have to learn how to design your own site. At least you should learn how if you want to get rich from escorting. Part-time escorts may be content with something a bit more modest, although even then your own website will attract more clients and increase your rates. If you have absolutely no interest in learning how to create your own website, then your best bet is to have an escort-referral site like Escorts4You (http://www.escorts4you.com) create a basic webpage for you.

Unless you are satisfied with a simple webpage, you will first need to determine where you want your site to be hosted. There are many options, including free servers and shared servers. Your ISP may provide you with server space as well.

Free servers are a tempting option because there is no cost involved. These include general servers like Geocities (http://www.geocities.com) as well as adult-oriented systems like Pridesites (http://www.pridesites.com). Whatever free server you elect to use, expect a series of annoying pop-up windows and tacky banner ads to be added to your site. These ads are how the servers make their money. Expect your website to run extremely slowly as well. To save on costs, free servers typically host more sites than normal, causing each one to run slowly.

Your ISP's server is likely to be a tempting option as well. They tend to run faster than free servers but may still require banner ads.

In either case, be sure you do not violate the terms of service (the rules) of your host. They are likely to erase websites without notice and, in the case of your ISP, may suspend your Internet access as well. Local rules may prohibit illegal activity, nudity, "obscene" content, or even links to adult sites.

Although the prices may seem fairly expensive, your most effective option for hosting your site may be a shared server like Verio (http://www.verio.com). Not only do some shared servers place few restrictions on content, they constantly maintain high levels of speed and reliability. There are a number of these servers that host adult content. Do a search for "web hosting" and you will find all sorts of possibilities.

As a side note, there is one other option webmasters may want to consider when your site grows to 600 or more megabytes per day of bandwidth. At that point, it becomes financially beneficial to upgrade from a shared to a private server. You will need a greater level of technical ability to do this, but it is not hard to learn. Of course, it takes many visitors each day to reach this level of bandwidth, but with time and effort an ambitious webmaster can achieve this result.

Once you contract with an ISP to host your site, it is time to begin building it. Precisely how you want your site to look is flexible, but you should always design your site to maintain interest in your services. That is where you will be selling yourself to your potential clients, after all. Discussions about your childhood are irrelevant, for example, unless your intention is to make yourself more "down to earth" in order to intrigue potential clients. My own website contains essays, a FAQ (list of frequently asked questions) about myself, information on my services, a picture gallery, a timeline of my history, a sex-advice column, and an online store. No matter how large your site, if properly done your investment should pay for itself many times over.

Many escorts have taken to using an adult verification service, or AVS, on their site. An AVS is a service that requires a person to pay to access restricted sections of a website. By joining an AVS, the user is able to access the restricted areas of all websites in the AVS's network. These sections usually contain nude pictures of the escort. The escort earns money each time visitors buy a membership with the AVS from his page.

I dislike the idea of using an AVS as a way to raise money. They do generate a small amount of income (perhaps a few hundred dollars per year), but they irritate potential clients in the process. In my opinion a far better option is to display the pictures for free while using them as a way to generate interest in your services. In the long run, this method is likely to generate more money than the AVS. Still, some webmasters prefer to make a small amount of money "for free" rather than work for a much larger amount. It is a matter of personal choice.

Another popular technique to make money on escort websites is to run banner ads. These are usually adult website advertisements or links to pages selling Viagra. As with an AVS, I have always found the use of banner ads to be shortsighted. You may earn a few hundred dollars per year, but you have done so at the cost of turning off potential clients. A neat and streamlined website will generate far more money in the long run.

One more tip for the aspiring webmaster: Do not put too many bells, whistles, and fancy graphics on your site. They may look and sound neat, but they slow down your webpage considerably. They may also annoy potential clients who require discretion. The last thing they need is to have their computer start blaring "New York, New York" while their wives and lovers are asleep. (Yes, I know of one escort website that actually plays that song.) No webpage graphics, however flashy, will ever substitute for a lack of interesting content.

**Site Traffic**

The largest and best-developed website will do no good if no one ever finds it. No picture gallery, however well-filled with professional shots, will generate the slightest amount of business if the site is not connected to the world around it. Fortunately, there are plenty of ways to bring traffic to your site.

*Search Engines* - When potential clients want to find escorts on the Web, many log onto search engines like Yahoo (http://www.yahoo.com). They type in a few keywords, such as "gay escort," press the return key, and presto! They now have numerous leads in their search for Mr. Right-Now.

Listing your site on search engines can be somewhat tricky. On one level, it is easy. Just fill out an online form, submit your information, and wait five minutes to five weeks for the site to add you to their general index of webpages. What is more complicated is that many search engines have their own list of websites that they recommend when someone searches the Web. The process of being added to this list is the same as being added to their general index of webpages but can take much, much longer due to an immense backlog.

For example, when I first filled out Yahoo's form, they indexed my site within several weeks. Users could then search for "Aaron Lawrence" and find my site, although it would still take considerable searching through Yahoo's information to find me. They finally added me to their official categorized chart of websites after two years of waiting. What a change it was! My website instantly picked up another three hundred visitors per day.

While this delay can be years, it can be sped up considerably. Many businesses such as Yahoo have a program where you can pay $200 for an accelerated listing. For more information on these programs, check the search engine's website.

There are a few other techniques for attracting more traffic to your site from search engines. For example, a number of services will submit your site to the major search engines. Do a search for "increase web traffic" to find them. They have mixed results and will often inundate you with e-mail advertisements, but they can help. Some search engines will also give higher listings to sites that use certain HTML coding (metatags) or that use their own domain name. Any good book on building website traffic should give you a number of ideas to try.

*Webrings* - Another popular way of bringing in traffic is the use of webrings. Webrings are a series of connected websites about a common topic, such as escorting, SM, gay pride, or any of a number of issues. In a webring, site A links to site B, which links to site C, which in turn links back to site A. Visitors can follow the ring from site to site, stopping to explore whatever piques their interest.

Joining a webring can be accomplished by going to the central website for the ring and filling out an online form. The site will then e-mail you the necessary HTML code that you must place on your website. You then download any graphics from the ring page that the code requires. Most webrings will guide you through the process. It may seem complicated, but it is actually easy and is worth the effort. Webrings generate a significant amount of traffic.

Some sites belong to as many as six or eight rings. In cases like these, the amount of HTML code and graphics can become cumbersome for users who are not interested in webrings. To get around this, some webmasters create a special webpage for their webring graphics. Ring travelers are then invited to enter or leave the site through this page.

*Link Sites* - There are many websites on the Internet dedicated to listing every gay adult website they can find. One good example of this is Men On The Net (http://www.menonthenet.com). These link sites provide a central location for people to find websites on a variety of topics. Either way, there are numerous escort sites that can be found on these pages.

Listings on these sites are usually free, although sometimes the pages require you to run a banner or link back to their site. Sometimes you have the option to pay a small fee in return for your listing to be printed in boldface or to be featured at the top of the page. Several listings for Link Sites can be found in appendix one.

Some pages of links are topical in nature. For example, All Worlds Video features pictures of men who have appeared in their movies, along with biographical information and links to their websites. If you have appeared in one of their movies, it may be a good idea to make sure their site features a link to your page. Themed Link Sites exist for a number of other topics as well. Try searching the Web and see what you find.

*Link Exchanges* - Link exchanges are different from Link Sites. A link exchange means "I'll link to your site if you will link to mine." They may be done informally, such as links between friends, or more formally through certain banner-ad exchanges. In these programs, your site always displays a random banner ad. Other websites randomly display yours as well. These generate traffic for your site, although probably not enough to offset the downside of adding a banner ad to your site.

*Amateur Picture Galleries* - One fun way to bring additional traffic to your site is to approach any of the hundreds of amateur male picture galleries on the Web. Offer to let them use your nude pictures on their site in exchange for a link from those pictures back to your site. Many galleries will agree, resulting in additional traffic for your site.

At some point in your web career, you may find your pictures have been stolen and are being used illegally on other websites. Rather than writing nasty letters to the webmaster, one approach is to supply them with even more pictures in return for a link back to your site. He may ignore you because copyright enforcement for pornography is virtually impossible on the Web. Alternatively, acquiring a link from his page may result in new clients from the additional traffic you receive.

*Other Methods* - There are plenty of other creative ways to bring in traffic to your site. One method I use is my syndicated online sex-advice column. It is released every other week and is distributed for free to a number of websites in exchange for links back to my site. These links bring in a considerable amount of traffic to my site. Be creative with your ideas. You never know which ones may bring you valuable business.

By now you should have plenty of ideas about how to advertise yourself online. Whether you are creating a simple e-mail account and profile or are building a massive Internet empire, you will quickly start attracting potential clients. To learn how to handle their inquiries, flip the page and keep reading.

## Chapter Nine
## Handling Potential Clients

*One of the most unusual phone conversations I have ever had was with from what seemed like an intelligent person. We worked out all of the details until it was time for him to provide me with directions to his home. He said he lived not too far away from Trenton, New Jersey. Unfortunately, he was unable to direct me to his home.*

*In an effort to be helpful, I asked him which exit off the New Jersey Turnpike he lived near. He wasn't sure, so I asked him what highways he lived near. He said he didn't know that either, but did know that I would have to get on Anderson Road. I pointed out to him that he lived eighty miles away from me, and that I had no idea where Anderson Road was. He tried to be more specific, but was not able to provide even the slightest amount of help.*

*I realized I was likely to become lost no matter what we figured out, I politely informed him I would not be able to visit him. I suggested he call me back if he ever figured out where he lived. It didn't surprise me in the least when I never heard back from him.*

Talk to anyone in the retail field and they will tell you that customer service is critical to the success of any business enterprise. Escorting is no exception to this rule. If anything, it is even more important. When you receive a phone call, e-mail, or instant message from a potential client, he may be someone who is willing to spend hundreds, thousands, or even tens of thousands of dollars for your time. If you are going to attract and keep him as a client, you must provide courtesy and respect from the moment of first contact.

**Your Phone**

For most escorts, the telephone is the lifeblood of their businesses. You will depend on it to arrange almost every transaction you make. Even if you arrange most of your appointments online, there will come a day when your business requires regular access to a phone. Fortunately, cellular phones have made this convenient and easy, even for escorts who are still living at home with Mom and Dad.

If you advertise your phone number either online or in print ads, be aware that you will receive phone calls 24 hours per day. This is particularly true for escorts living in cities. Even more annoying, a good percentage of late-night callers are drunk or high. If you take calls from these clients, be aware of what you may be getting yourself into. Many of these potential clients are horny guys who struck out at the bars, but others may be looking to play mind-games or may not have any intention of paying you for your time.

Many escorts set a policy for themselves regarding how late at night they will answer the phone. Others insist that late-night calls are a critical part of their business. You may want to consider your geography when deciding how late to answer your phone. I live an hour outside of New York City, so late-night visits into the city are not practical. Escorts who live in the heart of their city's gay community may be better-situated to tap into the late-night market.

**Answering E-Mail**

Answering e-mail is much like handling the phone, with a few significant differences. It takes hours or days to exchange information online, as opposed to a several-minute phone call. You are also likely to receive e-mail from people who find it less convenient to arrange a meeting by phone. For example, many married men prefer e-mail when contacting an escort.

Always remember that e-mail lacks the emotional and tonal qualities that voice conversations have, so they are more open to misunderstanding. If you are not a good typist or are new online, be extra careful to write back notes that are perfectly clear. Otherwise you may write vague messages that are perfectly clear to you but are confusing to the reader on the other end. Properly written, e-mail should leave clients with a comfortable feeling about you rather than a sense of wariness and confusion. If you are not a good typist, you should always run a spell-checker and proofread every message before sending it.

It is worth noting that e-mail has at least one advantage over the phone, in that it leaves a record of everything that was said. This is ideal for those escorts who wish to keep notes on their clients. At the touch of a button, entire conversations can be printed or saved to disk for later retrieval. While there is no doubt that these files can come in handy, they also open up possible complications later if anyone ever obtains access to them. Accordingly, you may want to keep as few records as possible and delete e-mails after they have been read.

## Conversations by Instant Message

Conversations via instant message (IM) are a unique hybrid of telephone and e-mail. They are relatively fast, and are "safe" for nervous people who are afraid to call an escort on the phone. Their primary downside is that the messages are easily misunderstood because of the faster pace of conversation and the highly informal style of writing. Always type slowly and clearly; otherwise you will confuse the other person.

There is little to say about instant messages that the advice for phone and e-mail conversations does not cover. As always, friendliness and courtesy are key to attracting clients. Complete sentences, proper grammar, and accurate spelling are important as well. Perfection is not required, but competence is expected. If you have difficulty typing messages, you may want to ask the potential client to call you.

## Handling Potential Clients

Your advertising will affect what people need to know when they write or call you. If you run a small print ad with a brief physical description and picture, chances are your clients will know nothing more about you when they contact you. If you have a more extensive presence on the Internet, you may receive calls from people ready to set-up appointments without asking for additional information.

When someone dials you on the phone for the first time, he is likely to be fairly nervous. There is a good chance he has never hired an escort in the past and in many cases may not ever have spoken to one. Callers like this will be anxious and unsure of how to handle the situation and will want you to take charge of the conversation. Even if the caller is experienced at hiring escorts, he may want you to do most of the talking so that he can get a feel for your personality.

Right from the start, you should put potential clients at ease. I sometimes make the conversation light and humorous for nervous clients by making a joke. ("Relax! I don't bite.") It is surprising just how many people appreciate this effort. It helps the callers relax, allowing us to continue our business discussion more easily. You should also always spend a moment asking clients how they learned about your services. Such information will be invaluable when evaluating the effectiveness of your advertisements.

E-mail works in a similar fashion, except that potential clients tend to talk about themselves more. On occasion you will even receive a message with a client's entire life story. Potential clients who e-mail you are likely to be less nervous as well. They do not have to experience the stress of calling an unknown escort and can take time to compose their letter at their convenience.

However the client approaches you, there are two ways of discussing business. The first is to provide direct answers only to the questions they ask. The second is to take control of the conversation and give a small "speech" on your services. The former method is useful for callers who have specific questions they want answered, but the latter is better for potential clients who want general information on your services. All escorts use both methods at times, but most have a preference for one method or the other.

My own preference is the second method, during which I give a short presentation to phone callers about my services. Over the years, it has evolved to answer all the questions clients commonly ask. Reciting the speech thousands of times has burned it into my memory. When I finish, they usually have enough information to make a decision.

My own sales pitch is as follows:

*"Well, I'm 24, five-foot-five and 120 pounds. I'm very boyish-looking and only look about 20 or 21. I have a smooth chest, and I'm pretty well hung. I got pretty lucky in that respect.*

*"Ratewise, I charge $350 per hour. I am not a stickler for time, meaning I don't sit with a stopwatch in my hand or anything. I just ask that people don't take advantage of that in return. I can accept credit cards, and I can take incalls as well as outcalls."*

Your image or the type of services you offer will also affect how you interact with callers. Bodybuilders may want to make references to working out, and SM masters will probably take a more dominant tone with their callers.

Regardless of the approach you use, potential clients should learn the following about you:

- An accurate description of your physical appearance.
- An indication of your personality.
- Your rates and any additional charges you may have (travel fees or night calls).
- Whether you offer incall or outcall services.
- Anything else they should know.

Of course, callers may know some or all of this already. Do not be afraid to repeat it all, because potential clients often use your speaking as a way of judging whether the two of you will be a good match.

How escorts handle e-mail frequently depends on their comfort level with the medium. Most online escorts are completely comfortable and are happy to provide information, details, and digital pictures. Others write only to ask potential clients to call them on the phone. The choice of how to handle your e-mail is up to you, but providing information through e-mail does help avoid losing the more timid clients.

Incidentally, many experienced escorts have a standard reply saved to disk. They cut and paste the response into the e-mail, pausing only to edit it to tailor it to the client's specific questions. Responding this way saves a great deal of time and effort and vastly improves the efficiency of e-mailing responses. Still other escorts send back friendly replies requesting potential clients check out their website. Once a potential client has done so and is asking for more specific details, the escort answers these questions and invites the person to set-up an appointment.

Whether to discuss sex by phone or e-mail is a difficult decision for people living in areas where prostitution is illegal. Talking about what you enjoy and are sexually willing to do helps your business but also exposes you to extra legal risks. Some escorts discuss sex openly. Others claim they provide only companionship. Still others make a compromise whereby they discuss a small amount of information about sex, but only after they talk to the potential client for a while and decide that he is "on the level." This last option is popular, but is also the worst of the three. It does little to protect the escort legally and does not attract clients as much as openly discussing sex.

If I elect to discuss sex with a caller, I add the following segment to my presentation:

*"Sexually, I'm pretty flexible. I enjoy kissing, cuddling, giving and receiving oral sex, and both fucking and being fucked. I'm both a top and a bottom in that respect. I'm also available both days and evenings."*

However you decide to handle discussions about sex, you must be ready for any legal entanglements you may encounter. We will talk more about legal issues in chapter eighteen.

Sometimes a potential client will ask if you "party." This is his way of asking you if you are willing to use drugs while you work. I cannot urge you strongly enough to turn people like this down. Not only are they unpredictable and dangerous but they are also at extremely high risk for cheating you out of money. I have also heard of law enforcement "sting" operations against escorts where the question is asked. If an escort replies that he does not do drugs, he is left alone. If he answers that he does party, the escort is then targeted for legal harassment and arrest. If you use drugs in your spare time, do not trust a client you do not know with that information.

You will also have occasional requests for bareback (unprotected) anal sex. I again urge you to turn down all of these clients. Barebacking puts you at greater risk for numerous sexually transmitted diseases. Even if you are already HIV-positive, you can make your health situation much worse. Peek ahead to chapter sixteen for more information about all of the STDs you can contract.

Once you have answered all of the potential client's questions, it is up to him to decide what to do next. Most of the time, he will thank you for the information and promise to call back later. Chances are you will not hear from him again, although sometimes you will. Sometimes the caller will let you know that you are out of his price range or will attempt to negotiate a lower rate. I highly suggest that you do not negotiate. It teaches clients that escort rates are flexible and sets a bad precedent in your own business. No matter what you charge, there will always be people who are not willing to pay it. It is perfectly all right to let them slip away from you, especially as your rates become more upscale. Remember that it takes only three clients at $200 each to equal what you would have made from four at $150. If you lose that fourth person, do not worry about letting him go. Sometimes you will keep all four, in which case you are well ahead of the game.

**Setting Up Appointments**

On occasion, a client will request a meeting to decide if he wants to hire you. Often he will mention a long-term arrangement or the possibility of taking you on a trip. It is an extremely bad idea to meet these clients unless they are willing to hire you for at least an hour. While there is no doubt that occasionally they are for real, the vast majority have other agendas that are unrelated to your business. In my earlier days as an escort, I met several of these people for dinner. In one case, the person turned out to be looking for an SM slave. Another time the client was looking for a kept boy. One particularly odd person would not believe I was for real. Even when I began showing him evidence that I was indeed an escort, he argued that I was involved in some bizarre police sting operation dedicated to trapping him.

In all my years as an escort, I have never initially met someone for free who later hired me. Serious clients do not request free meetings. If they desire something more long-term or unusual, they will hire you for an hour to get to know you. If they insist on meeting you non-sexually first, request they pay you for an hour of your time but with an agreement to apply the fee to your first hour of services together. If they will not agree to this, they are not worth your time and consideration.

Sometimes a potential client calls and is immediately ready to set-up an appointment. This may be for right away or may be for days or weeks later. Always have your calendar with you, so you can set-up appointments at any time. If you do not have your schedule handy, write the information down, and be sure to get their phone number or e-mail address so you can check your calendar and call them back.

When setting up an appointment, collect the following information from the client:

- The date and time of the meeting.
- His name. (A last name is helpful for hotel calls. Many upscale hotels will not connect you to a room without the guest's name.)
- The location.
- Directions (if necessary).
- A contact phone number or e-mail address.

I cannot stress enough how important this final point is. Having contact information encourages your clients to go through with their meeting. Nervous clients may otherwise find it too tempting to stand you up because they are completely anonymous.

Some clients will not want to give you their contact information because of concerns for their privacy, but I urge you to be persistent. The chances of the appointment falling through are much higher if you do not have a way to reach them. Often your client will give you his number if you agree to call only during certain times, such as just before the appointment or when his wife is at work. Having this phone number is also useful if you are forced to cancel, reschedule, or if you have trouble with the client's directions. Contact information for business travelers is less important. As long as you know your their full names as well as the hotels they are staying in, you have a way to contact them.

Whatever you do, be extremely wary of setting up an appointment to meet a client on a street corner, in the lobby of a hotel, a parking lot, or outside someone's apartment building unless you have full contact information for him. Absolutely never meet a new client like this unless he reconfirms the appointment just before you leave for the meeting. Even with a confirmation, without contact information the chances of a client actually showing up are much lower. If you are waiting for a client in public and he is late, wait for him no longer than 15 minutes after the agreed meeting time. If he has not arrived by that point, he is almost certainly not going to show.

One partial exception to this rule involves motel appointments. Often a client wants discretion and does not want the embarrassment of renting the room. Other times he does not want to have to wait for you to arrive after he rents the room. In either of these cases, it may be a good idea to meet the client in public nearby, then proceed to the motel together. Arranging to meet someone outside a diner is a perfect way to do this. Unlike standing alone in front of a motel, waiting for someone outside a restaurant is considered a perfectly reasonable thing to do. Once you reach the motel, he can hand you the money to rent the room. Wherever you meet the client, you should still have him reconfirm with you just before the appointment.

Sometimes the client will suggest you rent the room in advance of the appointment. If you do so, there is an excellent chance you will find yourself sitting in the room waiting for a client who is not going to show up. Avoid this problem by having the client hand you the money, then wait outside while you rent the room for him.

Sometimes clients will call and request immediate appointments, rather than scheduling for a later date. If your client calls you from his hotel room, you should always politely inform him that you have a policy of calling back to verify the location and room. Stress that while no offense is intended, you have been sent to fake appointments in the past. Do not think that people do not do this, either. Even the best escorts in the business wind up at fake appointments from time-to-time. Much to my embarrassment (and anger), I was sent on one the day I began writing this chapter. Had I spent two minutes confirming the information the caller gave me, I would have saved myself over two hours of wasted time and effort, not to mention tolls, gas, lost business, and aggravation. I have no idea why people play such practical jokes, but they do. Be careful to prevent this from happening to you.

If you are arranging an incall, you should inform your client that if he is going to be more than 10 minutes early or 15 minutes late, he should call you before he arrives. This renders you blameless if you are forced to turn him away at the door. If you have pets, you should also tell clients about them. The last thing you need is someone having an allergic reaction to your cat.

One other pitfall to avoid is that on occasion a client will underpay you because he thought the session was at a lower rate or for free. In this situation, you may suddenly become less sure of yourself as you wonder if you somehow failed to confirm the rate in advance. The client may also have thought that additional hours were on your time, not his. Most of the time these are honest misunderstandings, although ones that frequently result in you being paid only partially for the encounter. To prevent them, always confirm your rate when scheduling appointments, and make a clear note on your calendar reminding you that you have done so. If a client then tries to underpay you, you will be more confident when pointing out his error and demanding full payment.

## Arranging Trips

From time-to-time, you may receive inquiries about going on trips with clients. Usually these will be from clients you already know, but sometimes they will be from new ones. Escorts vary widely in their approach to such trips. Some barely charge a fee, viewing the trip itself as sufficient compensation. Others charge extremely high rates, since it takes them away from their day-to-day activities and involves a great deal of client interaction.

Be aware from the start that the vast majority of proposed trips never come to pass. It is highly unusual for a client to simply contact an escort and offer to show him the world. Most trips will be with clients with whom you have a well-established relationship. This is not to say that your first meeting with a new client will not be on a trip; it can and does happen. Rather, be wary of people you do not know who approach you with offers that sound too good to be true. The majority of them certainly are.

In setting your own prices for trips, you will want to speak with the prospective client about his expectations. Vacations that involve a great deal of relaxation time and relatively little work may warrant a slightly lower price. If you know the client to be "high maintenance," you may want to charge him a bit more. Generally speaking, you will want to charge at least your overnight rate for every 24-hour period of the trip.

When quoting a price to a client, it is a good idea to quote a rate per 24 hours as opposed to the trip as a whole. Otherwise you risk a client flying you out early in the morning and returning you late at night, so you lose an extra day in the deal. It is customary not to charge for travel time, although for unusually long flights you may want to work out a compromise. Also, avoid quoting prices per day, as it sometimes becomes confusing just what a day is. Another good way to avoid problems is to also confirm the total amount your client will be expected to pay you.

Once the trip is set, you may want to request a deposit. Some escorts are satisfied with confirmed plane reservations and do not ask for one. Other escorts request 10-25% of the fee in advance. If you have this policy, make sure the client understands this in advance. It is highly unprofessional to surprise a client with a deposit request once the tickets have been purchased.

Escorts vary in how they handle payment for the trip. Most are willing to accept either cash or bank (certified) checks. Bank checks have an advantage over cash in that the escort does not need to carry thousands of dollars on the trip and risk having it stolen or lost. Instead, the funds are guaranteed, and you can safely deposit the check in your account when you return home.

Escorts also vary when they request to be paid during the trip, with some requiring payment at the beginning and others at the end. In cases where you are meeting a new client, it is not a bad idea to suggest during the negotiation phase that the money be paid in the middle of your time together or in installments during the trip. You may want to allow your more trusted clients to pay you at the end.

Whatever you do, be extremely careful you do not allow yourself to be conned. I know one escort whose client promised to pay him at the airport gate at the end of the trip. The client dropped the escort off at the terminal, explaining that he would meet the escort after he parked the car. Tragically, the client drove off and left the escort with nothing to show for several days of work. Do not walk into such an easy-to-avoid trap. Always make sure you have the payment before you leave for the airport.

If your client paid you earlier in the week, you should always double-check that you have it before you leave for the airport as well. I know of another escort whose $2,000 bank check disappeared between the morning he was scheduled to depart and when he returned home. After numerous failed attempts to contact the client to ask if he left the check there, he was forced to conclude the client had stolen the check out of the escort's bag while he was not looking. A quick double-check before he left for the airport could have prevented this from happening.

Before your trip, you should make your client aware of any special requirements that you have, such as access to a gym or a vegetarian or kosher diet. Most clients will be helpful about reasonable requests, although an unusual travel schedule may make special requests difficult. Although clients will pay for your basic expenses during the trip, you should not expect them to pay for any additional requirements such as fees to use the local gym.

You should also join the various frequent-flyer programs as soon as you begin taking trips. Often clients are more than happy to place you on a certain airline as long as it does not cost any more. You would be surprised how fast you can earn free upgrades and flights.

Of course, not every inquiry will result in a trip or an appointment or even be from a potential client. Many people contact escorts with other intentions in mind. Most of these are harmless, but sometimes they can seriously complicate your life. In either case, the next chapter is dedicated to sorting out the other types of people you may be hearing from.

Chapter Ten
## Sorting the Other Calls

*About four months ago, I received several e-mails from men in the Philippines who wanted to become my pen pal. At first I thought they were just friendly people who had seen my website. Later on however, I learned I was incorrect. Two escorts I knew were also receiving numerous e-mails from Filipino men.*

*After several weeks of questioning our new fans, we learned that a magazine in the Philippines had reprinted pictures from our websites without our permission. They were being run in an advertisement about attractive men from around the world wanting to hear from their readers.*

*Since that time I have received letters from more than 50 Filipino men. I have sent each one an identical letter politely explaining the situation, and letting them know that I will not be able to be their pen pal. I still feel guilty every time I send out my standard reply letter, and wish that somehow this situation could have been avoided.*

Every escort knows that not every phone call or e-mail will contribute to amassing his fortune. For every client who hires him, the escort receives several more inquiries from potential clients who do not. Most of these are people inquiring about his services, but many of them are not. They can be loosely gathered into three groups; offers and requests, useless inquiries, and nutcases. It's not a bad idea to know who they are and what they want in advance.

## The Good Ones: Offers and Requests

There are several types of inquiries that involve offers and requests. They don't come along that often, but you will receive them from time-to-time.

*Advertising Opportunities* - Escorting advertisements are an important source of revenue for print publications and are critical for websites that sell advertising space. Often one print publication will start calling escorts that advertise in another and attempt to sell them advertising space. Sometimes they may even have special offers for new advertisers.

If you are unfamiliar with the publication or how well male escort ads perform inside them, ask the salesperson to fax or send you a copy of their escort pages. Contact several of their advertisers and ask how well their ads have done.

*Researchers and Interviewers* – Periodically you will receive phone calls from people wanting to interview you. These people may be writing anything from papers for school to articles for newspapers. Whether you help them is entirely up to you, but it is frequently a good idea to provide assistance when you can. Providing accurate information about escorting helps others learn and write about the validity of careers in the sex industry.

*New Escorts* - As stated in this book, it is common for a new escort to contact established professionals when they are in need of advice or insight. Just as you may need help on occasion, sometimes people will come looking to you for assistance. You may even still perceive yourself as a novice, but to the inexperienced escort you may be a skilled veteran of the trade.

Whenever you receive a phone call or e-mail from a new escort, it is always a good idea to be as helpful as possible when answering his questions. Even a few simple words of advice may be useful and in some cases help him avoid potentially dangerous situations.

Sometimes new escorts do not understand that an independent escort's advertisements are not those of an escort agency. They may call looking for work or wondering if you can find clients for them. In cases where the caller is completely inexperienced, you may wish to refer him to an agency where he can receive additional training and education about the industry. Once he reaches a certain level of professional maturity, he can make the break and become an independent escort. Referring new escorts to how-to books on the subject (like this one!) may be an excellent idea as well. Let him know if he would be welcome to contact you again once he has read through the book and gained a greater insight into the profession.

More information on books about escorting can be found in appendix three.

*Photographers and Pornographers* - Many escorts who live in major cities, especially London, Los Angeles, San Francisco, San Diego, and New York, will periodically receive phone calls from adult magazine photographers and video directors looking for models. Some of these invitations are offers from legitimate companies and are worth serious consideration. Others are from fly-by-night operations that should most definitely be avoided. Unfortunately, it is often difficult to immediately tell one type of offer from another.

The choice of whether to accept their invitations should depend on the company they represent as well as how comfortable you are with the public exposure of being in adult films and publications. More information about the adult video and magazine industries, and how to sort the good from the bad, can be found in chapter twenty.

## The Neutral Ones: Useless Inquiries

In his book *Hustlers, Escorts & Porn Stars*, Matt Adams claims that a skilled escort can determine whether a phone call will turn into a client within a few moments. I do not agree that an escort can always tell which potential clients will become real ones, but I believe Adams was correct that you can usually tell if a call is a waste of time.

Useless inquiries are those that waste your time without intending to cause you harm. Indeed, sometimes they want to do the exact opposite and help you with your business. The end effect is the same, in that your time is wasted and real business opportunities are lost. The people who make useless inquiries come in a number of forms, several of which are limited to the online world.

*Fans* - Fans are those people who invariably crop up around any online escort or porn star. For the most part, they are simply curious. They find it fascinating that you live in a world as exotic and exciting as they imagine the sex industry to be. Somewhat timidly at first, they rapidly become comfortable asking numerous questions about what life is like for an escort. "How did you get started?" "What was your ugliest client like?" "What are you going to do when you're too old to do this?" They have a never-ending list of things they want to know, and when one tires of talking to you, invariably there are three other fans standing in line. They are fun and an ego-boost to talk to but frequently have no interest in hiring the escort for his services.

Some escorts deal with fans by deleting their messages and refusing to write back. Others begin developing websites that answer the fans' questions, so they can refer them to the Web. A few particularly resourceful escorts have learned how to turn fans into a useful commodity by developing online stores on their website that sell merchandise or by using mailing lists to help arrange appointments as the escort travels around the country. Of course, those websites and e-mailing lists only serve to make the escort more appealing. This in turn attracts more fans, which begins the cycle anew.

Unless you choose to go the route of ignoring fans by deleting their messages, you should always be respectful of their questions. The careers of professional escorts are unusual, so it is only natural for people to want to ask questions. If and when their questions begin interfering with your business, it is entirely appropriate to decline to answer them on the basis of being too busy, and then return to your own work. Alternately, those of you aspiring to be career escorts may want to generate a list of these people to start building your own e-mailing list. Fans can be a useful source of information, so it is often a bad idea to offend them.

*Timewasters* - Timewasters are much like fans, except they lack any of the good points. They like having long conversations with you, frequently hinting they are about to set-up an appointment. Unfortunately, they never get around to actually setting up this elusive meeting. Some timewasters have long conversations about hosting a party and needing you to service the guests or about helping to haze fraternity initiates. Still others are persistent about building e-mail friendships. However long you talk to them, they always want to continue the conversation whenever you make a move to end it.

Unfortunately, talking to the timewasters gives them exactly what they want: attention. Precisely why they want attention is beyond me. They may be jacking off to their fantasies, or perhaps they are lonely people seeking attention. I honestly have no idea. What I do know is that they immensely irritate most escorts.

There is not much you can do to avoid timewasters. By the time you realize what they are doing, they have probably wasted your time already. Avoiding conversations with potential clients about unrealistic sexual scenes helps, but in general all you can do is cut them short and get back to work.

*Freebie Seekers* - Escorts receive numerous offers for sex, both inside and outside of their work. Since male escorts tend to be attractive and have well-developed sexual skills, it is hardly surprising that so many men want to have sex with them. Many people will pay the hourly rate and be done with it. Others feel a need to seduce an escort for free, even if they behave obnoxiously in the process.

The offers that you receive will vary widely. Many are rather unappealing offers from men who are simply too cheap to pay. Others are callers who offer you an erotic massage or oral sex with no reciprocation necessary. Sometimes the offers even come from other escorts or bodyworkers who like your pictures and want to "exchange services."

Whether you accept these offers is entirely up to you. Many escorts turn them down because they have lovers or prefer not having sex outside of their business. Others accept because they enjoy having sex or like the ego trip. It's up to you whether to accept the offers, but remember that you will still be expected to have an erection at your next appointment.

*Suitors and Friends* - Suitors are a variation of freebie seekers. The difference is that while freebie seekers only want sex, suitors are more interested in romance. You can always accept their offers to go out if you would like, but rejections should be handled politely. Courtesy is key, because you never know when one of these people may eventually decide to hire you.

Friends are similar to suitors, except that personality is emphasized more than looks. They are more interested in befriending you and want to spend time hanging out at clubs and the like. They are often lonely and closeted people in need of someone to guide them in their coming out. As before, the choice to meet them is completely up to you. Their offers are great opportunities to make friends but can also result in awkward meetings with strange people.

*Masturbators* - Escorts frequently attract the attention of horny men because of the sexual nature of prostitution. Some of these men have no interest in hiring you but instead want to masturbate while talking with you over the phone or Internet. They often begin conversations by posing as a client, because they know that few escorts are interested in phone or cybersex. They often give away their intentions by repeatedly shifting the conversation to sex. They will ask any number of sexual questions, all designed to elicit erotic descriptions from you.

One of the best ways to handle a masturbator is to ask him if he is jacking off at that moment. Rarely will an innocent client be offended by the question, while a guilty one will often answer the question truthfully. If a person admits he is masturbating, you can then quickly get rid of him by pointing out that you are not interested in cyber- or phone sex. The vast majority of masturbators will apologize at this point, leaving only a few pathetic souls begging for you to get them off.

I do not recommend you encourage masturbators. Doing so only makes them continue bothering escorts. It is difficult enough to handle a career in which your phone rings 24 hours per day without adding more unnecessary calls.

*Non-English Speakers* - Escorts near urban areas in the United States and the United Kingdom sometimes receive calls from people who speak only a smattering of English. Often these callers will begin by asking if you speak their language. In the case where the caller is new to the country, he may have mistaken your advertisement for a personal ad in search of romance.

How escorts handle these calls varies from person to person. Some of the more impatient and rude escorts simply hang up. Others draw from their limited reserves of Spanish (or whatever language) to have as meaningful a conversation as possible. Still others indicate they do not speak the language and end the call as quickly as can be done politely. As with all inquiries, handle these calls professionally. It is never easy living in a country where you do not speak the language. Courtesy is the least these callers deserve for their efforts. Whenever possible, refer these callers to escort agencies or community organizations that may be able to help them.

**The Bad Ones: The Nutcases**

I use the word "nutcase" out of an effort to avoid the use of obscenities in this book. For reasons beyond my comprehension, some people find a perverse delight in deliberately and maliciously causing problems for escorts. These callers are extremely skilled at causing stress, aggravation, and a loss of time and money. Fortunately, they can be avoided at least part of the time through constant care and screening on your part.

*Jokers* – Some people feel an incessant need to play practical jokes on escorts. These are often annoying but harmless in nature, such as calling and pretending to be recruiting for the *Jerry Springer Show*. Other times their jokes are more malicious, such as leaving messages on the escort's answering machine asking them to call innocent people or by calling or paging other people and asking them to call the escort. Unfortunately, there is little that can be done about them. Jokers who are foolish enough to send harassing messages via e-mail can be reported to their Internet service provider, usually by forwarding the message to postmaster@domainname. (The domain name is the second part of their e-mail address, such as hotmail.com or aol.com.) Other jokers are sometimes stupid enough to allow their phone numbers to show up on caller ID. In cases like these, calling them back and asking that they cease harassing you usually startles them into obedience.

*Fake Appointments* - The behavior of some nutcases can become truly vile at times. Sometimes they will set up fake appointments, either with the intention of sending the escort to a nonexistent address or to an uninvolved person's home. Fortunately, there are a number of ways you can cut down on these types of calls:

- Always obtain a contact phone number or e-mail address from your clients.
- Verify all phone numbers before the appointment.
- Do not agree to meet unknown clients on street corners, parking lots, or outside apartment buildings. This also includes the lobby of the client's hotel unless he has also provided you with his room number.
- Require appointments set more than a week in advance to reconfirm with you within 24 hours of the appointment.

Even if you take all of these steps, be especially careful of the following types of appointments:

- New clients.
- Appointments made more than a week before the appointment.
- Clients who arrange appointments from anonymous e-mail accounts like yahoo.com and hotmail.com.
- Calls from phone numbers where your caller ID reads as "anonymous" or "unavailable."
- Appointments where the client has behaved oddly or made unusual requests.
- Late-night calls.
- Unusually low-income destinations.

For these high-risk calls, you may want to use reverse-phone directories and services to verify your destination address. Your local phone book and the Internet can provide more information on these services.

Above all, trust your instincts. If you have even the slightest suspicion that something is not right, cancel the appointment. If you find yourself the victim of a fake call, chances are that you ignored the warning signs that it was going to occur.

*Saviors and Online Stalkers* – Saviors are people who try to convince you that what you are doing is inherently self-destructive. While most will stop arguing once you cease communication, a few of the more dangerous saviors will actually go so far as to try to ruin your business "for your own good."

Online stalkers are similar, except they lack the moralizing attitude of saviors. Stalkers are often particularly annoying fans or clients who brother you until you stop speaking to them. They respond as if they have been unjustly attacked, often counterattacking with surprisingly creative forms of retribution. For example, one online stalker on the Internet was famous for registering domain names with addresses similar to those of well-established porn stars. For example, registering aaronlawrence.net to impersonate e-mail sent from aaronlawrence.com. He would then use his domain's e-mail address to write letters to porn companies and directors canceling appearances and other agreements.

Both saviors and stalkers frequently report escorts to their ISPs and in rare cases to the local police. Sometimes they attempt to learn the escort's real name so they can publicize his name on the Internet or contact the escort's family regarding his profession.

Unfortunately, there is little that can be done to avoid these people. As long as their stalking does not leave the online world, your best approach is probably to ignore them until they lose interest and move on. Under no circumstances should you attempt revenge on these people. Always remember that they are looking for a fight and that you have more to lose than they do. Those two factors make purposely angering these people a dangerous idea.

If you are concerned that you are being stalked either online or in person, talk to other escorts whom you know. Some of them may have previously dealt with the person and may have helpful suggestions.

More information on the types of problem cases that meet you in person can be found in chapter fourteen.

Of course, these nutcases take up an extremely small percentage of your time. In fact, the vast majority of attention will be focused on running your business and meeting with real clients. From grooming yourself to counting your cash, the fun part is about to begin.

## Chapter Eleven
## Meeting Clients

*It is always a good habit for escorts to always carry a small bag with condoms and lube.* I used to go a little overboard with this, and carried a large black bag with several dildos, cockrings, adult videos, massage oils, and leather toys. Always in the spirit of being prepared, my bag also contained a toothbrush, toothpaste, mouthwash, clean towels, an extra pair of underwear, and anything else I thought might come in handy.

During one late-night appointment, a client and I had sex in the staff lounge of his company. Driving home after the appointment, I suddenly realized I had forgotten my bag on the office lunch table. Knowing he was married and not having his home number in any case, I left a message on his office voicemail letting him know of my error. Needless to say, he did not arrive in time to retrieve my bag. Whose bag that was became the mystery around the office the next day.

Thankfully the mystery was never solved, and no one ever figured out that my client was involved. It still gives me giggles though to think of everyone sorting through my bag in shocked amazement.

A successful meeting is one in which you charm the client, meet his needs, and make him feel desired and appreciated while giving him a great sexual experience. Learn this lesson well, because there are virtually no exceptions. This rule holds true for all occasions, regardless of your type and image. All escorts, whether upscale callboys, SM masters, or boytoys, need to know how to treat their clients properly. Precisely how you make a client feel desired and appreciated may vary, but the measure of success is still the same.

Bringing about this level of service is definitely not easy. A successful meeting is not nearly as simple as showing up and getting off. A high-quality escort makes a number of preparations before each appointment. Overlooking these steps is not always bad, but constantly maintaining high standards of service inevitably pays off in the long run.

**Your Appearance**

Your clients are extremely interested in your appearance. After all, clients hire escorts at least partially for their looks. Since they are paying for your time, it is important to look your best. Much of their first impression will also be based on your appearance. It is therefore extremely important for an escort to spend an extra few minutes getting ready for a client.

For starters, take a good look at yourself in the mirror. Do you advertise yourself accurately, or are you using outdated pictures? If you do not appear as advertised, you had better spare no expense in making yourself as attractive as possible. If your body is not as toned as it should be, or those love-handles have begun to show, you will want to improve yourself as soon as possible.

It may seem obvious, but getting ready for an appointment starts with taking a shower. Unless your client is one of those rare clients who likes his escorts a bit more "natural," make sure you wash and bathe thoroughly. Pay special attention to washing your butt, as this is one of the least hygienic parts of the body and can easily turn off a client. A good habit is to slide a soapy finger inside your anus to clean more thoroughly. It may be gross to bring this up, but it will make anal sex and rimming far more pleasant.

Some escorts will give themselves an enema before they work. While the advantage is that it makes things cleaner, the downside is that it irritates the rectum and increases the likelihood that HIV can be transmitted. Whether to use enemas is a personal decision, but you should be aware of the risks. You should also know that improper use of enemas or long-term overuse can cause medical problems, so be careful to follow the instructions carefully.

You may also want to spend a few minutes brushing your teeth. As with enemas, brushing your teeth slightly increases the chance of transmitting or contracting HIV. Escorts who want to play safely or who have HIV may want to rinse with mouthwash instead.

Do not forget to use deodorant as well, although if you are going to see a client who licks your armpits, you may want to skip it. You will want to avoid using cologne as well. Many clients do not like the scent, and cologne leaves a foul taste wherever you apply it. Some clients are even allergic to scents. Preppie escorts who feel it is a necessary part of their image should apply it only in small amounts.

Unless facial hair is part of your look, you should also make sure your face is freshly shaved. If your image is one that is boyish or youthful in nature, you should be especially careful about this. Nothing makes a young man look older than two-day old scruff. If you shave anywhere else on your body, you may want to touch up there as well.

You will also want to trim your body hair every week or two. Many escorts like to shave their balls and their ass. Some keep their chest and pubic hair short and trimmed. It is a good idea to trim these areas periodically, because unkempt body hair is a turn-off for many people. A good rule of thumb is to keep your chest and pubic hair between half an inch and an inch long.

When picking out your clothes to wear, take into account the location of the appointment. Incalls allow you to dress more casually, but outcalls to upscale hotels generally require you to be dressed better than usual. In either case, you should also make a point of wearing clothing that goes with your image. Jocks may want to wear a jockstrap, bodybuilders may wear obvious workout clothes, and masters should be clad in leather. Who you are seeing will obviously play a role as well, in that you may wish to wear an outfit that is likely to arouse your client.

You should also avoid wearing jewelry. Piercings may be acceptable depending on your look. Rings, anklets, watches, and neck chains should be removed prior to the appointment. Not only does it avoid the risk of having your valuables stolen, it keeps them from getting in the way during sex. Watches are useful for keeping track of time, but they are distracting and can scratch your partner. We will cover later in the chapter how to keep track of the time without a watch.

If you have two appointments scheduled that require you to wear different outfits, it is not necessary to compromise between the two. Simply bring along the second outfit and switch into it after the first meeting. Surprisingly few clients will ask why you are putting on different clothes. If they do, you can either tell them the truth or claim that you are going out with friends.

Escorts who travel to their clients by car may want to take advantage of another suggestion. Keep an extra set of work clothes in your car. This comes in handy when you receive requests to work at unexpected times and you are not dressed appropriately. You may be surprised how often this happens.

I have one more tip that may come in handy. On days you may be working or when a client takes you out to dinner, avoid eating onions and garlic. It makes your breath smell bad. A scampi lover myself, I learned this one the hard way.

**Preparing for Incalls**

Just as you have to prepare yourself for a meeting, escorts who offer incalls need to prepare their homes as well. Your location should be relatively picked-up and clean, and the bed should be neatly made. Special care should also be taken to make sure the bathrooms are clean, as nothing turns off a client faster than a moldy shower curtain. You will want to make sure there is a clock in your incall location as well. It does not need to be big and obvious. Even something as simple as a VCR clock may do. This will help you keep track of the time during your sessions.

Leaving out a few pieces of carefully selected clothing may be good for your image. If you escort as a wrestler, you may want to leave your wrestling uniform laying out. Likewise, clients who enjoy muscle-worship may enjoy seeing a jockstrap laying around a bodybuilder's weight room. Use your imagination here – it is not difficult to impress an already-aroused client.

Some escorts may want to leave out gay magazines for clients to examine. These may be news or social magazines, such as the *Advocate* or your local gay newspaper. These may also be adult in nature, in which case almost any porn magazine will do. Leaving out a few adult videos (in their boxes) is a good idea because many clients enjoy watching porn. If a client requests to watch a video, by all means put it on. It is easy to please a client engrossed in watching a video and will give him a better experience as well.

The vast majority of the time, it is not a good idea for escorts to work when anyone else is home. A few escorts with particularly large apartments or houses might be able to get around this, but in most cases the other occupant should quietly disappear as long as the client is present.

Unless you are expecting someone for a threeway, you should not admit anyone into your home when a client is present. It is also extremely unprofessional to interrupt a meeting to speak to anyone at the door. Finally, phones and pagers should be turned off if at all possible. Those who are left on should not be answered unless your client specifically requests you to do so.

The Male Escort's Handbook

## Your Bag of Tricks

Escorts who do outcalls usually carry a bag with them. This may be a knapsack or a small "fanny pack" worn about the waist. Whatever it looks like, you should have one to carry essential supplies. Your bag should contain:

*Condoms* - Every escort except those who provide only massage and masturbation services should carry condoms. If your client says he already has them, bring them anyway. You never know when a client may forget or when you will be seeing a second client the same day. Recommended types of condoms are covered in chapter seventeen.

*Lubricant* - Just as condoms are critical, so is the lubricant necessary to use them. There is a wide variety of good lubricants on the market, including I-D, Wet, ForePlay, K-Y, and Astroglide. Some of these lubes are better for anal sex, and others are more useful for masturbation. You may have your own preferences, or you are welcome to pick mine (Wet for masturbation, ForePlay for anal sex). Whatever you do, be sure to use the right type of lubricant with your condoms. Latex condoms require water-based lubricants, but polyurethane condoms can be used with oil-based ones. Whatever lubricants you use, they should not contain nonoxynol-9. (Nonoxynol-9 makes it easier to transmit HIV. We'll come back to that in chapter 17.)

*Massage Oils* - These are critical for bodyworkers and those who routinely provide massages but are much less important for other types of escorts. Numerous oils with a wide variety of scents are available on the market. Bodyworkers will always want to have at least one non-scented oil for those who are allergic to scents and perfumes.

*Sex Toys* - Lots of clients enjoy sex toys. These include dildos, butt plugs, vibrators, cockrings, tit clamps, ball stretchers, restraints, paddles, whips, and slings. Many escorts bring along a solitary cockring or dildo, but others carry enough for a small dungeon. Precisely what you bring along will vary depending on how your business evolves, but it is fair to say that the more exotic your services are, the more likely you are to need a wide variety of toys.

If you have a limited knowledge of sex toys, drop into any good sex shop or leather store. Their staff should be able to give you descriptions about how most toys work. Do not worry if you do not find all of the toys appealing. Unless you are providing heavy SM services, you will not need them all in your "toy collection."

*Videos* - A few escorts routinely bring along adult videos. If you have appeared in videos, it is not a bad idea to bring along a copy of one of them. You never know when your client may offer to buy it from you. Selling tapes is an easy way to bring in additional income.

*Toothbrush and Toothpaste* - Most escorts overlook this one, but it is a good idea to bring them along with you. Especially in cases where you are spending the night or going out to dinner, it is a good idea to make sure your mouth is clean. Smokers should be especially aware of this one, as many non-smokers strongly dislike kissing people who use tobacco. A small bottle of mouthwash in your bag may come in handy as well.

*Underwear* - Just as women carry a spare pair of panty hose in their purse, it is an excellent idea to carry a spare pair of underwear in your bag. You never know when one will come in handy (we all have bad days "down there"), and there is no substitute for an extra pair.

## Meeting Clients

Now that you are dressed, your bag is packed, and your meeting is verified, it is time for your appointment. If the directions seem particularly complicated and you have easy access to the Internet, you may want to check the directions with a website like MapQuest (http://www.mapquest.com). Your only other task before you leave is to write a note, leave an answering machine message, or tell a friend all of the contact information you have on the client. Just in case something goes wrong and you do not return, it will be invaluable in tracking down whatever happened to you.

Give yourself plenty of time to get to your destination. Being late is one of the most common ways escorts irritate their clients and should be avoided if at all possible. If you find yourself running late, call the client and let him know you are on your way. To an anxious and nervous client, every minute you are late seems like ten. It is also the courteous thing to do and will be greatly appreciated.

Before you walk in the door, glance at your cell phone or pager to see when you arrived, then make sure you turn them off to avoid distractions during your appointment. You should also look at your reflection in a mirror or window if possible and give yourself one last once-over. Be sure also to get over any bad mood you may be feeling, because from here on you are expected to be cheerful and professional at all times.

Inside the appointment location, you will want to take a look around for signs of trouble. Your client may actually be a gaybasher who has friends waiting for you, or there may be hidden police officers in the bathroom. You should check the door between hotel rooms as well; an unlocked door is a sign there may be police officers in the next room. Problems of this sort are rare but may happen when you least expect it. In any case, do not be too obvious when looking around; your examinations should be done discreetly.

In the event someone else is there, you should immediately demand an explanation of who the person is and why he is there. If you are even remotely concerned about the situation, you should immediately leave. It is not worth risking your safety over the encounter.

You should be smiling, friendly, and generally at ease. Many clients who are new to hiring escorts are extremely nervous at this stage. A few kind words can go a long way towards relaxing them. As you talk, your clients will ask a number of questions about you. Refusing to answer them is considered rude, so if you are not interested in answering a question, give a brief answer and change the subject. It is not difficult to change the subject politely without making a client feel as if he transgressed into your personal life.

On rare occasions the client may indicate you are not what he is looking for. Every escort is turned away on occasion, and it happens to the best of us. You should not take it personally, as it is impossible for every client to find you attractive. If you have advertised your appearance honestly and fairly, then you should request and expect a small fee for your time. In general, you should expect 15-20% of your fee. Exactly what percentage will be paid depends on how well the client likes your attitude, on your travel expenses, on the time of day, and the like. If you have blatantly advertised yourself in a false manner, you should expect to be paid nothing. (What were you expecting, anyway?)

On the subject of money, whether to require payment in advance is a subject of much debate in the escort community. With the exception of escorts who work for agencies, only hustlers, rookies, and less trusting escorts always require the money upfront. Most other escorts prefer being paid after the encounter. Doing so strengthens your position if the client turns out to be an undercover police officer (see chapter eighteen for an explanation why this is the case). Some experienced clients are sensitive to this issue and leave the money out in-plain-view during the encounter. This lets the escort know he will be paid and to avoid any fears of arrest beforehand.

Of course, not every client uses this technique. Sometimes the client will offer to pay the escort in advance or even just hand him a wad of money. In this case, it is a good idea to suggest he pay you later or ask him to set the money down on a nearby table or shelf. Avoiding the topic of money helps in countries where prostitution is illegal. Being paid after the encounter also encourages clients to leave a bigger tip. It is rare that a client tips an escort at the beginning of the meeting.

The downside of being paid later is that on occasion a client will not pay some or all of the money. Experienced escorts know in the long run that tips are greater than the losses to cheaters, so this is not as bad as it seems. There are exceptions. You should request the money in advance if the client:

- Appears to be drunk or high.
- Meets you in an unusually low-income area.
- Entertains you in his home, and his home is unusually cluttered and disorganized.
- Attempts to renegotiate the money when you arrive
- Has a history of underpaying you.
- Is otherwise downscale or not someone you would normally allow among your clientele.

The suggestions work. On at least one occasion, I have saved myself the trouble of being taken advantage of when a client admitted he didn't have the money. Several other times, I ignored the warning signs and lost out.

Once any initial money issues are out of the way, the client will frequently offer you something to drink. Many escorts will refuse these offers, because on rare occasions clients have been known to lace an escort's drink with narcotics. This is highly unlikely to happen to you, but it is still a slight risk. You are welcome to accept their offer of something to drink, but be careful not to drink too much alcohol. It is an easy mistake to become intoxicated with a client. Like any other job, you need to be sober to excel.

Escorts who smoke may be tempted to pull out a cigarette and light up. It is strongly advisable not to pull out your cigarettes unless the client lights one first. Many non-smokers allow smoking in their home, but they often dislike it anyway. If the visit is a particularly long one and you are staying with a non-smoker, you should inquire if there is a balcony or porch you may use. Once you do smoke, you may want to brush your teeth again. The time you use to smoke should not be put towards the length of the appointment unless the client is smoking as well.

Before the encounter begins getting sexual, you may also want to use the bathroom. This provides an excellent opportunity for you to make sure there is no one hidden there. Access to the bathroom is also useful if you need to clean yourself "down there" again. Try not to take too long in the bathroom; otherwise some clients may think you are getting high. Excursions to the bathroom have another hidden benefit. They allow you to look for a clock to check the time again. Knowing the exact time will give you a much better idea how to pace the encounter.

Occasionally you may arrive at the appointment sweaty or in need of a shower. In cases like these, it is a good idea to request a shower as soon as you arrive. If you need to take a shower when you arrive, let the client know that it will be done on your time, not his. If the appointment is in a motel or with a new client, it is a good idea to discreetly bring your valuables into the bathroom with you. You would hate to emerge to find yourself robbed.

Once you have relaxed the client and are ready to begin the fun, you will want the conversation to ease into the foreplay. Precisely how you do this will depend on your image, your services, your personality, and the particulars of the meeting. It will also depend on the client's experience with sex and escorting. The less experience he has, the slower and more gentle you will need to be.

As foreplay begins, you will begin removing your clothes. It is always a good idea to leave all your valuables in your shoes. This will prevent you from forgetting any of them later. As foreplay goes on, you will begin having sex and eventually will transition into afterglow. Foreplay, sex, and afterglow are covered in more detail in chapter thirteen.

Once the sex and afterglow are over, you should take a shower. Besides giving a chance to wash the lube off yourself, soap and water help prevent you from contracting certain STDs. It is also a good idea because you may have another call later on, even if you do not currently have one scheduled. For whatever reason taking a shower together is a good way to talk to your client for a while longer and get to know each other better.

Eventually it will be time to get dressed. Your client will usually pay you at this time. One technique used to earn a bigger tip is to be extremely affectionate and attentive as he counts the money. If he guesses you are after a bigger tip, make a joke out of it to distract him. A bit of humor is a good way to lighten the moment. Just make sure he does not believe that you are being affectionate for monetary reasons, or he will likely feel used and offended.

Many escorts do not count the money, although you may want to do so if there have been any problems during your session. Some clients consider it mildly insulting if you count the money, but others prefer you to do so to prevent any misunderstandings later.

If there is a financial disagreement, resolve it while you are still with the client. You should also make sure new clients pay you for the entire time. This may require an awkward conversation if the client has gone longer than he initially requested because he believed you were not charging him for any extra time. However you resolve the issue, it is important to always leave the meeting with the client understanding how business is to be conducted in the future. If you allow a bad precedent to be set, he will almost certainly continue to underpay you in the future.

Once he pays you the money, the meeting is over. Make sure you gather your belongings and take them with you when you leave. If the call is an incall, you will want to clean the sheets and towels you used. Be sure to use bleach (and a good stain remover if necessary) when you wash them for next time.

When you return home or your client leaves, you should update your financial records. If you let them slide for more than a day or two, you will find it difficult to remember important details. If you keep notes or records on your clients, you will want to update them at that time as well.

## A Few Notes on Time

When setting up an hour-long appointment, it is a good idea to expect to be there for an additional ten or fifteen minutes of non-sex time. The extra time is useful to relax an unusually nervous client or to take a long shower together at the end. If you find yourself using the bathroom for an extended period, such as after you engage in anal sex, you may not want to charge him for the time you are "indisposed." Escorts who charge upscale rates will want to be even more flexible about giving free non-sex time, but those who charge lower rates are justifiably more strict in their limits. Since clients frequently enjoy getting to know the escort, granting non-sex time is an excellent way to provide higher levels of service while increasing client loyalty.

Agencies may have their own rules about time. Agency escorts may be required to call in and officially start the clock once they arrive. In cases like these, it is not always a bad idea to spend a few minutes of non-sex time chatting with your client before you call in. You do not want to violate agency rules, but you also do not want to treat your client like a walking bank account. In cases where the agency is strict about time limits, you may want to apologize for the agency's rule. Hopefully the client will then view the annoying time limits as the agency's fault rather than viewing it as unprofessional behavior on your part.

Once the non-sex time comes to an end and the two of you are ready to start playing together, you should discreetly glance for a nearby clock. If no clock is available, hopefully you can determine the approximate time from what you read on your cell phone or pager before you arrived. Keep in mind that any clock you see inside the appointment location may be displaying the incorrect time. Some clients deliberately set their clocks early to help them wake up in the morning. A few sneaky clients even set their clocks back by ten minutes in the hopes of extending the appointment for free.

During the encounter, you will want to keep an eye on the time. You do not want to do this obviously, as it distracts the client and makes him think you are a "clock-watcher" who is interested only in getting paid and getting out. Escorting is much about illusion at times, and you must provide the feeling that you genuinely want to be there. If there is no clock in sight, you may be able to determine the time from commercial breaks on the television or by how long a porn video has been playing. If you are at a loss as to what time it is, ask during a downtime in the sex. Be careful about how you do that, because, again, it will make you appear like a clock-watcher. Generally speaking, if you need to ask the time during a one-hour appointment, the time is probably near an end.

If you are entertaining on an incall basis, occasionally you may run into trouble if appointments become dangerously close to overlapping. In a case like this, it is entirely appropriate for you to inform your client that you are expecting another guest. Whatever you do, make sure your clients do not meet each other. As awkward as it is for the client who is leaving, it is even worse for the client who is arriving.

From time-to-time, you will realize a one-hour meeting is going over the hour limit. If this happens, you may want to stop and discuss the matter with the client. It may offend some clients and may interrupt the mood, so care should be made to address the issue delicately. I suggest asking the client if he is aware that you are proceeding beyond the agreed meeting length. He will bring up any concerns that he has about money. This is much more polite then bluntly informing the client that his time is up and that you have to leave. Some escorts prefer not to bring the topic up in the hope that the client will pay for the entire time, but this can be risky. Once in a while, a client will underpay you, explaining he thought the extra time was for free.

If you are forced to cut short an appointment because of time, you should endeavor to do so in as professional a manner as possible. You may wish to give your client an orgasm, even if it means staying an extra five minutes. Doing so will end the encounter on a lighter note than simply leaving in the middle of the action.

One more thought on time. A few of your clients can be cunning when it comes to getting free time and services out of you. They will often be just as aware of the time as you are and will use it to their advantage by making requests at certain times. For example, five minutes before the encounter comes to an end, they may suddenly request that you top them. They know you won't be able to do this, finish, clean off, and get dressed in the remaining time. Fortunately, most clients are not like this, and similar requests are entirely coincidental. How flexible you will want to be with their requests will depend on your rates and your own style of business. The less you charge for your services, the more appropriate it is for you to be strict about your time limits.

**Trips**

When traveling, always carry spare money with you, both hidden on your person and in your luggage. If you are robbed or separated from your client, you will need immediate access to money. Having a calling card is also useful in this situation. Just make sure you have the proper access number if you are traveling abroad.

If you are traveling with someone for the first time, take extra care to watch out for yourself. I know an escort whose client unexpectedly abandoned him in the middle of a strange neighborhood outside Rome. Always make sure you have a back-up plan in the event your client pulls a stunt like this.

## Client Records

Although most escorts elect not to keep records of their clients in an attempt to prevent legal entanglements, a number of escorts like having client information at their fingertips. Sometimes these record systems are basic, such as the client's name, phone number, address, rate, directions to his home, and perhaps a few notes on his likes and dislikes. Other escorts keep entire histories of their clients, including appointment dates, activities they have done together, and a host of other personal information.

If you have a detailed record system, do not let your clients know about it. They have a legitimate concern for privacy. Detailed record systems should be kept absolutely confidential and in encrypted files whenever possible.

## When Things Go Wrong

On occasion you may find yourself in a bad situation. You may have a client who is drunk and cheats you out of money, or you may have a client who becomes extremely aggressive. Whatever the reason, your first priority is to get yourself safely out of the situation. Being paid money that is owed to you is a far distant second. No matter how upset you are or how unfair the client is being, it is not worth risking your safety for a few hundred dollars. Do not lash out at your client, vandalize his home, steal his possessions, or threaten him. Always remember that you stand to lose much more than he does, and a phone call to the police may land you both in trouble. There are also mentally unstable clients out there, and you never know when you are dealing with one. Get out of the situation and be glad you made it out alive. Not all escorts do.

If you recall the beginning of the chapter, you will remember it said a successful meeting is one in which you charm the client, meet his needs, and make him feel desired and appreciated while giving him a great sexual experience. Before we reach the fun part about sex, it is not a bad idea to take a good look at exactly who our clients are. That is what the next chapter is all about.

## Chapter Twelve
## Types of Clients

*Some time ago I found myself in bed with a young man named Daniel. He had a beautiful smile, a gentle touch, and a warm radiance about him that made having sex feel like making love. I was infatuated with him, and was so glad we were together.*

*Once the sex ended and the afterglow faded, it was time to clean up. We showered together and put our clothes back on. When the proper moment came, I opened my wallet and paid him for his time. Kissing him goodbye in the doorway, I handed him a nice tip. Being a client for once had been a wonderful experience, and worth every penny I spent.*

Just as there is no standard escort, there is also no typical client. Clients fall into a wide variety of shapes, sizes, and personalities and cross every racial, ethnic, and religious boundary. In fact, clients are even more varied than escorts. At the very least, escorts need to be attractive and able to meet the desires of others. Clients have no such limitations – they need only to be able to pay.

Clients also vary greatly when it comes to what they want from an escort. They want sex, of course, but the vast majority want more. They want their escort to be a friend, teacher, lover, therapist, and sometimes a confessor. In many cases, sex is only an excuse that clients use to have their other needs met. The skilled escort is able to identify and meet these needs, ideally before the client knows they even exist.

Of course, it is impossible to categorize every possible client you will encounter in your work. There are simply too many unique personalities and needs. Having said that, it is not all that difficult to identify a few basic types of clients and the needs common to their groups.

## Inexperienced Clients

*Some time ago, a 25-year-old graduate student saved up enough money to hire me for the night. He was a complete virgin with men and wanted his first experience to be with someone who could teach him all about male-male lovemaking. The entire night was spent entwined together, experiencing every common act of sexuality two men can perform together. He wrote me an e-mail two years later to let me know he was doing well and that he was now living an openly gay lifestyle.*

A number of clients hire escorts to teach them about gay sexuality. They range from the stereotypical young virgin all the way up to men coming out in their fifties and sixties. They vary in what they want to experience. Some have a desire to experience everything men can do together; others are more cautious in what they are willing to try. Many men even hire escorts to help them hone their skills at a specific act, such as being a bottom or giving oral sex. On occasion you will even find someone who considers himself sexually unskilled but is actually very good and simply needs a boost of self-confidence.

When working for inexperienced clients, it is important for the escort to take things slowly and let the client feel that he is in control of the situation. This is true even when the escort is "playing teacher" and leading during the encounter. The inexperienced partner needs to feel comfortable enough to request a new activity or stop one he is not enjoying. Every escort has his own way of making clients feel this way. One of mine is to smile and erotically inform an inexperienced client, "There is one rule of escort etiquette you need to know. You are welcome to try anything, touch anywhere, or have me do to you whatever you would like..." This helps set a supportive atmosphere where the client feels welcome to set the "agenda" if he wants to. It may seem obvious he would already know this, but remember that inexperienced clients may be overwhelmed with the situation.

If control is important for traditional forms of sexuality, it is even more so for inexperienced slaves hiring SM masters. Many inexperienced slaves have elaborate fantasies but have no idea how they feel in reality. Being fisted while bound and gagged in a sling may seem like a hot idea to the novice, but when presented with reality it may suddenly become much less fun. The use of "safe words" (code words or body movements that signal he is to be immediately released) is an excellent way to give clients a way out if they reach their limits.

Relaxation is another important issue for clients. Chances are that an inexperienced client will be extremely nervous and will need to talk before he begins anything serious. Some escorts are less than polite on this point, adopting strict time controls and starting the clock the instant the client walks in the door. A large portion of the appointment will be over by the time he is ready to begin exploring his sexuality. This leaves him with more of a cheap quickie than a true experience. Fortunately, most escorts (and certainly the more successful ones) are a bit more flexible about the time it takes the client to relax.

Inexperienced clients often bring needs to the encounter of which they may not be even aware. For example, they often have limited knowledge of how sex works and what is safe. Additionally, the escort will need to give constant reassurance that the client is learning to be a skilled lover in bed. Inexperienced clients are usually insecure about their sexual skills, especially concerning oral sex. Praising them for their skills will go a long way towards boosting their self-confidence. Many inexperienced clients may also be confused about their sexuality in general, so providing an opportunity to talk freely about their feelings may be a major milestone in their coming-out.

Those of you who read my first book, *Suburban Hustler,* will remember a story about a 19-year-old who hired me for his first same-sex experience. He left the encounter feeling anxious and confused about his feelings, and I never expected to hear from him again. Almost three years after our meeting, he dropped me an e-mail. It seems that while I had moved on from our encounter, he had grown to the point where he wanted to try it again. The moral of the story is that meetings with inexperienced clients are important in their lives. You may rarely think about them later, but they will be certainly thinking of you.

**Married Clients**

*Three years ago, I spent the night with a client in Connecticut. During the time between sex and sleep, he cuddled next to me and began talking about his life as a married gay man. "I really need to come out," I remember him saying, "but I don't want to hurt my wife." For better or for worse, he eventually did come out when his wife learned of his affair with another man. The marriage ended in divorce, and he later wrote me to say he was living with a male lover.*

Not every escort has a married man for his first client, but all have one within their first few encounters. They are so common that it would be virtually impossible to run an escort business without them.

Besides sex, the single most important service escorts provide married clients is discretion. Married men are almost always extremely concerned about what would happen if their families learned of their sexuality. In some cases, this would be a simple argument, but in others it may result in divorce and breakup of the entire family.

Besides discretion, married men need a great deal of convenience. A lack of free time is almost always a factor for married men, and those with small children have even less flexibility. Many married men simply do not have the ability to search for potential partners in bars, adult bookstores, or online. Being able to call to schedule an appointment may be their only option.

Location is an issue for married clients as well. Some married men have the ability to play on business trips, but others rarely travel with anyone but their families. Even if their wives work, many prefer meeting escorts outside the home. Escorts who offer incall services are the perfect solution to this issue, although not the only one. Occasionally married men suggest other options, such as having sex in their offices or cars. Flexibility in meeting your clients' needs is always important, but should not be without limits. As British actor Hugh Grant learned, having sex in a car is a great way to be arrested.

Beyond discretion and convenience, married men often need the simple luxury of a person they can talk to. Being married and in the closet often makes men lonely for someone they can speak with openly and honestly about their sexuality. Serving as an informal counselor and friend means a great deal to these clients, which makes them more loyal to you in turn.

Incidentally, you may remember back in chapter two that the quiz discouraged escorting for anyone whose ethics would not allow him to entertain married men. In spite of this, it is not necessary to give up your ethics about marriage entirely. I have turned down more than one married client because I did not like the way he was treating his wife. For example, one client wanted to see me while his wife was in the hospital for kidney dialysis treatment. Whether or not to take on a client in this kind of a situation is a personal decision, but I could not bring myself to accept so I politely turned him down.

## Young Clients

*It was 11:30 PM, and I was parked half-a-mile from his house on a dark street corner. I wondered if he was going to show up or whether it was a trap by young gaybashers. A few moments later I had my answer. A figure walked up to the passenger side of my car and lightly knocked on the window. I unlocked the door and watched a stunningly gorgeous guy sit down. In bed together an hour later, I asked him why an 18-year-old captain of his high school track team wanted to hire an escort. "I was feeling horny and didn't have anyone to get together with," he explained with a twinkle in his eye. "And besides, it's a school night..."*

Young clients are without a doubt among the most rare and enjoyable clients you will ever meet. Besides the fact they are often very attractive, they have an almost intoxicating sexual energy about them that demands constant attention. They are horny, eager to learn, and often able to bend into the most remarkable positions.

Humor aside, when being hired by a young client, always remember one simple lesson: young clients want sex, and they want it NOW. Like inexperienced clients, they may often need a bit of relaxing, but their hormones rapidly overcome their fears and launch them into action.

I have known clients as young as 16-years-old who have hired escorts and a few other escorts who claimed to have been hired by people even younger. Regardless of your willingness to play with younger guys, you should be extremely wary of the age-of-consent laws in your state or country. Being caught with someone underage is bad enough, but being an escort you would legally fare even worse. I recommend you become familiar with and abide by age-of-consent laws where you live. An excellent website that tracks these laws is Age of Consent (http://www.ageofconsent.com). It should also be noted that in the United States, age-of-consent laws for any arrangement made over state or international lines require that both people be at least 18 years of age.

Assuming the client is of legal age, you are likely to be in for a great deal of fast-paced and exhausting sex. He will likely be able to recharge quickly and can perform multiple times in a single session. If you attempt to match him orgasm for orgasm, you may find yourself quickly exhausted. It is not a bad idea to make the young client's pleasure the center of attention, thus saving the escort's orgasm for later in the encounter.

The key to meeting the needs of a young client is to remember that he may be fragile emotionally. Young clients easily become attached to their sexual partners, so they need extra assistance in keeping an escort-client relationship in its proper perspective. It is a good idea to charge a young client, even if you are tempted to do it for free. Charging a young client means he will remember the encounter as one in which he hired an escort. Having sex for free completely removes the business aspect from the relationship.

Of course, that does not mean you should not reduce the price for a younger client if you want to. Some escorts halve their rates for clients in college. Others become extremely flexible with the time once they are hired. Others simply ask clients under 21 to pay whatever they feel they can afford. Regardless of your approach, always keep in mind that a young client does not have much money. It is important to make money, of course, but the object is not to bankrupt young men.

**Older Clients**

*His name was George, and at 78 years of age he was my oldest client. I learned from him that being an "old man" was a mental state, not a physical one. Minutes into our first meeting, he indicated he wanted to top me, an act which obviously would not be a problem for him. Jutting forth from him was a surprisingly powerful erection. As we lay in bed together later, I commented on his youthful virility. He beamed as he thanked me, exclaiming "And I'm not even on Viagra!"*

As a group, older clients are far more relaxed, patient, and mature in their thoughts. Whereas young guys want to cram as much sex as they can into a single meeting, older clients often value the foreplay and the afterglow as much or more than the sex itself. Young clients are also very "spur of the moment" when hiring an escort. Older men are content to shop around and consider the issue, often for months at a time. Finally, younger clients are likely to hire an escort only on rare occasions, but older clients can become loyal clients because of their more stable financial situation.

When working for older men, it is important to keep in mind that they have their own specific needs. One of the largest and most significant is to feel reassured that they are still sexual beings. It is not hard to reassure them – a few well-timed moans can do wonders. Even more importantly, older clients want to be treated with dignity and respect. By the time men are in their sixties and seventies they understand they are not going to be asked to model for the cover of *Honcho* or *Freshmen*. In spite of this, they want to feel attractive and do not want to be treated like an "old troll." Treat them with respect and they will be loyal to you in return.

You will find that a certain number of your older clients are on medications or have had operations that affect their ability to maintain an erection. Clients like these need constant reassurance that they can still be sexual in spite of their situation. I often stress with these clients that sex is not only about having an erection or an orgasm. They genuinely want to feel sexual (who doesn't?), so it is not hard to help them maintain their confidence. However you handle the matter, keep in mind they are sensitive to these issues and require both patience and understanding.

## Collectors

*Thomas was one of the first clients to ever hire me. He seemed eager to set-up an appointment as soon as we began talking. The appointment was relatively easy but was notable because of how much he enjoyed talking about his experiences with other escorts. A few questions quickly determined that he had been with numerous escorts and that he had a virtual encyclopedia of knowledge about almost everyone who had worked in my area over the past several years.*

Many clients enjoy building long-term relationships with their favorite escorts, but some clients prefer just the opposite. These "collectors" enjoy meeting as many different escorts as possible and hiring them each for one or two sessions. They have little interest in building any long-term sexual relationships, although they may be more than happy to carry on friendships outside of the appointments.

Many new escorts will quickly find themselves being hired by several of these collectors. Some will be obvious, in that they enjoy discussing their meetings with other professionals. Others will keep their hobby to themselves and will be difficult to identify. In either case, they are generally friendly, easy to please, and are a great way for new escorts to gain experience.

If you find yourself hired by a collector, you should take advantage of the opportunity to learn everything you can about the escort scene in your area. From pricing strategies to the quality of your competition, collectors will be veritable fountains of knowledge on a wide variety of escorting issues. If a collector is willing to develop a friendship, it may be a good idea to ask for his business card or e-mail address. They make great contacts for additional information about the escort scene in your area.

## Overweight Clients

*I was a bit surprised when he opened the door. He had to be at least 350 pounds and was probably over 400. Definitely a "big boy" in my book, he was one of the largest clients I had ever met. He did have smooth skin, and I enjoyed spending the evening cuddling in his soft arms. It would have been impossible for me to put my arms around him, so I rested on my side and ran my free hand up and down his body. He enjoyed my touch and was greatly appreciative of my attentions - so much so that he tipped me an extra hundred dollars at the end of the evening.*

As an escort, you will meet many overweight men through your work. Many choose to hire escorts because they are tired of dealing with the constant attitude encountered at the bars, or they dislike having their "stats" (age, height, weight, etc.) constantly scrutinized online. For these men, hiring an escort is a matter of convenience. It saves them time, energy, and frustration involved with meeting people on their own.

When working with larger men, make a special point of treating them with courtesy and respect. The gay community has a strong beauty standard towards being toned and muscular. Showing heavier clients a good time while making their weight a non-issue will go a long way towards bringing them back a second time.

Other needs of overnight clients are more sexual in nature. You can read more about those in chapter thirteen.

## Lonely and Closeted Clients

*Steve was in his early thirties when he started hiring me. He was surprisingly youthful and cheerful in appearance, with only a few extra pounds causing him any concern. I realized quickly that he would not be a long-term client. He was ready to "explode" out of the closet and only needed someone to serve as the catalyst for this. After two overnight meetings, I suggested he hire me to spend the night together and then accompany him to the New York City Gay Pride Parade. Watching Steve take pictures of the event from the sidelines made me realize I had done something special. I had given him the opportunity to become proud of himself as a gay man and had brought him to the point where he would be able to continue coming out on his own. Sure enough, it was the last time he ever hired me, but not the last time I ever heard from him. We have continued to be friends for over two years since the parade.*

Another group that you will see frequently is lonely clients. Although these men can take any form (we all become lonely at times), I am referring to middle-aged gays who live a closeted lifestyle. They often have few gay social outlets and even fewer supportive friends with whom they can talk openly. For a variety of reasons in life, they have chosen a path that leaves them alone most of the time.

As you might expect, lonely clients usually want companionship as much or more than sex. They often want to take an escort to dinner to learn more about him. They frequently call or e-mail the escort after their meeting, to thank him for their time together. They call or write to stay in contact more often than most clients. Their gay identity makes them feel socially isolated, so the escort is a valuable lifeline to the rest of the gay world.

There are several ways an escort can help meet the emotional needs of lonely clients. Having a selection of gay newspapers and magazines available during incalls is a good idea. A closeted client may have never seen a gay newspaper. Another way is to introduce clients to each other or to your friends with whom they have common interests. Referring closeted men to coming-out groups and support networks is also useful, although particularly helpful escorts will go a step further and obtain specific information about the groups for them. Referring particularly troubled clients to psychologists and other to therapists may be useful as well.

When seeing lonely gay clients who are deep in the closet, care should be taken to make sure they are not spending more than they are financially able. At one point in my career, I had a client spending well over $1,000 per week on me - money, I later learned, that he was not able to afford. Eventually I was forced to place him on a budget that allowed him to hire me for one hour every three weeks. He was unhappy with my limits but grew to accept them as he worked himself out of debt. In a case like this, it is entirely possible the client will simply switch to seeing another escort. That is a risk I was more than willing to take, because at least then I would not be responsible for his eventual financial collapse. An escort should provide sexual services, not serve as an emotional drug dealer.

On occasion a lonely client will attempt to "force" you into becoming his friend by constantly badgering for your attention. It is often difficult to handle this type of client, because the alternative may be to let him know you are not interested in being his friend. That is extremely hurtful and is something most escorts are not willing to do. In a case like this, repeating to the client that you see people only through your work is a polite way of handling the situation.

Fortunately these clients are few-and-far between. As a group, lonely clients who are deep in the closet can be among the most rewarding experiences you will have as an escort. Helping someone come out is a great way to feel proud of your work as an escort, not to mention it can make you a lifelong friend in the process.

**Couples**

*Eric and Jacob had been lovers for almost 30 years when I met them. The two were going through a phase in their relationship which involved revitalizing their sex life, so they invited me to join them for an evening of fun. They had clearly thought about the issue and had developed what they considered a fair system for "sharing" me. The first half-hour was spent in the bedroom having sex with Eric. When the time was up, Eric politely left, and Jacob joined me for the next 30 minutes. After that, Eric returned and the three of us spent the next hour playing together. It was an enjoyable evening for all of us and one we repeated several times until Eric's death from cancer. Our evenings remain among my most treasured memories as an escort.*

Although couples make-up only a small percentage of clients, they are interesting because they are such a different experience than most encounters. Couples have more diversity of their physical types, sexual requests, and interpersonal dynamics than any other type of client.

The vast majority of couples that hire male escorts are gay, but occasionally straight couples hire them as well. Couples may be romantically involved or may just be friends who enjoy playing together. And while both people are usually excited about the encounter, occasionally the dynamics are not as healthy because one partner has pressured the other into agreeing to the encounter. You may be aware of this before the encounter begins, or you may find out as the appointment proceeds.

No matter what the makeup of the couple, the escort needs to make a concerted effort to learn everything he can about the situation. Spending an extra few minutes talking to the clients after you arrive is an invaluable way to learn what they are looking for, and how to meet those needs. It is rare when an escort is able to play therapist with a couple because they are both present and are less likely to open up as much as a solitary client. The escort should therefore concentrate on the sexual requests, rather than any needs he perceives deeper in their relationship.

During the threeway, it is important for the escort to make sure both parties feel a part of the encounter. It is particularly easy for one partner to feel left out, especially if the person was opposed to the idea of an escort in the first place. It can happen even more easily if the escort is considerably more attracted to one client than to the other. Fortunately there are a number of ways to address this possibly contentious issue. Those can be found in chapter thirteen in the discussion on sex.

## Clients With Medical Issues and Disabilities

*Dick was in his mid-thirties when he was injured in an accident at work. As he used a welding torch one day, his clothing burst into flames causing severe burns across his back. Several years later he hired me for his first same-sex experience. Visually the burns were barely noticeable, but the lifelong medication they required made his body hypersensitive. He explained that he often found sex to be painful, as if someone were "hitting his dick with a hammer." The pain required that I touch him only at certain times or in certain ways. We saw each other about 20 times over the period of a year, during which he and his doctor adjusted his medication several times. At the end of the year, he was able to enjoy sex without any major adverse side-effects. He was grateful that I had been patient and helpful during this process.*

Most escorts who have been in the business for any length of time have been hired by a client with a disability. Many of them hire escorts for the usual reasons, such as discretion, convenience, or because they are horny. Others hire escorts because they feel isolated by virtue of their disability. Regardless of why they are hiring escorts, it is important to treat clients with disabilities with the dignity and respect that any human being deserves.

There is little that can be said that holds true for all people with disabilities, other than that they want to enjoy their experience with an escort as much as possible. When hired by someone who has a disability, be upfront about your lack of knowledge about his condition if that is the case. Few clients will have a problem discussing their issues with you, especially when you make it clear that you are asking because you want to be able to serve them better and because of your own curiosity.

There may come a day when you are faced with a client with a medical situation that makes you uncomfortable. In a case like this, you should make as proactive of a suggestion as possible under whatever guise is necessary to solve the problem. For example, one client I met who used a wheelchair smelled strongly of urine. I suggested we take a shower, under the rationale that it would be a fun way to begin foreplay. He agreed, and we spent the next half-hour washing each other thoroughly. However you handle the issue of a client in a situation like this, you should do so in a manner that is respectful and maintains the dignity of the client.

There may be rare clients who have conditions that you are simply unable to handle. For example, I had a client who had a hernia the size of a bowling ball between his legs. His penis and testicles were buried within the mass. If this or any other situation is beyond your ability to handle, you should apologize politely, make whatever suggestions may be appropriate (such as having surgery for the hernia), and leave. In a case like this, you should not request to be paid for your time. If the client offers to pay you, refuse the money, even for your travel expenses. The client already feels deeply hurt by the meeting. There is no need to take his money as well.

Fortunately, the vast majority of clients with disabilities and medical issues are just like everyone else. They may use a prosthetic limb, a wheelchair, or a pacemaker, but sexually and mentally they have the same desires as other people. When you have specific questions about a client's health, ask him. It is an opportunity to learn, and as long as your questions are asked respectfully, everything should work out fine.

## Deaf Clients

*I do not recall how Geoffrey initially contacted me, but we have now been seeing each other every few months for several years. The fact that he is deaf and I am not sometimes presents some challenge regarding our ability to communicate, but we both value our relationship on business, sexual, and personal levels. This is important because we have begun taking small trips together and are scheduled to vacation in Key West next spring. All of this would not be possible if I had initially dismissed him like so many other escorts did.*

Although deaf clients are relatively rare, they are a group with needs unique enough to deserve mentioning. I place these clients in their own group rather than with people with other disabilities because their issues are different. The challenges deaf clients face occur when setting-up an appointment.

Because deaf clients are not be able to hear over the telephone, they use a teletypewriter, also known as a TTY or TDD. A TTY is a small keyboard and screen that hooks up to a telephone. Users dial normally, then place the phone in a plastic inset on the TTY. The user can then type his message into the phone, which in turn is printed on a screen by the TTY on the other end.

Most of us do not have TTYs, so phone companies offer a relay service in all fifty states and in some other countries. The relay service involves a deaf person typing their message to a trained communications assistant (CA), who then voices the message to a hearing person. The CA knows the deaf person is done speaking when he types GA, short for "go ahead." The hearing person then speaks their message back into the phone to the CA, who types it into the TTY for the deaf caller. The hearing person says "go ahead" when he is ready for the deaf person to resume typing. The conversation continues back-and-forth like this until it is completed. It is a slow process, but it provides an invaluable aid to those who may otherwise be unable to hire an escort.

If you receive a relay call, it will begin with the CA indicating the nature of the call and then offering to provide you with instructions on the service. Although any conversation you have with a CA is confidential, many escorts still feel uncomfortable discussing sexual acts or arranging appointments this way. One way of dealing with this is to request the client write you an e-mail or a letter directly to arrange an appointment. Another is to discuss appointments and fees, but to refuse to discuss any overt sexual acts on the telephone.

Using a relay service is awkward for hearing people not used to the deaf community, and can be uncomfortable when arranging an (illegal!) escort appointment. An ambitious and open-minded escort can turn this to his advantage. Deaf clients who do not utilize the Internet have few escorts to choose from because so many escorts refuse to discuss arrangements through a relay service. When approached by a deaf client, even small amounts of courtesy and respect go a long way.

Occasionally you will receive relay calls when you are running out the door or are on another phone line. In this case it is entirely appropriate to tell the operator that you are unable to talk and to ask the caller to call back later. It is a good idea to do this if you are in a hurry, because once you are on the phone using a relay service, the call will almost certainly take at least five-to-ten minutes.

Other times you may receive calls from deaf callers who are interested in becoming friends or pen pals, but not hiring you as an escort. As with many callers for whom English is a second language, the person likely mistook your escort advertisement for a personal ad. There is no easy solution to turning such a person down, because you do not want to hurt the other person's feelings. Explaining that the ad is about prostitution is one method but can be awkward because of the presence of a relay operator. Probably the best suggestion is for the caller to write you an e-mail instead. If he does not have access to the Internet, he can create a free e-mail account through the computers at his local library and Hotmail (http://www.hotmail.com). You may also want to suggest he visit the Deaf Queer Resource Center (http://www.deafqueer.com). It's a great resource for getting in touch with other deaf gay people.

For more information on TTYs or relay services, consult your local phone book.

Meeting deaf clients works like most any other appointment. Whenever you meet a deaf person, you may wish to briefly discuss his hearing. Some clients will be able to speechread, but others will need you to write messages down with pencil and paper. In either case, have fun with your meeting

Of course, clients are not limited to just one group. You may see an inexperienced client who is much older, for example. Or may see a particularly overweight younger guy. You'll have to consider all of a client's physical attributes when meeting his needs.

By no means are these the only types of clients, either. There are so many men out there that it is impossible to place them all into a few brief categories. Even years into your career as an escort, you will continue to meet new and different types of people.

Whatever your client is like, he will be eagerly looking forward to hopping into bed with you. Although you can probably handle yourself at that point, the next chapter is filled with pointers on how to improve even the most skilled lover's abilities in bed.

## Chapter Thirteen
## The Hard Way

*One client of mine had an extremely rude personality. He kept making comments about anything he didn't like. Unfortunately, every time he went down on me he somehow made the head of my dick become painfully sensitive. I completely lost my erection at his touch. Every time I managed to become partially hard, he would go down on me and do it again.*

*"You're not a very good escort if you can't stay hard, are you?" he finally asked.*

*I was infuriated and was ready to walk out on him. In anger and frustration I finally gestured at him saying, "Of course I'm not hard. Look what I have to work with!"*

*To my surprise, he laughed uproariously. It was then that I realized he wasn't a rude person, he simply had an extremely sarcastic sense of humor. As long as I threw his insults right back at him, we would get along fine. My theory was correct, and we have remained friends since that day.*

When a client hires an escort, he is usually looking for a number of services. He may want convenience in scheduling, discretion, or even a person to talk to. Of course, clients always want sex too. It is the basic service of the escorting profession, and that which keeps us in business.

Only on extremely rare occasions will a client not be interested in sex. I have had over 1,200 appointments in my career, of which only two did not involve sex. Both of those involved me telling stories about my work and my experiences. Cases like those are virtually nonexistent, so you should expect to have sex at least once during every appointment.

In the unlikely event that you are new to male-male sex, rest assured that you will gain experience fast. Be up-front about your relative inexperience. Most clients will be happy to teach you what they know. If you are nervous and in need of a good book on the subject, check out Jack Hart's *Gay Sex: A Manual for Men Who Love Men*.

Even if you know what you are doing, you will have plenty of opportunities to learn new techniques. Even veteran escorts with years of experience can always learn something new. Learning as many skills as you can will make you a better escort as well as an excellent lover.

### A Word on Attractiveness

People often ask an escort how he can stand to touch "really ugly clients." The answer is that an escort has a different definition of "ugly" than most people. When you meet a client, you should be able to identify attributes about him that you like. If he does not have a beautiful body, then perhaps he has nice eyes. If he lacks nice eyes as well, he may have a cute smile, a good sense of humor, or a pleasant personality. In the rare cases when you cannot find anything to compliment, you should not be working for him.

Ironically, you will need to be extra-professional when you are with an extremely attractive client. It will be tempting to give in to your own desires and place your agenda over his. This is a pleasant challenge to have, but is a challenge nonetheless.

### Types of Sex

Sexuality is incredibly diverse, with a wide range of turn-ons and practices that people enjoy. For the escort, this presents the unique challenge of having to become skilled at many techniques, positions, and styles.

For the most part, clients are interested in the same four basic types of activities: affection, masturbation, oral sex, and anal sex. Not all escorts offer all four services. Bodyworkers offer massage, masturbation, and occasionally oral sex but only rarely kiss or have anal sex with their clients. Other escorts define themselves exclusively as a "top" or a "bottom" in anal sex and are not willing to perform in both roles. What you are willing to do is up to you. Just remember, the less you are willing to do with your clients, the less business you will have.

When a client arrives for an appointment, ideally he will be aware of any sexual limitations you have. In countries where prostitution is illegal, you may not have felt comfortable discussing sex acts in advance. In either case, you should make sure the client understands that your lack of willingness to perform a given act has nothing to do with him, even if it does. Doing otherwise is hurtful and may understandably upset your client. If you are not willing to kiss less attractive clients, by all means do not tell them the real reason. Instead, stress how deep and personal the act of kissing is for you. Tell him that you could not imagine ever kissing someone with whom you were not in love. He will still not like it, but at least he will not take personal offense at your actions.

Beyond the basic types of sex, there are plenty of others that are less commonly practiced. These include bondage, spanking, role playing, sadism, masochism, cross-dressing, watersports, fisting, and the heavy use of sex toys. Whether these acts are common in your work will depend on how you advertise your services. As an escort, you will periodically receive inquiries in most of those areas. Accept only the acts that you are comfortable performing.

Occasionally, you will arrive to meet a client only to discover he would like to experiment sexually in a way that makes you uncomfortable. In cases like these, it is a good idea to let the client immediately know of your reservations.

You should do this in a positive manner, explaining that the act is not a service that you can provide with any skill. You should not express any disgust you may feel for the activity, unless it crosses ethical lines to the point where you feel you must leave. Do not agree to do anything you will dislike just because it pays well. Doing so is one of the fastest ways to burn yourself out.

**Styles of Sex**

In addition to types of sex, there is also the matter of style. Styles of sex are difficult to define but can be thought of as personality traits when in bed. For example, some escorts prefer being passive, and others are more aggressive in nature. Some escorts also enjoy talking during sex (either intellectual conversation or dirty talk), and other escorts are almost silent. The same can be said for how "into" the sex escorts become. Some are calmer; some prefer it wild. There are many more styles that can be easily identified.

Each client has his own preferred style as well. Ideally, your advertising and personality on the phone should be sufficient for a client to decide if you would be a good match. Unfortunately, this is not always the case, so be prepared to alter your style during the appointment. Always try to determine early in the encounter what style the client is looking for. In cases where it is not possible to do so, do your best, and observe how he responds to you in bed. Remember that it is your responsibility to match the client's style and not the other way around.

On occasion, a client has a style that you may find unpleasant. For example, he may enjoy manhandling and throwing you around the bed. If you are gentle or small in stature, you may not be able to deal with this. The best way to solve the problem is to ask him politely to stop. If he does not change his behavior, then you will need to decide whether to and stand up and leave or to stay and suffer. It may take more than one request before he realizes that his actions are bothering you.

It is extremely rare when the client's style of sex is beyond your ability to match. In cases like these, your best bet is to apologize and leave. Monetary disputes need to be solved on a case-by-case basis, depending on the details of the incident, the length of time you have been together, and the like.

### Determining the "Agenda"

When clients show up for an escorting appointment, they may or may not have an agenda of acts they want to try. (This is not a written agenda, although once I had a client show up with one. He periodically interrupted the encounter to check items off the list. Honest!) Some clients will mention acts they enjoy to the escort, and others will be silent regarding what they like. It is up to the escort to find out what a client wants to do, since he is responsible for making sure the client has a good time. An hour can be a long time to fill when servicing a particularly distant and unresponsive client.

Most clients are pretty good about discussing sex once they relax and begin fooling around. Even if they have trouble saying what they like, a few experimental touches or licks on various parts of their bodies may help determine what they like. If a client grinds his ass into your crotch, chances are he likes butt play. Similarly, if he moans when you go down on him, he loves having his dick sucked. Watch for both obvious and subtle clues as to what he may like.

As stated before, occasionally clients do not provide any verbal or physical indication of what they like. In cases like these, try asking your client about the best sex he ever had. The answer can give you a clue as to what he likes. If he is still vague and unhelpful, you will have to guess as best you can. Often, times I inform the client that I am not sure what he wants me to do and that I am completely guessing. Techniques like this help an escort live up to his obligation to do his best and excuse him if a client does not have the best possible time he could have.

**Erections**

Obviously, it is critical for a male escort to be able to obtain an erection during an appointment. It would be great if you were able to produce one throughout the entire encounter, but this is often not necessary. Clients understand that you have sex on a regular basis, and that you may not be attracted to him the same way that he is to you. Still, you should be able to maintain an erection for at least part of the encounter.

Unfortunately, there will come a day when you have difficulty staying hard. It may be from sexual exhaustion or a lack of chemistry between you and your client. On a day like this, you have your work cut out for you.

When you find yourself in a situation where your erection is not up to par, one of the best techniques to use is "sleight of hand." Distract the client so he does not know that you cannot stay hard. For example, if you are struggling to obtain an erection, take advantage of the moment by going down on him. While he is enjoying himself, you can pleasure yourself with your free hand. Alternately, you can give the client a massage, masturbate him, or do any of a number of other activities that may occupy his mind. As soon as you find yourself "rising to the occasion," make him aware that you are hard and let him play with you. Done correctly, the client may not ever realize you are having any difficulty.

Another method that you may find helpful is to wear a cockring or tightly hold the base of your dick. (A cockring, in case you are wondering, is a leather, metal, or plastic ring that goes around your dick and balls.) By restricting the flow of blood through the veins, blood is trapped inside the shaft, helping to make it stiff. Other people find that cockrings only distract them and make getting an erection more difficult. You should test your own body's reactions well in advance of this situation.

The most ideal solution to the erection problem is to head it off before it occurs. Conserving sexual energy is one way to do this and will be covered later in the section on orgasms. Another way is to let clients requesting last-minute appointments know in advance that you are sexually tired. Some will choose to reschedule the appointment, but others will invite you over anyway. In either case, the client will greatly appreciate your honesty, and you will be spared embarrassment when you are unable to stay hard.

Another popular method is to use Viagra. This is particularly useful when you know you will be visiting a client whom you find less attractive. Many escorts will not consider this alternative because of side effects and risks. The uses and limitations of Viagra are discussed in more detail in chapter seventeen.

If you absolutely cannot stay hard, be honest with your client and offer to reduce your fee at the end of the session. We all have off days. Most clients understand this and will not hold it against you. Some will even insist on paying you the full rate.

On the flipside of the erection issue, there will also be days when your client is the one who is having trouble. Fortunately for you, this is a lot less stressful. As before, there are plenty of possible causes and solutions for this problem. For starters, some clients have medical conditions that prevent them from becoming fully hard. Many medications also have this side effect as well, including several drugs for depression and high blood pressure. In cases like these, there is likely to be little you can do to give them an erection. Viagra may help, but that has to be a decision they make in conjunction with a doctor. Under no circumstances should you ever give Viagra to your clients. Not only is doing so highly illegal; it is also extremely dangerous. Mixing Viagra with the wrong medication can be a fatal mistake.

Other clients may have difficulty achieving an erection because they are nervous, tired, or have other things on their mind. In these cases, letting time pass, sleeping, or talking for a while may help solve the problem. If you are seeing your client for an overnight or several-hour session, you may want to do something else for a while. A back massage can do wonders for alleviating the tension of the moment. Sometimes the problem may not be the client at all. If you have been having intense sex for more than an hour or two, the client may simply need a few minutes to recharge.

If your client's trouble is that he loses his erection once he puts on a condom, he may need a bigger one. This is particularly the case with longer or thicker dicks. Cockrings may also come in handy for these men, although they are likely to do little for people who cannot maintain an erection. Whatever you do, don't bareback. It is not worth risking your health just to give your client an ego boost.

The easiest solution to the whole lack-of-erection dilemma is to do something else. If your client cannot stay hard long enough to play top, then switch to another activity. Many clients will happily allow you to service them and may be able to respond better to another activity.

**Orgasms**

Many hustlers and straight-identified escorts are willing to orgasm only from masturbation and oral sex. They are not interested in reciprocating for a client. Professional escorts are usually the opposite. They encourage the client to have an orgasm but try avoid having one themselves if possible. The reason for this difference is simple. Hustlers are usually uncomfortable having sex in the first place and want to touch their client as little as possible. Professional escorts prefer saving their sexual energy for later appointments.

Unless you are one of those rare men who easily cums more than once, it may be a good idea for you to avoid having an orgasm if you can. This is frequently not possible because many of your clients will have a strong desire to watch you lose control. Other times, you may be too excited to hold back. Whatever the reason, be mindful of your work schedule. If you know that a client likes to watch you blow your load, you may not want to schedule another appointment after that.

Fortunately, there are techniques you can use to save your sexual energy. Many escorts will encourage the client to service him earlier in the encounter, reserving the later time for acts that involve taking care of the client. Some escorts will also use the time to their advantage, aiming the client's orgasm for five minutes before the end of the session. In that way, time constraints make it more difficult for a client to get the escort off.

An excellent technique for avoiding an orgasm is to lie down next to the client after he cums. Ideally, this is done in such a way that your dick is not readily accessible, such as by affectionately lying down on top of the client. Spend the next several minutes cuddling with him as he basks in the afterglow of the moment. By the time the client begins to rouse himself, frequently his sexual mood has diminished and he is more interested in cleaning up than getting you off.

Yet another technique to avoid having an orgasm involves feigning sexual exhaustion. This is easiest when done after a sex session that has lasted for several hours. As the client begins directing his attention towards your orgasm, lie back in mock exhaustion and talk about how intense the encounter has been. Sometimes the client will agree and will choose to cuddle with you affectionately instead of helping you get off. Other times, he will request you masturbate yourself to orgasm instead, in which case you may need to oblige. No technique for saving an orgasm is 100% perfect.

The most controversial way to avoid an orgasm is to fake one. It is generally possible only when you are topping your client, although I have heard of escorts who manage it using saliva and precum during masturbation. When faking an orgasm during anal sex, moan while making thrusting motions as if you are close to cumming. Thrust harder and harder until you "peak." After the "orgasm," collapse on top of the client in exhaustion. Lying on top of him for several minutes while pretending to gather your strength helps make your performance more believable.

When removing a condom after faking an orgasm, care should be taken so the client does not see that there is nothing inside it. This can be done by casually blocking the client's view with your hand. If possible, hand the client a nearby towel at the same time you are removing the condom. Doing so will distract him, especially if you suggest he use the towel to clean himself off because the condom is "a little bit messy." Most clients become self-conscious at that point and become more interested in cleaning than examining the condom. You should then throw out the condom in such a way that it is not sitting in plain sight in a wastebasket. You may want to flush the condom down the toilet so he will not be able to examine it later. If you do this, be sure to wrap the condom in toilet paper first. Otherwise it may fill up with air and not flush easily. Faking orgasms should be used only as a method of last resort because of the chance of being discovered.

**Bottoming**

When it comes to bottoming, the golden rule is, "if it hurts, stop!" This may mean telling your partner that you need a break or more lube or may involve refusing to provide bottoming services in the first place.

If you do not mind bottoming, be aware that eventually a client will reach your limits. If you find a client approaching this point, use positions that are comfortable and will delay the hurting as long as possible. When the time finally comes that you need to stop, do not be afraid to say that you have reached your limit. Most clients will completely understand and will be happy to do something else.

If you have been thoroughly topped, it is always a good idea to make a quick bathroom run when you are done. Do not rush out in a panic but politely excuse yourself and head for the door. Not only will it give you a chance to wash yourself off to prevent STDs it will also give you a chance to use the bathroom to clean up.

## Mess

Whether you are topping or bottoming, occasionally there will be a bit of a mess. Some men use enemas in advance to prevent this from occurring, but many do not choose to use that option (or even know it is possible). Even if both of you have prepared in advance, it is possible to have an off day. However the mess occurs, dealing with it is part of the job.

If anal sex becomes messy, simply treat the issue with a polite detachment and clean it up with a nearby towel. Fold down any soiled sheets on the bed as well. If necessary, either you or the client should use the bathroom to clean up. For particularly off days, you may want to suggest both you and the client take a shower and then try other activities when you return to the bedroom.

## Sex With Overweight Clients

When working for overweight clients, you should remember a few simple tips. The more the client weighs, the more difficult it is for him to bend and move around the bed. In fact, particularly heavy clients may find it difficult to do much more than lie there while you move from position to position. Regardless of their ability to move around, it is not a bad idea for you to take the initiative and to encourage overweight men to lie back and relax. They are likely to find the position more comfortable and will enjoy having you service them.

When it comes to topping overweight clients, the key is to find a position that works for you. If your client lies on his back, you may find it difficult to hold his legs in the air for any length of time. Having him place his butt on several pillows may take much of his weight off you. Topping your client while he lies on his stomach may be a useful position as well. Some escorts even find it easier to stand on the floor while topping a client who is lying sideways across the bed.

Escorts with smaller endowments may have difficulty topping larger clients because the smaller dicks are not long enough to reach through to the hole. Even escorts with medium or large dicks will have trouble with particularly heavy men. Pulling their buns apart may help some, although it will not work for everyone. A good solution in this case is to finger a client, then rub your dick up and down the crack of his butt instead. Don't lie and say that you are in him, but instead claim you like the feeling better this way.

## Threeways

There are two types of threeways you may experience in your work. The first involves working with another escort, and the second involves servicing two clients. Handling the first is easy. Always make the client the center of attention, unless he specifically wants to watch the two of you. As long as you remember not to ignore the client, you will almost certainly do fine.

As stated before, working with two clients can be a bit trickier. One of the downsides of this type of threeway is that it becomes easy for one of the clients to feel left out of the encounter. This is particularly the case for a couple in which one partner initially opposed the idea of the threeway. Care must be taken at all times to make sure they are both feeling like they belong. If one person begins to feel left out, you should spend some extra time making him feel like an important part of the encounter.

Unless the couple specifically wants you to service one person while the other watches, you should divide your attention equally between both partners. If you are going to spend time exclusively pleasing one person for any reason, make sure the other is aware that you have not forgotten about him. I often do this with a friendly smile and a kiss. Doing so assures he does not perceive he is being ignored.

**Virgins**

Much of what virgins want during sex is to explore their vast and confusing feelings. This is difficult to manage in one encounter, although a few hours together can go a long way towards this goal.

When having sex with a sexually inexperienced client, you should proceed slowly. Spend time explaining what you are doing, to help him understand what is going on. Feelings you take for granted may be new to the client. He may need time to stop and think because everything is happening so fast.

For example, you are probably used to being anally penetrated. Even if you do not like the feeling, you have almost certainly tried it before. A virgin client has no experience at this. When sliding your finger inside him, he is likely to feel a sudden need to use the bathroom. He does not actually need to do so (at least we hope not!), but his lack of experience makes the sensation confusing. Talking about what you are doing and what he is feeling is an excellent way to overcome this. Encourage him to ask questions about what you are doing, and answer them as best you can.

On the subject of anally penetrating virgins, it is an excellent idea to do so in extremely slow fashion. Experienced bottoms know their own limits and are able to relax their muscles, but virgins are completely new to this. Virgins also have an added disadvantage of not knowing what positions they find comfortable. It will take months or years of practice and experimentation for them to learn what they like.

When "warming up" virgins who want to play bottom, it is a good idea to spend some time slowly fingering them. You may want to avoid penetrating them for the first minute or two. Slowly relaxing them over a period of several minutes will allow their muscles to open up considerably more than if you attempted to penetrate them right from the start. The last thing you want is for a virgin bottom to find the experience painful, so every precaution should be taken to help them enjoy the encounter. Once they are relaxed, then you can finger them. When they are sufficiently opened up after that, you can try giving them the real thing. Be sure to remember that the virgin will probably tense up just before you enter him.

Virgins, especially young ones, have a habit of cumming quickly. Depending on the length of time you will be together, you may want to help them hold back. Longer meetings give you more flexibility in this matter, as they allow plenty of time to recharge. The interlude between sex sessions is also an excellent time to cuddle and talk.

Another issue for virgins is that of sexual self-confidence. As an escort, you can help them develop this by complimenting their sexual skill no matter how they are in bed. They will learn to be better lovers over time, but what they need at first is the confidence to continue their sexual exploration. A perfect opportunity to do this is when the client starts sucking you for the first time. He will almost always stop and ask you how you like his oral skills.

Smile by way of answering, compliment him, and urge him to continue. You will earn a place in his heart for doing so.

## Sex and Psychology

Alas, not every client will be an expert or even adequate in bed. A few clients are walking sexual disasters. In cases like these, sex can be irritating, uncomfortable, and sometimes even painful.

The standard classic approach is to speak to your client about your concerns. You cannot very well say that he is lousy in bed, but you can urge him to do things differently. Most of the time he will listen, although sometimes he is so caught up in his own fantasies that he does not even realize what he is doing.

One idea you may want to try involves using the behavioral psychology principle of positive reinforcement. This is when you reward a client for using a sexual technique he needs to learn. A reward can be a moan, a kiss, a gasp of pleasure, or a compliment on his skill. Carefully use these every time the client does something right in bed. The right training may do wonders for his skill.

Fortunately, clients in need of sexual training are infrequent. The vast majority of sex with clients proceeds without a hitch. Still, there are plenty of other pitfalls to watch out for when meeting clients. Some clients are drunk, some are abusive, and a few have even more sinister things on their minds. As hard as you try to screen them in advance, periodically these clients slip through. What to do with one of these clients is exactly what the next chapter is about.

Chapter Fourteen
**Problem Clients**

When an escort arranges an appointment with a client, everything will probably work-out fine. Unfortunately, "probably" does not mean "always." You will run into a variety of problem clients in your work. Some of these will be irritating, but not necessarily dangerous. Others are the sort you dread to encounter, clients who are aggressive, abusive, and violent.

When learning about these groups of problem clients, it is important to keep in mind that they are not necessarily mutually exclusive. Someone who is drunk may also cheat you out of money, for example. So when you find yourself meeting someone who is problematic in one way, be aware that he may be difficult in other ways as well.

**Drunk or High Clients**

*I knew he was drunk a few moments after I arrived. He seemed harmless enough, and I was eager to earn another few hundred bucks, so I chose not to leave. I had dealt with drunk guys before, and nothing serious had ever happened. I wanted to get to know him, so I kept him talking for several minutes. "Oh, it's a nice neighborhood," he said at one point. "I like living here, and the people are nice. Except for the niggers." I looked at him in surprise, not believing what I had heard.*

> *"But I'm prepared for them,"* he declared with a gleam in his eye. *"If they ever come over here, I'm ready to protect myself."*
> 
> *I could only stare in shock as he removed a gun from underneath the couch and pointed it directly at me.*

The most common of the five types of problem clients are those who are under the influence of alcohol or drugs. You can encounter them at any time during your work, but it is particularly likely late at night. Fortunately, it is not hard to cut down on these clients. Not answering your phone after midnight is one way. Informing potential clients that you do not do drugs is another.

Precisely what will happen when you meet a drunk client will vary. The most common outcome is that nothing out-of-the-ordinary happens. You work for them, they behave a little oddly, and then you go home. Other times, the client will begin behaving extremely erratically. These clients may become abusive, threaten to call the police, or cheat you out of money you are rightfully owed. It is your decision how to handle these clients. Just be sure to stay sober when you are with them. If and when they finally go nuts, you are going to need your wits about you.

## Abusive Clients

> *I knew he was into spanking when we agreed to meet. I was new to escorting at the time, having met perhaps a dozen clients at the most. In my naïve world where everyone was nice to each other, it never occurred to me that perhaps I should not take him on as a client. I hated being spanked, but I wanted the money. What I did not know was that his fantasy was to spank someone so hard that they would become angry and spank him hard in return. So when I made it clear he had reached my limits, he deliberately crossed them again, and again, and again...*

One of the most common questions people ask escorts is, "Aren't you afraid for your safety?" When they ask this question, they are referring to abusive clients, those who willingly inflict bodily harm on an escort. Some only do so on a minor level and stop before things become too serious, but others have absolutely no concern for your health and welfare.

Hopefully, there will never come a day when you meet this type of person. Unfortunately, they are one of the deepest pitfalls of our profession, so be prepared for them. What to do if you encounter one of these clients is covered in chapter fifteen.

**Cheaters**

*I began dressing myself after we finished having sex. He vanished into the other room for a moment before he returned with a wad of bills. I counted the money only to find it was $60 short. "I thought you liked the sex," he explained with a guilty look on his face. "So I didn't need to pay you everything..."*

Sometimes a client will have a good reason to want to pay you less than your normal rate. If you were unable to stay hard, for example. In this case, his request is fair and should be considered. Other times, there may be an honest misunderstanding about the fee. This can be the case when a one-hour appointment unexpectedly goes into additional hours.

Most of the time when a client underpays you, he is deliberately doing so. Precisely why clients do this is something I have never understood. Perhaps they feel as if they are above being honest, or perhaps they think they can behave however they want because they are "only" hiring a prostitute. As covered back in chapter eleven, there is little that can be done about these people. Your best bet is to identify likely cheaters in advance, have them pay up-front, assert yourself about any money that you are owed, and avoid letting the situation escalate out of control. Once you are home, you can achieve a small amount of justice by warning other escorts in your area to avoid the person.

## Unattractive / Unhygienic Clients

*I stood in the middle of a motel room watching him remove his clothes. I did not like the client, and I found him extremely unattractive. I considered myself a professional, so I had forced myself to hide my true feelings while acting pleasant and friendly. When he pulled down his pants, I saw a hernia the size of a bowling ball between his legs. It was so large that his genitals were lost within it. I blinked several times as I tried to figure out what to do. If I had to touch that thing, I was sure I would throw-up.*

I list this group in the chapter on problem clients not out of disrespect or to imply that they are dangerous. As a group, these clients are not harmful. An unattractive client may coincidentally be problematic in other ways, but there is no correlation between the two.

Precisely what is too unattractive or too unhygienic for an escort will vary widely. Like everyone else, escorts have different tastes and physical requirements for their sexual partners. For the most part, escorts are able to take a great deal of ugliness in their clients before they begin having a problem, and even then a pleasant personality can make the situation workable.

The difficulty is when a client is so unappealing that it is beyond your ability to handle. In one such case, I was hired by a client who was, shall we say, extremely anally unclean. He sat down on the bed and left a large brown stain on the sheet. He seemed completely unaware of his condition and was serious when he talked about wanting me to finger and top him. I was so disgusted that I could not continue. The idea of asking him to bathe never even entered my mind. I apologized, refused his offer to pay me for my time, and left.

When faced with the prospect of unpleasant encounters, you need to make a quick decision. You can stay and make money for the hour, or you can politely apologize and leave. In either case you have an obligation to do as little harm to the client as possible. Indeed, you should help the client if you are able. Politely explaining how he can solve his problem often helps. In the case of the man with the hernia, it would be entirely appropriate to urge him to see his doctor. The other client should be urged to bathe thoroughly and to learn to check his personal hygiene.

At some point, you should consider whether the problem is one the client could have avoided. In both of the above examples there were easy solutions to their dilemmas. Other clients are not so fortunate, having conditions that are long-term or permanent. In cases like these, extreme care should be taken to avoid causing mental harm. As an escort you have the right to choose with whom you go to bed, but as a human being you have an obligation to treat others with dignity and respect. If you cannot cope with someone's condition, politely explain that the fault is yours and not theirs, and then leave.

If you terminate a meeting with a client because he is too unattractive or unhygienic for you to handle, then you should not accept payment, even if he offers it to you.

**Mindgamers**

*One client I used to see had a fixation for controlling the lives of others. He would frequently call for last-minute appointments, and if I was scheduled to see someone else, he would offer me large sums of money to skip the other appointment and see him instead. At one point, the client developed a habit of calling me on my cell phone at all hours of the day and night. When I explained that I could not afford to speak to him all the time, he offered to pay the entire bill so I would not have an excuse to avoid him. Eventually his controlling behaviors grew too strong for even my patience. By that point he had found a new escort to manipulate, so he gladly let me go.*

In your work you may encounter clients who enjoy playing mindgames. Many of these people are relatively harmless and can be stopped by terminating the relationship. Others are more erratic and dangerous. These people should be dealt with using extreme care.

I have encountered several erratic clients over the past few years. I wrote about one in my book *Suburban Hustler*. He was devoid of all emotion and played a series of mindgames during the encounter in an effort to degrade me. He expressed absolutely no interest in the sex, insulted my looks and my services, and even offered me a role in a kiddy-porn movie. I finally walked out on him in disgust. Some time later, a reader of my book called to say he recognized the client in the story. I learned they had been neighbors when the reader was a teenager. According to the reader, the client engaged in all sorts of eccentric behaviors, such as shouting sexual comments at the reader.

If you escort for any length of time, you will certainly meet people who play a variety of mindgames. A few will hire you only once, but others will bother you numerous times over a period of weeks or months. If a client begins engaging in eccentric behavior that makes you uncomfortable, break off the appointment and the relationship. No amount of money is worth the stress these people can inflict.

Incidentally, in the first example of the controlling client, I would reschedule the other appointment so I could see both clients and make a nice profit. I called it the "idiot surcharge." He acted like an idiot, so I surcharged him. Clients who play mindgames can be highly lucrative, but are highly risky to deal with in the long run. In retrospect, the thousands of dollars I made off him were not worth the stress he gave me.

Sooner or later you are going to run into clients like these. Hopefully your experience will not be a bad one, and will teach you to appreciate your regular clients all the more; however, things can and do go wrong. When they do, the situation may be potentially life-threatening. The next chapter is dedicated to the idea that escorting safely requires more than using condoms in bed.

Chapter Fifteen
## Protecting Yourself

*Some time ago I was attacked by a client of mine. I wrote about it in my first book. Not long after the book came out, I learned the client did the same thing to another escort. This escort fared worse than I did, coming out of it raped and with a black eye. He left the profession for a year at that point. What frightened the two of us was not our experiences; we both survived what happened. What scared us was knowing that this man is out there continuing to prey on young men, and his next victim may not be so fortunate.*

The key to staying safe in an encounter is to prevent the situation from ever going bad in the first place. Some of this is done by screening your clients as best you can. If they seem unusually odd, then you should be "busy" anytime they request an appointment. It is better to be safe than sorry.

Talking to other escorts about your clients is another excellent way to learn whom to avoid. Although you have an obligation to keep the names of your clients private under normal circumstances, this does not hold true if you are concerned about your safety or well-being. There is nothing wrong with disclosing information to another escort if it means protecting yourself or others from danger. If you are a member of an Internet listserv of escorts, you may want to ask if anyone is familiar with a person. You would be surprised how often someone will know him.

You may also want to visit blacklist websites as well. Blacklists are invitation-only lists of clients who have cheated and assaulted. They tend to be short-lived because as word gets around of their existence, clients on the list begin harassing the webmaster until he eventually removes it. Still, they are an excellent resource when they exist. I advise asking around to learn about them.

As mentioned back in chapter nine, refuse any client who asks if you "party" or do drugs. Mixing drugs and prostitution vastly decreases your ability to protect yourself, and can be an express trip to the morgue. You may like to party in your spare time, but you need to avoid doing it in your work. You need your wits about you when you escort. Drugs are not the way to do that.

Consider how tough it would be to call the police and tell them a client raped you while you were working as a gay prostitute. Now imagine how it would look if you had to admit you were on drugs at the time. It is not exactly the best way to gather sympathy and support. Avoid that fate before it happens to you.

When meeting a client, always make sure you leave detailed information in your home or with a friend about who they are and where you are meeting. In the case of an incall, make a point of leaving information about the person coming to see you. This can be done by leaving details on your answering machine, writing a note on your desk, or telling a roommate or lover.

One popular technique commonly used in suburban and rural areas involves meeting a client in a public parking lot. Make a point of calling a friend or your answering machine either as you or the client arrives. Read the client's license plate to the person on the phone. Hopefully the information will never be needed, but it is nice to know that you can be tracked down if need be. Make safety precautions like this a part of your routine. They are as much a part of this job as any other.

Be careful if you arrive at a client's home only to find that things do not seem quite right. In one case, I drove to Philadelphia to meet a client for an overnight visit. He had an extremely difficult time providing me directions and wound up sending me to a nonexistent address. When I called him at home, he directed me to an apartment building two blocks away. I showed up and rang the bell, then waited for almost a full minute before he answered the intercom. He sounded somewhat disoriented.

In retrospect, I should have left at that point. Instead, I went up to his apartment because I was greedy for the money. As it turned out, it worked out fine. (Sort of. He was highly strange and seemed to be living in a group home. I never did figure out how he came up with the money to hire me.) My greed and irritation could easily have been my undoing. Do not be as stupid as I was. If your instincts tell you something is wrong, get out of the situation fast.

Many escorts use cellular telephones to their advantage through a system of code words. When calling home to a lover or friend, they have a series of words plotted-out in advance to mean different things. For example, talking about "sixty-nining" might mean everything is fine. Cracking a joke about whips and chains, on the other hand, might mean that something is wrong and the person should call the police. Other codes may mean the person should call the escort back in five minutes to check on him, or they should call the doorman or hotel desk and ask them to check on you. A properly given code at the right time can be a lifesaver in an emergency.

Of course instincts and code words are not infallible. There will be days when your judgment fails and you find yourself in a bad situation. That is where the tough part begins.

Whenever you meet a client, always remember that your first priority is to be able to get out of a bad situation safely. No amount of money, drugs, or anything else is worth risking your life. **If you think you are in a dangerous situation, leave immediately.** Abandon your belongings if you have to. Credit cards can be canceled, cell phones can be shut off, and clothing is easily replaceable.

Your health is not so easily repaired, so do not take chances that you may regret later.

If you find yourself facing an unstable client that is rapidly losing control of his behavior, try to disarm your opponent verbally. This means not arguing with him and not giving him any reason to become upset. Police officers use these techniques in their work every day to avoid escalating a situation. If an angry client accuses you of stealing his stash of crack (this happened to a friend of mine), offer to help search for it instead. It may buy you the time you need to get dressed and escape.

On occasion, a client will block your access to the exit. This may stop you from leaving, but it has advantages as well. As long as he is standing in front of the door, you can step back and wait him out. At worst you have delayed a confrontation. At best you may be able to diffuse the situation peacefully.

On other occasions, an angry client may pick up the phone and threaten to call the police. This may not be a bad way out of a situation in places where prostitution is legal. If he does call the police, you are unlikely to be charged with anything serious unless you vandalized his apartment or brought illegal drugs to work with you.

In places where prostitution is illegal, you need to take this threat more seriously. A client who calls the police is likely to get both of you arrested. Diffusing a situation like this will depend on the exact circumstances. Whatever you do, do not give in to any demands that make it more difficult to leave, such as removing your clothes or returning to the bedroom. You are better off facing the police than putting yourself in a position where you may be physically assaulted.

If you ever have reason to believe the client has drugged you (if you are quickly becoming sleepy or disoriented, for example), you should immediately go to the nearest bedroom or bathroom and lock yourself in. Once you are inside, use your cellular phone to call for help. If at all possible, do not try to make this call while you are still in the same room as the client. If he has in fact drugged you, he will know you are calling for help. Expect him to do everything in his power to delay your call. Pretending you have to use the bathroom is a ruse that just might work.

In cases where a client becomes insanely violent and attempts to hurt you, there is little advice I can offer you. I have heard that Jeffrey Dahmer's only victim to escape did so because he kept reminding Dahmer that he was a human being with thoughts and feelings just like everyone else. Supremely-ill people like Dahmer reduce people to objects in their mind, so reminding them of your humanity may help.

Finally, many escorts have a system in which they call a friend or lover to check-in and say they are okay. Employees of escort agencies usually have to do this as well. A good idea is to have a system where if you do not check-in by a certain time, such as half an hour after the appointment ends, a friend will call the client's phone number to check on you. Just be sure not to fall asleep or lose track of the time, as you do not want to scare your friend if he cannot reach you.

Aside from problematic clients, another pressing concern for escorts is the issue of STDs. That's a subject you will find covered in the next chapter.

## Chapter Sixteen[*]
## Sexually Transmitted Diseases

*Early in the second year of my escorting, I contracted crab lice twice in as many months. I guessed that I had been exposed to them by one of my regular clients. An examination of my records revealed a man who had hired me just before both outbreaks. The next time we met, I made a point of examining him for crab lice early in the appointment. Sure enough, I found them. He was extremely embarrassed, but my "it can happen to anyone" attitude helped him retain at least some of his dignity.*

*Unfortunately the next time I saw him, I noticed that he still had crabs. Somehow he had failed to completely rid himself of them. I pointed them out again, which embarrassed him far more than the first time. He never did hire me again after that.*

As escorts, we understand and accept the risks of our careers. We know that there are dangerous clients, we are aware that law enforcement officials sometimes target escorts, and we know that there are plenty of sexually transmitted diseases waiting to strike the unwary. We seek to minimize these risks as best we can, but understand they cannot be entirely eliminated.

Unfortunately, we also have the bad habit of preferring not to think about the dangers in our work. It is much more

---

[*] The material in this chapter was obtained and verified by Stephen E. Goldstone, M.D. I highly recommend his book *The Ins and Outs of Gay Sex: A Medical Handbook for Men.* Be sure also to check out his website (http://www.gayhealth.com).

pleasant to count our money while pretending that the dangers do not exist. Take the case of STDs: We know that we should learn exactly how they can be transmitted, but how many of us have actually taken the time to do this? It is much easier to use the same guidelines that protect us against AIDS/HIV. After all, isn't that the most serious of the diseases? It seems logical that the same precautions should in turn protect us from lesser diseases.

In reality, this is not even remotely the case. Activities that are 100% completely, absolutely, definitely, and undeniably safe when it comes to transmitting the AIDS virus can transmit other STDs. For example, rubbing your naked crotch right up against your partner's buns cannot spread HIV, but can easily pass along genital warts.

Surprised? I was too when I learned this. In fact, the reality of escorting is that you cannot have sex and completely protect yourself against STDs at the same time. Play often enough and sooner or later you will contract something. No amount of making sure your partners are "clean" will protect you, either. You cannot always tell when your partner is infected with an STD, and he will not always be able or willing to inform you.

There are ten primary STDs that should concern you. These are crabs, scabies, HIV, hepatitis, syphilis, gonorrhea, herpes, genital warts, nongonococcal urethritis, and molluscum contagiosum. Each has its own symptoms, causes, long-term effects, and treatments. Many also make it easier to transmit and contract other STDs. Worse yet, there are high correlations between having one STD and having another at the same time. The lesson here is that if you contract one STD, you should always see your doctor to check for others.

Unfortunately, doctors often misdiagnose STDs, especially in the mouth. This is in part because the symptoms of many diseases are similar, but also because doctors frequently assume that their male clients are all straight. When visiting your doctor for any possible STD-related symptoms, make sure you mention that you have sex with men.

You may receive a few strange looks, but that is far preferable to a misdiagnosis. Of course, a far better solution would be to find a gay doctor who is hip to the issues facing both gay men and sex workers. We will talk about how to do that in chapter seventeen.

Whenever you are diagnosed with an STD, you should find out when it will be safe to go back to work. Many STDs have a limited time period during which you can infect your partners, during which you should not be seeing clients. If you intend to work in spite of a possible infectious condition such as HIV or herpes, you should talk to your doctor about what you can do to minimize putting your partners at risk.

When reading the following sections, keep in mind that these are short summaries about each disease. People with compromised immune systems may suffer more severe symptoms or require different treatments. When considering your own health issues, talk to a qualified medical practitioner who is knowledgeable about both gay and sex-worker issues.

**Crab Lice**

Technically speaking, crab lice is not a disease. In fact, crabs are small insects that are transmitted via skin-to-skin contact, as well as by sharing towels, bed linens, and the like. They can usually be found in your pubic hair region, including your crotch, stomach, thighs, and butt. On occasion they can even be found in facial and armpit hair. They are about the size of the tip of a pencil and have the appearance of small specks against your skin. You may also see small brown dots of lice poop against your skin. Crab lice eggs can be found "glued" to the hairs of your body as well.

Unless someone spots them, chances are you will realize you have them when you begin itching. The itching starts in approximately two weeks after exposure if it is your first infestation. Future ones cause your body to begin itching almost immediately. If this is your first experience with crab lice, you may want to use a pair of tweezers to pick up and examine a louse up close. Such an education will be invaluable in recognizing them in the future.

Treating crabs is relatively easy. There are a number of over-the-counter medications available at your local drug store that are excellent for this purpose, including RID, Nix, and Kwell. They can be purchased in either shampoo or lotion form. Carefully follow the directions, and then use a special comb for removing dead lice and eggs from your body. Regular combs will not suffice; lice combs are much more fine. The itching should stop within a few days. A second treatment may be necessary, depending on how effective the first was.

Some people also have the habit of using a pair of tweezers to scan their bodies for any lice that the comb and shampoo may have missed. You may want to do it yourself, or may want to ask a partner for help. This approach is useful in clearing out any surviving lice but should not serve as a substitute for regular treatments. If you find any lice during your search, grab them with the tweezers and burn them with a cigarette lighter or candle flame.

Immediately after you treat yourself, you will want to wash your clothing, bed linens, towels, and the like with special anti-lice detergents (usually sold right next to the anti-lice shampoos). To kill any surviving lice, be sure to iron your clothes or dry them on high heat. You will also want to set-up an appointment with a doctor to be tested for other STDs. One-third of all people with crab lice have another STD as well. Considering the amount of sex that escorts have, there is an excellent chance you will be in that third.

As unpleasant as it may be, you will also want to inform any recent partners about your condition. They may easily have contracted crab lice from you and can give them back the next time they see you. This is especially true if you have worked with another escort. Your regular clients may overlap, and you would hate for the crab lice to be passed around, and around, and around...

## Scabies

Scabies is another form of insect that causes itching, only in this case they burrow below your skin and reproduce. Their movements under your skin leave a series of lines that may be visible. They can affect your genitals, arms, stomach, hands, and especially the skin between your fingers. Treatment is typically applied in cream form and can be purchased over the counter. Clothing, towels, linens, and the like must also be washed in hot water and dried with heat.

As with crab lice, they can be transmitted through close physical contact or by sharing towels and the like. In the event you ever contract scabies, you stand a good chance of having another STD as well. Make an appointment with your doctor and be checked, even if just to give yourself a clean bill of health.

## Syphilis

Syphilis is the first of the ten STDs here that has the dubious honor of being potentially fatal. Fortunately, this rarely happens in developed countries. Unlike crab lice and scabies, syphilis is a bacterial infection that is transmitted sexually, and on occasion by skin-to-skin contact. Using a condom for anal and oral sex helps but is not foolproof. You can minimize your risk of exposure by washing yourself thoroughly with soap and water after sex, especially where bodily fluids touched you. You can contract syphilis on your penis, in your mouth, on your scrotum (the sack that holds your balls), and in your anus.

The first symptom of syphilis is usually highly visible - a painless red sore (or occasionally, sores) located wherever you contracted the disease. This can occur up to three months after the time of infection. If the disease was contracted anally, the sore may be difficult to see without proper medical equipment. If the sore is inside your body, it may actually be painful. The sore may also cause bloody bowel movements, diarrhea, and a thick, gelatinous (mucus) discharge.

Wherever it is located, an untreated sore will heal itself within three-to-eight weeks. Unfortunately that does not mean that the syphilis is gone. The syphilis then enters a second stage causing a variety of symptoms including a skin rash, fever, swollen glands, tiredness, joint pain, and a runny nose. Left untreated for long enough (another 10-20 years), the disease may eventually enter a third stage and attack the nervous and circulatory systems, possibly causing death.

Fortunately, that fate is easily avoidable. A shot or oral dose of antibiotics can easily clear up the infection in either of the first two stages. The tests are relatively simple and painless and can be done by most doctors. As with all STDs, having one means you may have another. Have your doctor run the usual series of tests.

If you are diagnosed with syphilis, it is extremely important that you notify your partners. Doing so goes a long way towards eradicating this unnecessary disease. Did you know that many countries have already done so? Canada has reduced this disease to virtually nonexistent levels, but the United States still has a ways to go. We have over 101,000 new cases reported annually. Considering that male-male sex is estimated to cause half of these, we have a responsibility to do our part to eradicate this disease.

## Gonorrhea

If you think syphilis is a problem, consider gonorrhea. There are over ten times more cases of gonorrhea than syphilis reported annually. That is not including the estimated one million more cases that are not reported either.

Like syphilis, a bacterium causes gonorrhea. It can infect your mouth, throat, anus, or urethra (the tube inside your dick). The exact symptoms vary according to where you are infected. If you contract gonorrhea in your urethra, you will probably begin to feel pain when you urinate two-to-five days after exposure. It is also common to have a green or yellow discharge coming from your penis. You may observe this, or may notice the stain in your underwear. If you contract oral gonorrhea, you may experience a sore throat, swollen glands, pain when you swallow, or a redness in the back of your throat. The symptoms of anal gonorrhea include a slight pain when you defecate. You may notice a slight discoloration or trace of blood as well. You may also be leaking discharge from your anus.

On occasion men can contract gonorrhea and exhibit no symptoms. This is exactly why it is a good idea to be tested if you are ever diagnosed with other STDs. You may be infecting your partners, but have no idea that you even have the disease. Left untreated, the bacteria can infect other parts of your body causing a wide variety of more serious difficulties including joint and tendon infections.

If you suspect you have gonorrhea, you should inform your doctor when he examines you, especially if he is not experienced with gay patients or sex workers. You should also have yourself tested for the bacteria in all locations. Treatment involves antibiotics, either given through an injection or taken orally.

The quick incubation time for gonorrhea makes it easy to determine whom you may have exposed to the disease. If you are diagnosed with gonorrhea, you should immediately inform all partners you met within a week before the onset of symptoms.

## Nongonococcal Urethritis (NGU)

Nongonococcal urethritis is a bacterial STD that infects the urethra. Rather than being a specific bacteria, NGU refers to a whole category of infections. You may be familiar with one of the more common infections, chlamydia. Symptoms for NGU are similar to those for gonorrhea in the urethra, but tend to be less severe. Men with NGU may produce a discharge ranging from thick-and-white to thin-and-clear. The key symptom to look for is a stain on the front of your underwear. You will also experience pain during urination.

You can contract NGU by topping without a condom, although receiving unprotected oral sex more commonly passes it. Symptoms begin approximately one-to-five weeks after you are exposed to NGU. Fortunately, the disease is not serious (although highly uncomfortable) and can be easily treated by a doctor. As always, the presence of an STD may indicate that you have been exposed to others as well.

## Herpes

Herpes is different from syphilis and gonorrhea in that it is caused by a virus, not a bacteria. That means that there are no treatments available that can directly kill the virus. What medications do exist are designed either to prevent the virus from reproducing or to help your body respond better when fighting the disease. Like HIV, your body lacks the ability to rid itself of the virus.

Herpes is actually not one disease, but is one of many strains of the herpes simplex virus (HSV). Most have nothing to do with what is commonly thought of as herpes. Two strains, HSV-1 and HSV-2, are in fact the causes.

For the most part, what spreads herpes is kissing, oral sex, rimming, and anal sex. You can be either the "giver" or the "receiver" in any of these acts and still be exposed to the virus. Occasionally herpes can also be passed through nonsexual skin-to-skin contact as well. This is of special concern to those masseurs/bodyworkers who may not otherwise expect to be exposed to STDs. During sex, the virus can also cover fingers, condoms, sex toys, and the like. Washing your hands and toys with soap and water as often as possible is an important part of preventing the disease.

If you are exposed to herpes, your first symptoms may feel like a mild cold, including a minor fever and an aching feeling. About a week later you will develop a burning sensation and a group of small, clear blisters where you were infected. These blisters may become painful as they enlarge. You are highly contagious at this point, especially when the blisters break. Touching other parts of your body can infect those areas as well. Be careful to wash your hands thoroughly with soap and water after touching the blisters. After several more days, the blisters will break and turn into small pink sores that eventually heal.

Do not assume that you are over the disease at this point. Herpes is a lifelong condition, and from time-to-time you will have outbreaks of these sores. You are likely to have several attacks in your first year, with the attacks slowly decreasing in frequency and severity. The location of these attacks will depend on where on your body you contracted the disease. They may be in various places in your mouth, around your anus, or on the head, shaft, or foreskin of your penis. You may also have other symptoms depending on the location of your infection. These can include a bloody discharge from your anus, bleeding and pain when you pass a bowel movement, pain when you swallow, cold sores, redness in your throat, or swollen glands in your neck.

It is easy for escorts to go into a panic every time they have a canker sore. Fortunately, you can usually tell the difference between a canker sore and herpes. Canker sores are usually solitary and white in color, whereas herpes sores in the mouth are usually in groups and are red once the blisters break. Of course you should not be working with canker sores either. Having one of those makes it a lot easier to contract all sorts of nasty STDs.

Although herpes is a lifelong condition, there are a number of medications that can help. Often these must be taken at the first sign of an outbreak. Talk to your doctor for information about these options. Although you are primarily contagious during outbreaks, you should also know that you can still pass the virus to your partners even when you do not have any sores.

Protecting yourself against herpes is difficult. It helps to use a condom for both oral and anal sex and to avoid kissing and rimming. Unfortunately, if you adopted all of those requirements you would be going a long way towards putting yourself out of business. At least one step though is not problematic – discreetly examining your client's penis for sores before you become more intimately involved.

Sadly, even all of these steps are not enough. Herpes is one of those risks we take as escorts. We hope that it will never happen to us, but in the end it is a real possibility.

### Genital and Anal Warts (HPV)

Genital warts, technically referred to as condyloma acuminatum caused by the human papillomavirus (HPV), is yet another of those incredibly annoying but non-fatal STDs. Men who have sex with men have this virus in shockingly high numbers. Up to 65% of HIV-negative men have the disease, and over 90% of people with HIV! According to Dr. Goldstone, one of the country's foremost experts on gay medicine, it is virtually impossible for an escort to escape HPV infection no matter how hard he tries to avoid it. Fortunately, HPV can only be fatal if it develops into anal cancer (more on that in a bit).

HPV is actually a whole series of viruses. Several of these are responsible for what we call genital warts. The warts are not in fact the disease, but rather are the human body's response to the virus. That means many of you will have the virus on parts of your body and still show no symptoms. As Murphy's Law might have predicted, you can contract the virus from seemingly safe parts of your partner's body. You can even spread the virus from one part of your body to another part as well.

HPV can infect a number of areas of the body, including your scrotum (balls), butt, thighs, the shaft and head of your penis, and the entire pubic region. You can also have HPV warts inside your urethra, and on both the inside and the outside of your anus. As with herpes, the virus can be spread both sexually and through skin-to-skin contact. The virus is also easily spread to your partner or to other areas of your own body by fingers and sex toys during sex. Sadly, condoms do not provide adequate protection against spreading genital warts. If your partner tops you while wearing one, it will protect you against only those warts that are covered by the condom. Warts on the inside of your anus can spread using your own bowel movements as a method of transmission.

Because HPV does not always cause genital warts, you will not always know when you are infected with the virus. You may grow warts within a few months of exposure, or you may not grow them at all. Even if you have the warts treated, you may still have the virus and grow new ones years later.

Visible warts may be white, or may be slightly lighter or darker than your natural skin color. They usually occur in patches, so if you spot just one there may be more on the way. They may itch as well. In the case of anal warts, they may not be visible at all. Instead, anal warts may cause pain after you pass a bowel movement or after bottoming during anal sex. They may also cause some bleeding out of your anus, and may even cause a painful anal fissure (tear in the anal lining).

Because of the extreme frequency of HPV in gay men, you should immediately set-up an appointment with your doctor if you even remotely suspect that you have genital or anal warts. Regardless of where you may have them, your physician should check both on the surface of your skin and inside your anus. You can even be a strict top and have anal warts, as gay men are several times more likely to have warts in their anal canals than on their penis. If your doctor cannot or will not examine the inside of your anus using a special scope, find a doctor who will. Regular screenings are the single-best way to protect yourself against genital warts.

Treatment of genital and anal warts varies according to where you are infected. You should not attempt to treat them with over-the-counter wart removers. Those are meant for a different type of wart, and can be dangerous if used for genital warts. Let your doctor treat them instead using a cream, an injection, or a minor surgical procedure.

**Anal Cancer**

Although technically not an STD, anal cancer is worth mentioning here because of its unique relationship to HPV. As might be expected in a chapter with so much bad news, anal cancer can be dangerous and potentially life-threatening.

As stated before, HPV is a whole series of viruses. Unfortunately several of these strains predispose you to develop anal cancer. Inside your anus, normal cells may turn into abnormal cells of three varieties: atypical, low-grade dysplasia, and high-grade dysplasia. Atypical and low-grade cells are not immediately dangerous, but they must be tracked long-term in case they develop into high-grade cells. The high-grade cells are a more serious medical problem, as researchers estimate they will develop into anal cancer about 10% of the time.

Even if you have never been diagnosed with genital or anal warts, you may still have contracted the dangerous strains of HPV. In this case your cells may be becoming more and more abnormal without you even being the slightest bit aware. The best way to combat this is to be screened for it using a Pap smear.

Yes, you read correctly. I mean a Pap smear, the test commonly given to women to check for cervical cancer. This test is used because HPV is thought to be the same disease that causes cervical cancer. The results will determine whether you have normal or abnormal cells, and if abnormal, of which type (atypical, low-grade, or high-grade). If your cells are normal, then you need only be checked again in three years (one year if you are HIV-positive).

Pap smears are not painful, but they are slightly uncomfortable. They involve the doctor scraping the cells inside your anus with a dacron swab. He will also place a small amount of vinegar inside your anus before he looks inside you with a special scope. (In case you're wondering, vinegar makes it easier for the physician to see the warts.)

If the Pap smear confirms you have abnormal cells, your doctor will want to biopsy a small bit of your anal lining to confirm how abnormal the cells have become. The Pap smear does not hurt, but is hardly pleasant either. Expect to feel some discomfort and to have some blood in your bowel movements afterwards. You will need to refrain from bottoming and escorting for several days after the procedure.

If the tests confirm that you have high-grade cells, then you will want to have the cells removed before they become cancerous. Your doctor will guide you through that process. If your cells are atypical or low-grade, you should have follow-up Pap smears every three-to-six months in case the cells become high-grade.

One final note on anal cancer. Many doctors are not well-educated about gay health concerns. If your physician does not understand why you are requesting this procedure, explain the link between HPV and anal cancer. Alternatively, GayHealth.com (http://www.gayhealth.com) has an excellent article for physicians on the how's and why's of an anal Pap smear. Print it out and bring a copy with you. If he refuses to do the procedure, find a new doctor.

## Hepatitis

Hepatitis is another potentially deadly virus on the list. Hepatitis is a series of six viruses named Hepatitis A, B, C, D, E, and G. (Don't ask me why there is not an F. There just isn't.) Hepatitis A, B, and C are all immediate concerns. Hepatitis D, E, and G are rare.

Many times you may contract and successfully fight off a hepatitis infection while not showing any symptoms at all. In cases like these, you will probably only learn of your infection through a blood test at a later date. On occasion, the infection is much more dangerous and can lead to long-term liver damage or death. Of those with hepatitis, 30% never have symptoms, and only a few have symptoms that can be life-threatening. Most people will become sick from hepatitis, but their immune systems will overcome it. These people typically become ill for several weeks and experience a range of symptoms including jaundice (the yellowing of the eyes and skin), loss of appetite, and nausea. In all cases, the carriers are contagious before they begin to show symptoms.

Hepatitis A is most commonly passed through feces that are accidentally ingested orally. For gay men, this is most commonly done through rimming, although it can be done accidentally if you finger an infected person's anus and then later handle food or touch your mouth. Approximately two-to-six weeks after exposure, you will begin to show symptoms. At that point you are extremely contagious, even through kissing. Typically the disease runs its course in six-to-eight weeks, at which time your liver returns to normal. Hepatitis A is rarely life threatening.

Hepatitis B and C are different in how they are transmitted, with the additional downside of being more serious. Both can be spread through bodily fluids such as blood, and perhaps through semen and saliva. Experts have had difficulty determining how B and C are passed along sexually, but there is no doubt that multiple partners vastly increases the risk. Both the B and C strains of hepatitis have a large window period before you start to show symptoms, ranging from two weeks to six months. Like hepatitis A, during this time you are extremely contagious.

Sometimes your body is not able to fight off a hepatitis infection. This is called chronic hepatitis. It typically does not happen with hepatitis A. In hepatitis B it happens about 5-10% of the time for people with normal immune systems, but 90% of the time if you are HIV-positive. Hepatitis C is far worse, with 90% of normal immune systems becoming chronic, as well as almost 100% of compromised immune systems. A chronic infection needs to be treated with interferon and other drugs, otherwise the disease can slowly destroy the liver and eventually cause death.

Treatments for hepatitis are limited, but your doctor can guide you through what is available. By far your best strategy is to avoid contracting the disease in the first place. Luckily, there is an absolutely wonderful option available: immunization. With just a few shots you can become immune to both the A and B strains. For hepatitis A, a single shot with a booster after six-to-twelve months generally does the trick. The hepatitis B vaccine requires three shots over six months. You should also receive a booster one year later. A combination vaccine of three shots for both A and B is available. Always remember that vaccinations for one strain of hepatitis will not protect you against the others. You need to be vaccinated for both A and B. There is no vaccine for hepatitis C yet.

If you are accidentally exposed to hepatitis, you should contact your doctor immediately. Immunegloublin treatments given quickly enough after exposure may render you temporarily immune to hepatitis. This is not a substitute for vaccinations, but can be helpful in the right situation.

**Molluscum Contagiosum**

Molluscum contagiosum (MC) is yet another virus that you can contract. Fortunately, it is not as dangerous as any of the other viral infections, as the virus is not a lifelong condition. Left alone, your body will usually fight it off in two-to-four months, although it can take years. Some reoccurrences can occur, although it is not known whether these are a result of the virus hiding in the body, or if they are from new infections.

MC is traditionally passed through direct skin-to-skin contact with the infected area of the body. That means it can be contracted easily through sex as well as through massage and touching. It most often affects your anus, genitals, thighs, and stomach, although it can also affect your face, back, and arms.

Approximately one-to-three months after you are exposed to MC you will develop obvious symptoms. These are sores that look like pimples with small depressions in the center. Over time they can grow to about the size of a pencil eraser. Typically the sores are in solitary patches, although they may be found in more than one place on your body. If you squeeze a sore, a semi-solid white slime comes out.

As with all STDs, see your doctor if you suspect you have MC. He will remove the sores using one of several simple procedures. You should not delay going to the doctor in the hope they will go away. Although this is possible, they also might not and you may spread them all over your body. The sores can also become infected, which gives a greater chance of permanent scars being left behind.

## HIV

HIV is the virus that causes AIDS. It is believed to have only been in the United States since the 1970s, yet most escorts can scarcely remember a time before it. HIV is a virus that gradually breaks down your immune system.

In fact, two different strains of the same virus can cause AIDS. Human immunodeficiency virus-1 (HIV-1), and HIV-2. In the United States, HIV-1 is the primary culprit, and HIV-2 is almost nonexistent. Other countries have different balances.

Contrary to popular belief, HIV is actually a difficult virus to contract. Unlike many of the other STDs you have read about, HIV must enter your bloodstream to infect you. No amount of HIV on the skin will do the trick. Unless you have a cut or a sore, your skin is the perfect barrier to protect you.

Passing the virus into your bloodstream is most commonly done through giving or receiving unprotected anal sex ("barebacking" or "raw sex"), or by sharing needles. You can also contract HIV through oral sex, although it is extremely difficult to do so. Theoretically kissing can exchange the virus between two people, but this is extremely unlikely most of the time. Having sores in your mouth, on your cock and balls, or near your anus makes you more likely to contract HIV as well, because they give the virus a much easier path to reach the bloodstream. The same goes with having other STDs. If you or your partner have an STD, the chance of passing HIV becomes much higher.

The first sign that you are infected with HIV is acute viremia. Symptoms include a rash, muscle aches, and a fever. All of these occur soon after infection. As the years go by, your immune system will become less effective, making you vulnerable to a host of other infections with a variety of symptoms. Eventually your immune system degrades to the point where one of the opportunistic infections can kill you.

By far the best way to protect yourself against HIV is to insist on the use of condoms for all anal sex. In the case of oral sex, it is a good idea to use them as well. The risks are less that way, so you will have to make that decision for yourself whether to choose on the side of safety or business.

Your next-best ally in the fight against HIV is testing. When you are tested, you are actually being checked for your body's antibodies to HIV, not for the virus itself. In fact, an HIV test is actually two tests, the ELISA and the Western blot. The ELISA is good at determining whether you have the HIV antibodies, but it also has the bad habit of occasionally showing a false positive result. A false positive result is when the test says you are HIV-positive when in fact you are not. If the ELISA says you have the HIV antibody, a Western blot test is immediately performed. The Western blot is much more accurate and will help screen out the ELISA's occasional mistakes.

Recently a new test has come on the market called the Murex rapid test. This test is extremely fast, with results available in as little as ten minutes. Unfortunately, false positives occur in this test as well. If the Murex says you are positive, then a Western blot is done. In that case it takes an extra day to before your results are available.

There is also an oral test called OraSure that can be done. This checks your saliva for antibodies instead of your blood. Results from an OraSure test may take up to a week before they are available. The OraSure requires a Western blot test for confirmation purposes.

Finally, there is a home-based HIV testing kit available from the Home Access Health Corporation. Available for $40-55, the kit allows you to anonymously test yourself for HIV. You mail in a small blood sample, and call to receive your results in three-to-seven (depending on the type of kit you buy). The test can be purchased online as well as numerous pharmacies including Wal-Mart, Eckerd, CVS, and Rite-Aid. More information on this kit is available at http://www.homeaccess.com/hiv/main.html.

Unfortunately, all of these tests check for antibodies and not for the actual virus. Antibodies can take two-or-more months to appear after you are infected with the virus. During this time you may test HIV-negative even if you have the virus. Regardless of the type of test you prefer, as an escort you should be tested every three-to-six months. Male escorts are one of the highest possible risk groups for HIV, so you must protect yourself accordingly.

In the event you suspect that you may have been exposed to HIV, you should see your doctor immediately. There is a strategy of treating new HIV infections that involves taking medications for several weeks after transmission, but the treatment must begin within 72 hours of exposure. This is primarily used for medical providers who are accidentally exposed to HIV, and is still being studied for sexual exposure. Still, it is better than doing nothing at all. Either way, this is not a substitute for safe sex.

Regarding drugs and HIV, many drugs including poppers have the effect of lowering your immune system, making it more likely that you will contract HIV if you are exposed to it. Furthermore, drugs make it a lot easier to be caught up in the "heat of the moment" and to ignore condoms. Drugs are a no-win situation when it comes to escorting, so do not use them in your practice.

As for treatments for HIV, there isn't any. At least not any treatment that will cure you. Once you have HIV, you will have it for life.

STDs are among the largest drawbacks to escorting. There are dozens of bad points about STDs and no good ones. Still, potential health hazards are not the end of the world. In the next chapter we will cover a few more health issues and then plot a course of action to stay as medically safe as realistically possible.

## Chapter Seventeen
## Maintaining Your Health

*Some time ago I received a phone call from someone asking how he could get into the escort business. He explained he was desperate for money to pay off a $1,500 phone bill a houseguest had left him. I gave him some basic tips on cyberhustling, and asked that he keep me informed how his business progressed.*

*Two months, thirty clients, and several thousand dollars later, he called to let me know he had raised all the money he wanted to and was leaving the business. Several days after that, he called me again to let me know he had been diagnosed with genital herpes. I expressed my sympathy that his two months in the business had ended this way. His reply was that I didn't need to feel bad. He had been having sores for several years. It was only now that he had seen a doctor about them.*

*Hanging up the phone gave me a queasy feeling. I wondered just how many of his clients now had herpes, and how many escorts in turn would catch it from them.*

When it comes to life, there is little that is more important than maintaining your health. Few people disagree with this, yet we often prefer not thinking about the risks of our actions. How many of you have ever had unsafe anal sex with someone you did not know very well? You knew perfectly well you should use a condom, yet you purposely did not. For whatever reason, you placed your life and your health in jeopardy for a quick thrill or a few bucks.

I do not bring these issues up to be accusatory, and I am certainly not in a position to moralize on this issue. What I am trying to say is that you need to consider what you are doing when it comes to your health. As you read in the last chapter, you are already taking plenty of risks with your health. If you are going to add to them, you need to think long and hard before doing so. Sooner or later your number will come up, and your doctor will have some bad news for you.

**Finding an Escort-Friendly Physician**

There are plenty of reasons to find an escort-friendly physician. He is more likely to diagnose your conditions correctly. He will be more open to listening to your concerns about how your work may be affecting your health. Perhaps most importantly, you are more likely to see your doctor if you feel your needs are understood and being met.

Many escorts have more than one physician: a gay doctor for sex and escort-related issues, and a straight one for other problems. This is a tempting option for escorts that live in rural or suburban areas and have a difficult time finding a knowledgeable gay doctor. If you elect to take this route, be careful when you decide to see the straight doctor, and always tell him as much as you can. Often what may seem to you to be a cold or the flu may in fact be the first symptoms of a viral STD. A straight doctor may misdiagnose you because he does not know about your escorting career and your sexuality.

Fortunately, finding the right doctor can be surprisingly easy. For starters, your insurance company or HMO may keep a list of gay and gay-friendly physicians. HMOs in particular are always looking to send you to doctors within their network, so do not hesitate to call and ask for a referral.

Gay and lesbian organizations are also a wealth of information when searching for a doctor. Many gay information lines maintain lists of doctors for just this purpose. Print publications (such as the ones you use to advertise yourself) often have gay-friendly doctors listed as well. The Internet is also an excellent place to search. A number of organization websites list gay and gay-friendly physicians around the world, including the Gay and Lesbian Medical Association (http://www.glma.com). In particularly large or progressive cities, there may even be clinics that specialize in health care for gays and lesbians.

Alternately, word-of-mouth can be an excellent source of advice. Ask your gay friends who their doctors are, or talk to other escorts online to learn who they see. Consider calling your local hospital and asking it to refer you to someone. They may have a list on file or may put you in touch with their HIV specialists. Those specialists in turn may be able to recommend you to a gay-friendly general practitioner.

If you have never been vaccinated for Hepatitis A and B, give your new physician a call. This is also an excellent opportunity to have a Pap smear done to check for signs of anal cancer. You may even want to be tested for HIV as well. Just be sure to tell the office in advance what you want to do at the appointment, so they can make sure that they have the vaccinations on hand. It also allows them to refer you to someone else for the Pap smear if they do not have the necessary medical equipment.

**Insurance**

Health insurance is increasingly becoming a major headache. In some countries, socialized medicine helps alleviate this problem, but in the United States it can be a major problem. As an escort, one of the first things you will want to do is check on your insurance coverage. Depending on your situation, you may be insured through your parents, a significant-other, or another job. If none of these apply, you will want to immediately obtain a health insurance policy.

Remember, as an escort you have no health benefits and you receive no sick pay. If you are injured or become ill as a result of your work, you cannot count on having an income. Add a pile of medical bills on top of that and you may be in trouble. This has been the downfall of more than one sex worker. Do not let it happen to you. Insurance is expensive but is also necessary. Considering the health risks that escorts face in their profession, there is an excellent chance that you will be using the coverage at some point.

**Viagra**

The release of Pfizer's anti-impotence drug, Viagra, was intended to revolutionize the sex lives of men with erectile dysfunction. As a side effect it changed the sex industry as well. No longer do porn actors struggle to become hard on the set. Now with the pop of a pill their troubles are solved. The same can be said for escorts and Viagra. On those days you are worried about staying hard, Viagra can provide a helping hand. It works, too. I'll be the first to admit that I have tried it.

Of course, the drug has some major downsides. Two hours after I take a 50mg tablet of Viagra, I have a splitting headache. Other side effects can include blushing, a rapid heartbeat, and a blue tinge to your vision. Worse yet, the drug becomes potentially deadly when combined with nitrate-based medications and poppers (amyl nitrate). This is important, so let me make this perfectly clear: **Never mix Viagra and poppers unless you want to die.**

It is illegal to take Viagra without a prescription, but there are plenty of websites that will give you an "online consultation" allowing you to receive a legal prescription. The catch is that you also have to order Viagra from them. It is expensive this way, but two days after filling-out their form you can have a bottle on your doorstep. The federal government is slowly moving towards shutting down this online industry, but for now the option remains available.

If you order from one of these services, be extremely careful about doing so. The consultation they give you is nothing compared to what you should be receiving from your doctor. You may be taking an incorrect dosage, or your regular doctor may prescribe you a nitrate-based medication or other drug that has a potentially fatal interaction with Viagra. Furthermore, the U.S. Food & Drug Administration has never approved the use of Viagra for people without impotence problems. Taking them when your body is normal may result in unforeseen long-term effects.

It is also worth stating that distributing Viagra to your clients is a federal offense. Should your client have an adverse reaction to the drug, you may find yourself in immense legal trouble. If a client asks you to bring along Viagra, politely decline to do so.

Of course it remains your decision on how you want to handle Viagra. At some point in your business someone is bound to offer you a pill. Take it at your own risk.

**Steroids**

Outside of legitimate medical purposes, adult men typically use steroids to "bulk up" and build muscle. In surprisingly short amounts of time steroid-use can make a person considerably bigger. They are commonly abused on bodybuilding circuits where blood tests are not performed and are just as prevalent among "muscle boys" of the porn and escorting industries.

Ask someone who is poorly informed about steroids, and chances are he will tell you they are safe and are illegal only because of an irrational and conservative government. He is dead wrong. Steroids have a wide variety of side effects, some of which can be potentially deadly. These include an irregular heartbeat, high blood pressure, nosebleeds, stomach problems, nausea, vomiting, and infertility.

Steroids also harm the liver, kidneys, and prostate, and have the bad effect of increasing your risk for heart attacks and strokes. If that is not enough to frighten you, keep in mind that steroid use also causes bad acne and impotence as well.

In short, steroids are an effective way to bulk-up, but are also a great way to screw-up your health. When considering the use of steroids, keep two things in mind.

First, just as women often suffer from anorexia (a mental disorder in which they cannot become thin enough), some men suffer from its opposite. In Male Body Dysmorphic Disorder ("bigorexia"), men have obsessive thoughts that their size is too small. They feel a need to constantly exercise, to check their appearance in mirrors, and to use steroids. Their dedication to their bodies is such that they may even continue exercising even after a major injury such as a dislocated shoulder.

Second, escorts who do not use steroids will almost certainly never be able to match the bodies of those who do. Fortunately, that is not critical in this business. Clients do make looks an extremely high priority when first considering escorts, but personality almost always becomes a more important factor as they begin actively shopping for Mr. Right-Now. Do you need proof of this? Glance ahead at chapter twenty-two. Count the number of times the escorts advise being friendly and respectful to your clients. Compare that with how often they say you need to look good at all times. You might be surprised at the result.

Obviously, this is not something that affects all escorts. If you use steroids and are utterly dedicated to your exercise routine, you might want to see a professional psychologist for a "mental check-up." Otherwise, skip the steroids and stick with a personal trainer.

## The Uses and Limitations of Condoms

As was mentioned in chapter eleven, you should always carry three types of condoms to each appointment. First, you should carry the basic nonlubricated variety with the reservoir tip. These are used for anal sex. Second, you should carry nonlubricated condoms without the tip. These are better for oral sex, since the lube tastes bad and the tip can make some people gag. Third, you should carry extra-large condoms for your better-endowed clients (or perhaps for yourself).

As stated before, you should use latex condoms whenever possible. Polyurethane condoms are an acceptable alternative, but you should **never use "natural" or lambskin condoms.** Those will not protect you against most STDs and HIV.

When you are working, you should carry all three types of condoms because you never know when you will need them. For example, even if you do not require condoms for oral sex, having them available may prompt the client to use them. It may not be so hot as what you are used to, but it lowers your risk of contracting STDs from that client. In our work, there will always be another hot dick to suck. We do not suffer from a lack of sexual opportunities, so play orally safe whenever you can.

One way to suggest to clients that you use condoms for oral sex is to allow the client to watch you sorting through your bag. If you peak his curiosity, show him your assorted cockrings, condoms, and the like. Mentioning that you have condoms specifically for oral sex may prompt him to request using them, especially if you have flavored ones. Clients often find those too intriguing to pass by.

Regardless of the types of condoms you use, be aware of their uses and limitations. They are great for protecting yourself against HIV, but are only somewhat helpful at preventing syphilis, gonorrhea, hepatitis, herpes, and genital warts. You can contract those five diseases even if you use condoms for oral and anal sex. Condoms are also completely useless in protecting you against crab lice, scabies, and molluscum contagiosum.

As a side note on lubricants, it was once thought that you should always use a lube containing nonoxynol-9 for anal sex. This chemical is a spermicide and was found in lab tests to kill the HIV virus. Conventional wisdom has shifted, and now researchers disagree with their earlier opinion. The amount of nonoxynol-9 in lubricants is not enough to kill all of the HIV in semen. Furthermore nonoxynol-9 may actually irritate the lining of your rectal walls making it easier to contract HIV. You should therefore make sure your condoms and lubricants do not contain nonoxynol-9.

**Working with STDs**

As your escorting career progresses, some of you will contract an STD. This may be something simple and treatable, or may be more serious in nature. You may even be diagnosed with more than one STD at the same time. Whatever you catch, you will invariably have appointments on your calendar. It will be highly tempting to keep those meetings, even if you are unsure if it is safe for you to work.

However tempting the money may be, you should not have sex with any of your clients if you suspect you may be contagious. As an escort, you have an ethical obligation to do no harm to your clients. At the first sign of any symptom, you should set-up an appointment to see your doctor. Discuss your concerns about infecting your clients with him. He will educate you about your medical situation and will be able to help you arrive at a decision as to when you can return to work. Working with an STD is a bad business decision in any case. One review on the Internet stating you knowingly worked with an STD may cost you thousands of dollars in business.

You may find yourself having contracted an STD that cannot be cured. Take the case of herpes. There are many escorts with herpes who work in spite of their medical condition. They often lie about their condition to their partners, justifying their actions on the basis that clients "know the risk" when they hire an escort. In fact, clients rarely know what the risks are. When you read through chapter sixteen, you may have been surprised to learn how easily STDs can be transmitted. Unless your clients are physicians, chances are they have no idea what their risks are.

If you test positive for HIV, the decision to quit or to remain escorting becomes a difficult one. Some escorts choose to hide their positive status. Others elect to retire from the business. However you decide to handle the issue, know there are three other options you may want to consider.

First, many bodyworkers in the business are HIV-positive. They offer erotic massage services sometimes followed by masturbation. As far as HIV is concerned, working like this is completely safe for the client as long as you do not have a cut or an open sore on your hands. If part of your work routinely involves rubbing your body against your client's, then your body must be free of sores as well.

A second option may surprise you. There is a steadily increasing number of escorts who have elected to work as openly HIV-positive escorts. They state that they are positive in their print and online advertisements and usually clarify their status to all potential clients. I interviewed one escort with HIV that informed me that only 10% of his business indicates being positive as well. Another 10% claim they are negative, and the other 80% never volunteer the information. In no case does he offer unsafe sex (barebacking) as a service, and he does not allow his clients to lick or swallow his semen. Financially his business is still successful, and he works several times per week (sometimes more than once per day).

A third option is to only accept HIV-positive clients. This would limit your business but would certainly keep you from worrying about accidentally infecting your partners. Do not offer bareback services if you have HIV. There are many diseases you can contract through barebacking, and your compromised immune system cannot fight off infections like it should.

However you choose to handle the issue of STDs, remember that you have an ethical obligation to do no harm to your clients. Talk to your doctor and devise a strategy that will allow you to maintain as normal a career as possible while still protecting those around you.

## A "Protection Strategy" For Your Health

Obviously, there is a great deal of information on your health that as an escort you need to know. Fortunately much of it can be condensed into a series of steps designed to help protect you against STDs.

*First*, before you so much as talk to your next client, find a gay/sex-work-friendly doctor. A doctor who is clueless on these issues is better than none but may also misdiagnose your symptoms.

*Second*, if you have not been vaccinated for Hepatitis A and B, set-up an appointment to have them done. Have your doctor test you for HIV as well. If money is an issue, you may want to utilize the free HIV-testing services available in your area.

You may also want to obtain a clean bill-of-health as far as other STDs are concerned. Ask the doctor to give you the complete battery of STD tests, including a Pap smear for anal cancer. If you cannot afford all of the tests and do not have insurance, have your doctor refer you to a clinic where you can have this done at low-cost or for free.

*Third*, buy lots of condoms. Unless you only provide your clients with masturbation and massage, you are going to need them. Be sure to buy all three types previously discussed.

*Fourth*, read appendix four, the quick chart of visible signs of STDs in your sexual partners. Study it every day until you memorize the information. Come back to the chart often and refresh your memory.

*Fifth*, be prepared to say "no" and to walk away from a client if you are in doubt about his health. Make an effort to tactfully examine all of your clients as you remove your clothes and begin foreplay.

*Sixth,* if you ever rim your partners, make sure they are as anally hygienic as possible. Requesting your client to wash himself "down there" with soap and water is perfectly reasonable before you begin. Not only will it make the experience more pleasant, but also it will cut down on your risk of contracting STDs.

*Seventh,* take a shower after every sexual encounter. Wash yourself thoroughly with soap and water. If showering is not possible, use the sink to wash your genitals, anus, and hands as best you can. Be sure to wash your skin anywhere that came in contact with semen or other bodily fluids.

*Eighth,* at the first sign of having an STD, cancel all of your appointments until you meet with your doctor. If you are diagnosed with an STD, be tested for all others. Continue avoiding your clients until your doctor gives you a clean bill-of-health to return to work.

*Ninth,* visit your doctor every three-to-six months for another HIV test. Ask your doctor to give you another Pap smear every three years (every year if you are HIV-positive).

As a working escort, you will have plenty of health decisions to make. Should you use Viagra? Will you perform unprotected oral sex in your work? Who will you see when you need to visit a doctor? There are plenty more questions that can be asked as well. These are all questions you should be able to answer.

As you know, escorting involves taking a series of risks. Dangerous clients are one. Medical risks are another. In the next chapter we will explore legal concerns for working escorts. Hopefully in our lifetime prostitution will be recognized as a valid career entitled to legal protection. Until that time you can either move to Amsterdam, or turn the page and begin learning how to handle the reality of today's society.

## Chapter Eighteen
## Legal Issues

*I was watching the New York City Gay Pride Parade when a familiar face marched by. I realized that he was a client of mine, and one who would not mind me saying hello. In front of a thousand onlookers I ran toward his contingent and gave him a hug and a kiss. He and I shared a knowing smile about our meeting, but to the rest of the world we were only two friends greeting each other. The irony that I was kissing a member of the Gay Officers Action League was lost on everyone but the two of us.*

One of the most serious hazards of escorting is the risk of legal harassment and arrest. Even in areas where prostitution is technically legal there are often other laws that make the work of an escort difficult. While these laws do have the pleasant side effect of keeping prices up, they ultimately harm those of us who choose to sell our time to those in search of adult companionship.

**Prostitution Laws**

How Western nations prohibit prostitution varies from country to country, but in general the rules are the same. To convict an escort for prostitution, the state must be able to prove:

- An agreement was made,
- The agreement was to engage in a sex act, and

- The agreement involved a fee for performing that act.

The way to protect yourself against successful prosecution is clear. When running your escort business, you must avoid allowing the police to gain evidence of one of the three points.

Unfortunately that is easier said than done. Before you meet a client, you always need to establish an agreement (point one). Unless you are willing to do it for free, you are going to have to negotiate a fee (point three). That means the safest way of avoiding prosecution is by publicly maintaining the illusion that your services do not involve sex. That is why prostitutes commonly refer to themselves as escorts. An escort is someone who accompanies his clients and provides companionship. The reality is completely different. With a few rare exceptions, men do not hire escorts solely for nonsexual companionship.

There are many ways escorts advertise their services without specifically mentioning sex. They often post nude pictures of themselves, talk about how sexual they are in their personal lives, and describe their sexual fantasies in great detail over the Internet. Other escorts have a more simple approach. They place their ads and then refuse to speak about anything sexual. All of these steps do help but are not foolproof ways to protect yourself. For one thing, escorts are often only cautious on the telephone. Arresting officers are skilled at convincing escorts to talk about sex in person. All it takes is one slip to provide the officer the evidence he needs to establish point two.

Of course, all this is assuming that the officer tells the truth. There are many documented cases of officers who have violated both the law and their department regulations by lying about what happened. Unfortunately, if an officer decides to lie, there is little you can do to defend yourself.

Worse yet, in some areas a prosecutor may begin charging escorts even if the evidence is flimsy. Many prosecutors are elected to their positions, and may be prosecuting even the weakest cases against escorts as a way of demonstrating politically they are able to "clean up" their community. Even lower-ranking prosecutors will often aggressively pursue cases in order to advance a political career or to curry favor with a superior.

In some communities, police often use harassment to deter escorts from their work. They arrest the escort before they have enough evidence for a successful prosecution. The charges are dropped almost immediately, but not before the escort is subject to all the indignities of arrest. Even worse, in many communities the names of those arrested become public knowledge, resulting in the escort's name being printed in the paper. Even if the charges are dropped, the escort will have a permanent arrest record for the remainder of his life.

## More Laws

There are plenty of other laws an escort can easily violate. For example, New York City and parts of Australia require masseurs to be licensed, a process that often requires long periods of formal training. Advertising massage services without a license can subject the escort to arrest. For the same reason that prostitutes refer to themselves as escorts, erotic masseurs sometimes refer to themselves as bodyworkers: To avoid legal harassment.

Escorts in some parts of the world are also at risk of violating laws regarding "living off the immoral earnings of another." These laws exist in a number of states in the United States as well as in the United Kingdom. While designed to combat the owners of brothels and escort agencies, they can easily be used against independent escorts and their businesses as well. Significant-others of escorts should be especially wary of these laws. While it is unlikely they will ever be targeted for legal harassment, you never know until it happens.

One of the most serious laws to be concerned with is the issue of tax evasion. Prostitution, whether legal or illegal, is a taxable source of income. Failure to truthfully report your income can result in heavy fines and possible jail time. Remember the gangster, Al Capone? That's how the government finally prosecuted him. Precisely how to handle your money to avoid tax problems will be covered in chapter nineteen.

**Finding a Lawyer**

The first lesson when it comes to finding a good lawyer is to do it well in advance. You are far better off having your legal defense planned out before you need it, rather than sitting in jail wondering how long it will take before someone finds a lawyer for you. The sooner you have your own legal counsel, the better off you will be.

When finding a lawyer you want to make sure you have access to one that is supportive of sex workers and their issues. By far the best way to do this is to ask around. Ask other escorts to refer you to a good lawyer. Many cities have organizations for sex workers with up-to-date lists of recommended attorneys. Gay information lines work in much the same way and can be useful as well.

If you do find yourself in legal trouble, beware of "ambulance chasers." In many countries like the United States, it is unethical for a lawyer to approach you and offer to provide legal counsel. There are a variety of lawyers who ignore this and hang around the courthouse (or hospitals – remember Danny DeVito and Matt Damon in *The Rainmaker?*) looking for people with no legal counsel. They usually strike up a conversation with a person in obvious need of legal assistance, and then casually mention they work in the legal field. They then wait for the person to inquire about legal services. They often may provide referrals to companies specializing in bail bonds, because they receive a kickback from their referral (more on bail bonds in a while). In any case, they will be more than happy to represent you, but you are likely to receive substandard legal counsel from them. Remember that they are hanging around the courthouse because they do not have enough work at their office. That is not a sign of a good lawyer.

However you find a lawyer, keep his or her number with you at all times. Make sure two or three friends also have the lawyer's number as well. If you are in jail, you will want to call one of these people. He or she will in turn call your lawyer for you, or if that person is not available, they will find someone else. You do not want to be spending your own precious phone time talking to a lawyer's answering service if he is on vacation in the Bahamas.

You may want to contact the lawyer in advance of an arrest to establish a relationship. This can be as simple as just a phone call to confirm that he provides legal defense services for escorts. You will want to introduce yourself and mention the name of the person or organization that referred you. Some people will act as if it is strange that you are calling, but others will be friendly and chatty. In either case you will have a good idea about what their personality will be like when dealing with you. If the lawyer also provides personal services, such as wills, living wills, durable power of attorney documents, and the like, you may want to hire his firm to do a bit of legal work for you. You can establish a good working relationship that way.

In some cases, you may want to hire a lawyer on retainer. Some retainers involve paying a set fee in advance for a specific set of contracted services. Others involve you putting a certain amount down with the lawyer in advance. Whenever you have legal questions or need assistance, you can contact your lawyer, who will then draw from the account. If you can find a good lawyer willing to utilize this type of arrangement, by all means do so. It establishes an excellent working relationship that you may need later.

However you find a lawyer, you should take care to speak theoretically when initially discussing your business. Lawyers are obligated by law to only provide truthful information as part of your legal defense. They cannot knowingly submit false evidence on your behalf. If you make it clear to your attorney that you have a career as a prostitute, he may find it difficult to convince the prosecutor that this was an isolated incident. Ask your lawyer how to proceed with this sort of theoretical discussion. Under no circumstances should you lie to your attorney (or worse yet, lie while under oath). Doing so can make a bad situation much worse.

### Special Issues for Agency Escorts

Back in chapter five, I mentioned that when you are looking for an escort agency to work for, it is a good idea to find one that provides legal counsel for its employees. Having the escort agency's attorney is better than having none at all, although a good agency attorney is not a substitute for having your own legal counsel.

When a lawyer works for you, he has an ethical obligation to work for your best interest. In cases where you are arrested while working for an agency, your best legal interest may be to provide evidence against the escort agency. In this case, you would provide information for legal efforts against the agency in return for a lesser sentence or a complete waiver of the charges against you. It is not necessarily honorable to do so, but it may be a legal option for you. In cases where the agency is paying for your lawyer, there is a conflict-of-interest that may affect your ability to receive sound legal advice regarding this option.

In order to represent you, the agency's lawyer would ask you and the agency management to sign a form stating you are aware of the conflict-of-interest. If you choose to sign this document, be sure you know what you are doing. You have no way of knowing the ethics of your new lawyer, and where his priorities lie. There is a chance that the lawyer is going to balance your interests with those of the agency. Then again, the lawyer may be an excellent one and may be able to avoid legal trouble for both yourself and the agency at no cost to yourself. The decision is yours to make.

Regardless of your choice of legal representation, if you are arrested you should always use your phone call to contact someone outside of the agency, such as a friend or a lover. Let them contact the agency instead. Many agencies will offer you legal counsel, but others are not so honorable. Instead of hiring a lawyer on your behalf, a less scrupulous agency might spend the next few hours destroying records that acknowledge you were ever an employee. You are much better off having a friend on the outside track the agency's progress as they find counsel for you.

**If You Are Arrested**

Some of you reading this book can and will be arrested in the future for prostitution-related crimes. In the event something goes wrong, you need to be prepared for what to do.

If your client whips out a badge, **do not resist arrest.** This includes running away, fighting back, and arguing with the officer. Your situation is bad enough; resisting arrest can only make your situation worse. Even if the officer does not cross the line into police brutality, he can still snap those handcuffs extra tight. If you would prefer a ride to the station with at least a small amount of comfort and dignity, do not antagonize him unnecessarily.

When you are arrested in the United States, the officers will read to you your Miranda Rights early in the proceedings. These rights include your right to remain silent, the right to an attorney, and so on. The process of being arrested in other countries will vary. If you are not sure what your rights are, ask. Be wary of the answers however. Just because your rights may be read to you does not mean the officers will explain their true meaning.

If you have the right to remain silent, you should exercise this right. As the Miranda Rights say, "anything you say can and will be used against you in a court of law." The message here is simple: **Shut up and say nothing!** Answer basic questions such as your name and address, but do not discuss any facts relevant to your case. This includes why you have condoms with you, what you were doing at the appointment location, and anything else related to your escorting and your appointment. You should inform any arresting officers that you are exercising your right to remain silent until you speak to an attorney.

Incidentally, the right to remain silent applies even when you have not been placed under arrest. From time-to-time an officer may identify himself and begin to question you. You are legally required to provide identification to the officer, but beyond that you are not required to answer his questions. If you choose to answer them, you are waiving your right to remain silent. If you do not wish to answer any questions, a good suggestion is to say to the officer, "I am in a hurry and do not wish to answer any questions at this time. Am I free to leave or am I being detained?" In this case the officer will either have to arrest you or have to let you go. I cannot urge you strongly enough: **Do not discuss any details of your case with a police officer.**

When an arresting officer questions you, it will be highly tempting to try to talk yourself out of the situation. Do not attempt to do so. You will be making your situation worse. Under no circumstances should you lie to the officer. What you say can be used as evidence against you, and lying will make your situation more serious. Once an officer places you under arrest, no amount of pleading or storytelling is going to remove those cuffs.

## At the Station

Once the officers walk you to their vehicles, you will be transported to a police station for booking. In larger cities it may be done at a precinct building or at a central booking location. At the station you will be fingerprinted, photographed, and interviewed for identification purposes. You may be asked if you want to make a statement on your behalf. You should refuse this offer. As with before, do not discuss your case with anyone but your lawyer.

You should know that police are skilled when it comes to convincing escorts to talk. Sometimes they will sit you down, give you a cup of coffee, offer you a cigarette, and start chatting with you. They will explain how some "stupid" people play hardball, but that only hurts them because it angers the prosecutor. If you would be willing to make a statement, they will "put in a good word for you." Other times they will play a game of "good cop, bad cop." This style of interrogation involves one officer giving you a rough time, only to be summoned away and replaced by another officer who plays the part of the friend. Do not fall for either maneuver. Remember that anything you say can and will be used against you. Your silence is your best legal defense.

You will be taken to a phone at some point and given the opportunity to call someone. Use this call wisely: Call a friend or family member who can bail you out of jail. Be careful not to discuss the details of your arrest on the phone. It is doubtful that you are being recorded, but your conversation is certainly not private. If you are allowed to use one of the department's phones, be aware that in many stations all phone conversations are recorded.

Once you have made your phone call, you will be taken to a cell where you will remain until your arraignment before a judge or until you are bailed out. While you are in the cell, you should not speak about your arrest to anyone else. Discussions with cellmates are admissible as evidence, and you would hate to help the police because you were frightened and depressed.

Local laws and the nature of your charges will affect what happens next. For minor crimes, many areas have a set bail schedule. Bail is a sum of money that you pay to make sure you show up for trial. If you show up, the money is refunded. If you do not, the money is forfeited to the court and a warrant is issued for your arrest. If the charges are more serious, you may be held without bail until a judge arraigns you. This may take several days depending on where you are.

An arraignment is when you are brought in front of a judge, read the charges, and given the opportunity to plead "guilty" or "not guilty." If you have not been able to obtain legal counsel by this point, a court lawyer is temporarily appointed to guide you through the proceedings. He almost certainly will not be representing you beyond this point, so be wary about how much you confide in him. He ethically cannot disclose what you tell him, but the quality of his representation will not be the same as having a "real" lawyer acting on your behalf.

Before the arraignment, the prosecutors may approach your legal counsel to offer a plea bargain. Plea bargains are typically offered for minor crimes such as prostitution-related offenses, to save time and money for the overburdened judicial system. Under such a bargain, you plead guilty in return for reduced charges or a lesser sentence. To encourage you to accept the offer, the prosecutor may tell you that the offer is only good if you plead guilty immediately.

If you have not retained your own lawyer by that point, you should be wary about accepting any agreement. If you are not completely satisfied with the offer that they give you, plead "not guilty." There is so much pressure on prosecutors to avoid trials for minor cases that your regular lawyer should be able to obtain you an identical or better offer.

On occasion, the prosecutor may offer you an "adjournment in contemplation of dismissal" (ACD). An ACD does not exist in all 50 states, but where it is available you may want to strongly consider it. An ACD is not an admission of guilt. Rather, it is a temporary adjournment of the charges against you. If you are arrested again within a certain time period (six months in New York City), the charges may be reinstated against you. Even if you do run afoul of the law again, the bureaucracy is on your side – the initial charges often never resurface. An ACD is usually only offered if a person has no prior arrests.

Barring unusual circumstances, you will have to stand before the judge at your arraignment. Contrary to television's *Night Court*, the judicial system tries to be an orderly process. You should not attempt any theatrics, make political statements on behalf of the decriminalization of prostitution, or complain about how the police treated you. Let your lawyer do his job of representing you, and when addressing the judge do so in a courteous and polite manner.

If you enter a plea of guilty, you will be sentenced either on the spot or at a later date. The sentence may involve a fine, probation, community service, or jail time. Your criminal record will be permanently changed to reflect the charges against you. You will also be subject to minor court charges and other fees.

If you plead not guilty, a trial date will be set. If bail has not previously been determined, the judge will then set it. The amount of the bail will be determined by your risk of flight, the severity of the crime, and your prior criminal record. The court has several options for bail. You may be released on your own recognizance, in which case there is no bail. You may be required to pay a certain amount of cash (checks may be acceptable), secure a bond from a bail bondsman, or a combination of the two. Other forms of payment besides cash may be acceptable as well. If you are indigent (financially poor), the court may waive bail and appoint an attorney to represent you for the remainder of your case. You will need to prove to the court that you in fact have little or no income, so expect your tax and financial records to be scrutinized.

Bail bondsmen provide the full amount of the bail in return for a percentage (usually about 10%) of the total sum. This saves you from having to raise the entire bail upfront, but has the disadvantage of costing you money in the long run. As with all bail monies, if you elect to run rather than show up for your trial, the bail money is forfeited to the court. In that case, the bail bondsman may send bounty hunters after you. Do not expect life to become any easier at that point.

**What Happens Next**

If you have been lucky enough to secure an adjournment or if the charges were dismissed, then you are in good shape. If you are awaiting trial, then you will need fast legal advice. Hopefully you have secured a lawyer before this point. If not, hire one fast. Go back to the part about finding a lawyer and think about how smart it would have been had you done this beforehand.

Once you have a lawyer, the two of you will plan a defense. This may involve your lawyer approaching the prosecution and striking a deal. If the case against you is particularly weak, you may choose to go to trial. In either case, you are going to have to head back to court.

Once you are finished, hopefully you have been lucky and the charges were dropped or you were acquitted. Failing that, hopefully you were able to strike a plea bargain that you can live with. Prostitution charges are often reduced to "massaging without a license," for example. If worse comes to worst, I hope you will not spend time in jail. Whatever happens, remember you chose to enter the profession willingly. Laws against prostitution and sex work are unfair and unjust, but they are a reality of life.

However your case ends, the police now know who you are and what you do. There is an excellent chance they will periodically call and check up on you. If you fall back into the old habit of agreeing to have sex for money, you may wind up in handcuffs again. You will find that the judicial system is not nearly as friendly the second time around.

Fortunately, the majority of you will be lucky enough to avoid these nightmares. So enjoy your work and the money it brings in. Do not forget to pay your taxes either, because the Internal Revenue Service can make your life a living hell. How to handle your money and placate the government is exactly what the next chapter is all about.

## Chapter Nineteen
## Managing Your Money

*I have a European friend that works as an escort outside of his native country. He liked to save as much money as possible, and then launder it during periodic visits back home.*

*During one such trip he carried several months worth of cash in his suitcase. It was well above the legal amount of money he could carry into the country, but he was confident he would have no difficulty smuggling it in. Unfortunately, a customs employee randomly selected his belongings to be searched. They found the money and immediately confiscated it under the country's laws. The money was never returned, and he was forced to continue home with nothing to show for months of work.*

There are many rewards to escorting, but few are as enjoyable as playing with piles of money. Often you will find yourself counting thousands of dollars at a time. Of course, the pain of financial responsibility go along with the joy of collecting cash. Few escorts have trouble making money, but many find handling investments and taxes to be a confusing experience at best.

### Handling Your Money

One of the first things you should do as an escort is to buy a sturdy and fireproof lock box. Besides being perfect for keeping papers safe, it is an excellent place to lock away your cash from the prying eyes and hands of others. As you develop a steady income, you should also find an extra hiding place for your money. In this space you should keep $2,000 or so. This money is to be used for emergencies, such as if you need bail money. If you are ever arrested in your home and the police seize your lock box, you will be glad you have your hidden stash.

Career escorts should also build their bank accounts until they have saved at least three months worth of living expenses. If something should ever happen and you cannot escort for several months, this money will keep you from being evicted or going hungry. Having a "nest egg" saved in advance is far preferable to begging your clients to help pay your bills.

Whatever you do with your money, use it wisely. You will not be young forever, and your escorting income will not always be there. Legendary porn star and escort Joey Stefano learned this lesson the hard way. At his peak in the early 1990's, he estimated his earnings to be over $110,000 per year. By the time he died of a drug overdose several years later, he was financially in ruins. Do not make his mistake. Use your money to pay for college, buy a house, or save for retirement. Do not spend it excessively on drugs, parties, vacations, and other frivolous expenses.

As you deposit your money in the bank, be aware of any important laws in your country regarding the reporting of large or suspicious cash transactions. For example, in the United States all cash transactions of more than $10,000 must be reported to the federal government; furthermore, current federal law requires banks to report suspicious transactions. This includes both single transactions and patterns of activity over longer periods of time. As an escort, it is important to be careful of this because it is easy for banks to become suspicious that you are handling drug money. The tellers are not necessarily the ones that will cause problems for you, either. It is often the bank computers that perform this task. You are probably fine as long as you are paying taxes on all income that leaves a paper trail, but it is something to keep in mind.

Throughout the year, you should also make a point of saving at least 25% of your money in a special fund for taxes. When taxes come due, you are likely to owe a great deal of money at once. For career escorts, this amount can easily reach $10,000 or more. Having this money saved up can make tax day a lot easier to handle. Depending on the tax laws in your country, you may want to save even more.

Be wary about what you tell your clients about your finances. Many states allow for people to anonymously report those who are cheating on their taxes. Having you audited is an ideal way for an angry client to make you miserable.

## Checking Accounts and Credit Cards

Many career escorts choose to establish business accounts with their bank to make their finances easier to manage. The legal requirements of doing this vary widely, but typically you are required to file a notarized form with your county or state government. There are many books and kits available on starting small businesses that can guide you through this process. Fill them out as if you were starting a "consulting business." Once your business is registered, you will be able to open a checking account and obtain credit cards in your business's name. Running your expenses through these accounts makes sorting out your business finances at tax time much easier.

Registering your business and opening up a business checking account are also necessary steps if you ever wish to accept credit cards. The process may vary, but generally you go through a company that operates as a middleman between the card companies and your business. There are a number of companies that do this, of which Cardservice (http://www.cardservice.com) is one of the biggest and best.

Unfortunately, the process of accepting credit cards is not an easy one. Few escorts will want to bother with the trouble and expense. For starters, you are required either to lease or to buy the electronic equipment necessary to accept credit cards. A number of models are available that vary in price, function, size, and convenience, but in general you can expect to pay $800-$1,500 to buy one outright, and slightly more over several years if you choose to lease. Once you obtain the equipment, expect to pay another $100 in initial fees to establish your account. Beyond that, the card companies and middlemen typically charge you 20-cents per transaction, 2-4% of the total charge, and an additional monthly fee of $10 or so as well.

Assuming that the initial expense is not a problem, you may still have difficulty being approved to accept credit cards. Card companies will not knowingly allow their cards to be used for illegal activities and will immediately terminate your account (and possibly notify the authorities) if they discover you are using them for your business. Even in countries where prostitution is legal, card companies often avoid being used with adult businesses. The easiest way around this is to have a secondary business of some sort. When establishing an account with the middleman company, use the secondary business as a cover for your escorting career.

There are a few more difficulties as well. You cannot say that you are running a secondary business if one does not exist. The middleman company will require proof that you are actually running one. This may include visiting your website, receiving copies of part or all of your business taxes, and seeing the letterhead and promotional materials for your business. Middleman companies are helpful and flexible with this process, but do not want to cause problems for themselves with the credit card companies.

When filling out the forms, you will be asked to indicate the transaction amounts that you expect to charge. You should indicate an amount that reflects both your hourly and overnight rate. The card companies at first may also ask you to submit copies of invoices supposedly submitted to your clients. You can create these using various financial software packages. *Quicken* software is great for this.

As a side note, escorts that accept credit cards do not carry machines with them. They write down the credit card information and then type it in manually when they return home. A few others call a lover or roommate who punches it in manually over the phone.

## Taxes: The Big Decision

One of the most important decisions you will make in your escort career is whether to pay taxes on all, some, or none of your income. In the United States you are required to pay anywhere from about 15% of your annual earnings up to a third or more. Taxes can be even more significant in other countries. The financial benefits of cheating on your taxes are great, but so are the legal penalties.

As with any taxpayer, there is a chance you will be audited. The chance is not high, but if you are sloppy about your record keeping, or if you make mistakes while filing your taxes, your chances increase significantly. Even if you fill out your taxes honestly and correctly, you can still be audited. There is no foolproof method to avoid an audit. Being caught for tax evasion can result in heavy fines and possible jail time.

You should keep your financial goals in mind as you decide how to handle your money. If you are saving your money to buy a home, you will need to establish a high level of income to qualify for a mortgage. If you are going to school, reporting a high level of income can jeopardize your student loans. Consider your situation carefully as you plan your tax strategy.

Regardless of your income, there are a number of deductions and tax-deferred investments that you can use to save money and reduce your tax burden. We will come back to those later.

## The Advantages of Spending Cash

Anyone who has ever filed taxes in the United States knows that it is no fun. The forms are complex, the language is confusing, and the process of filing can drive a man insane. Escorts have it even worse. Because you are not paying withholding taxes along with every paycheck, at the end of the year you may owe a great deal of money. For career escorts, this total can easily surpass $20,000 or more. If you have not saved a portion of your money throughout the year, you may be in serious financial trouble.

When it comes to avoiding taxes, many people begin thinking about taking suitcases of cash to the Cayman Islands or opening a Swiss bank account. While I have no doubt that these things are possible, I do not have the faintest idea how to go about them. If you decide to start sneaking money out of the country, be aware that you are required to report to the U.S. Customs Service if you are taking more than $10,000 with you at a time. If you do not report this money, you run the risk of having it seized by customs and being fined for your actions.

If you choose to hide your income, by far the most effective way to do this is to spend as much cash as you can. Buy food with cash; buy birthday gifts with cash; rent hotel rooms while on vacations with cash, and so on. Use cash for every expense that does not leave a paper trail. You should even avoid shopping online, choosing to spend your money in stores. Shopping online requires a credit card, and payments leave a paper trail that can be followed by an auditor. When you report your income on your taxes, you would then leave out anything you spent in cash.

It is easy to see your financial savings. Suppose your income tax bracket is 25%, meaning you are required to pay 25% of your yearly income in taxes. If in a year you charged $5,000 on your credit cards you will not only have to pay your credit card bill, you will also have to pay another 25% in income taxes on that amount. That brings the total to $6,250. Were you to spend the money in cash in stores, you would only pay an additional 5-8% sales tax (depending on your area), bringing your total to about $5,300. That saves you almost $1,000. The worst possible thing you can do is to use your credit card in stores. In that case, you pay both sales tax and income tax on the money, and your bill goes up to $6,625.

Obviously you can save thousands of dollars by cheating on your taxes. It is highly illegal, and I neither recommend or condone it. Still, it remains an option. Use it at your own risk.

**Taxes in the United States**

As you may know, when you prepare your taxes you are required to fill out Form 1040. As part of the 1040, there is another form called Schedule C (Profit or Loss From a Business). Schedule C asks you a number of questions to determine your total business income, and then offers you a number of areas in which to make deductions. Determining your income is the easy part. Legally, it is all of the money you earned from your escorting that year. Many escorts choose to report only the income they have run through their bank and investment accounts, but others report their full earnings. As always, this is your decision to make.

Deductions take a bit more time to compute, but can legally save you thousands of dollars. Deductions are all of the legitimate expenses you have made during the year. These include:

- A "mileage deduction" of about 32 cents per mile that you have driven your car for work.
- Other transportation costs incurred in your work (plane tickets, cab fare, tolls).
- Lodging while on work-related trips, as well as 50% of the food expenses.
- Advertising and promotional expenses.
- Office expenses.

- Parking fees.
- Work supplies (massage oils, condoms, lubricant).
- Telephone service fees and phone calls.
- Hi-tech expenses (computers, cell phone) that are purchased primarily for work purposes.
- Business phone calls and charges.
- Business-related purchases such as this book or tax-preparation software.

You must be able to document any expenses that you wish to take as business deductions. This means you must have receipts to prove that you actually spent money on them. If you are audited, any deductions you make without proof will be disallowed, possibly causing you to be fined for underpaying your taxes.

One of the largest Schedule C deductions you may be able to take is the home office deduction. If you have part of your home that is only used for work purposes, you may be able to deduct expenses related to that area. Be careful if you do take this deduction. People who take the home office deduction have a higher audit rate. If you have been particularly creative on your taxes, you may not want to take this deduction. An audit could cause you no end of nightmares.

One of the best deductions you can make on your taxes is savings for your retirement. Under certain circumstances, you may be eligible to open an Individual Retirement Account (IRA). This can typically be done anytime up until the end of the tax year's April 15$^{th}$ deadline. The income you invest (up to a certain maximum) is tax-deferred, meaning you can deduct it off your table income right now and then pay the tax when you collect your investment at retirement and in a lower tax bracket. More importantly, if you are filling out a Schedule C, you have the option to place approximately 15% of your net business income into a tax-deferred investment called a SEP-IRA.

To set-up a SEP-IRA, you need only open an account with a brokerage firm. If you know absolutely nothing about doing this, find an accountant who will walk you through the process. Trust me, you want to invest as much money as you can this way. When you hear clients and escorts telling you to "invest your money wisely," this is exactly what they are talking about. Besides putting a nice chunk of money in your retirement account, it also has the effect of saving you even more money on your taxes.

There may be other expenses you can deduct on your taxes depending on your situation. For example, if you are self-employed and pay for your own health insurance (as opposed to being insured through another job), this is partially deductible elsewhere on your taxes. Be sure to check with an accountant or at least read the fine print on the tax forms before taking deductions like this. You would not want to accidentally take incorrect deductions, or miss ones to which you may be entitled. Tax-preparation software is helpful in claiming these deductions, but there is no substitute for the services of a professional accountant.

Another more legally questionable way in which you can save significant amounts of money is by having your clients vouch that the money they pay you are gifts, rather than income from your escorting services. Under 1999 tax law (the most current as I write this), you can claim up to $10,000 in gifts per giver per year. This means you do not have to pay taxes on the first $10,000 you receive from any client, so long as he is willing to say that the money was a gift and was not payment for services rendered. Obviously, if you deposit tens of thousands of dollars into your account and insist it was all gifts, you will raise a great deal of suspicion in an audit. Still, if you have two or three clients who spend significant amounts of money on you, this is an opportunity to consider. Best of all, gifts are not reported and not deducted on your taxes because they are never reported as income in the first place. This means the IRS is far less likely to ever learn of the money's existence.

One illegal variation of this involves making a cash payment to a friend in exchange for an equal or slightly smaller gift in return. For example, if you have $9,000 in cash, you can give it to a friend in exchange for an $8,500 check back to you. He gains $500 in the deal, but you are now able to deposit the money in your personal bank account as a gift. The savings in taxes easily surpasses the $500 you are losing. Just be sure the check he gives you is valid; you would hate to have his check bounce. You should also make sure your friend does not deposit all of the cash into his account. Should he ever be audited, the IRS may learn of the illegal exchange.

There is one more important lesson you need to know about taxes. The first time you fill out a Schedule C for your escorting business, the tax on that income is due April 15$^{th}$ as usual. After that you are required to pay your escorting taxes quarterly, based on the income from the previous year. Worse yet, the first quarterly tax installment is also due on April 15$^{th}$. Confused? Consider this example.

Suppose you began escorting in 2000. You fill out the Schedule C, and after deductions you earn $20,000. For the sake of simplicity, assume your tax rate on this amount is 25%. So on April 15, 2001, you owe the government a $5,000 check for your 2000 taxes. If you escort during the year 2001, the government requires you pay your taxes quarterly instead of all at once in 2002. The first payment due date is April 15, 2001, the same day you have to pay your 2000 taxes. At that time, you are required to pay 25% of the Schedule C taxes you made in the 2000 tax year. In this example, that comes to an additional $1,250. You will also owe that amount on June 15, 2001, September 15, 2001, and January 15, 2002. (Do not ask me why the quarters are not all three months apart, because I don't know. These are IRS requirements. They are not intended to make sense).

You will also want to make sure you understand your state tax laws. Many states require their own income taxes be paid quarterly as well.

If all of this tax information seems confusing to you, find yourself a good accountant, or at least use tax preparation software for your computer. I use TurboTax and think it's great. Taxcut is another good one.

One final note: If you work with an accountant, be sure you tell him you are an escort rather than a prostitute. Unlike lawyers and clergy, what you tell your accountant is not legally confidential. Furthermore, be careful what you tell your accountant if you practice "creative finances." Accountants understand that people want to pay as few taxes as possible, but they risk their own licenses if they knowingly help people submit false taxes. One common standard used by accounting firms is to report income honestly, but to take deductions like crazy. Keep that in mind when preparing your own taxes.

**Taxes in Other Countries**

It is impossible to cover how taxes work in every country. If you escort outside the United States, you should speak to an accountant about how to handle that country's taxes.

In the end, money remains both one of the happiest and most depressing factors of the escorting business. Making it is wonderful, but paying taxes can be so depressing that you wonder why you even bother. Still, there are lots of ways for the enterprising escort to strike it rich. That is precisely what the next chapter is about, how to nudge that income level even higher.

## Chapter Twenty
## Branching Out

*Following the success of my role as "Howie" in* The Dream Team, *I began actively looking for more video opportunities in the porn industry. To my frustration, I had a difficult time finding work. The California-based industry has little enough interest in twink actors, and use them even less if they have to fly them in from New Jersey.*

*So when I began e-mailing with Noah Walker, a twink porn star in the Kevin Clarke movie,* Something Very Big, *I was excited to finally have someone to ask for advice. Ironically, before I could ask for his help, I received a note that began, "Aaron, I was wondering if you could give me some advice on finding porno work..."*

For all the money that escorts earn, sometimes it does not seem like enough. Those vast piles of cash do spend quickly. If you are feeling the pinch of greed (or ambition as we greedy folks like to think of it), then dabbling in other sex-related fields may be just the thing for you. Even if you are happy with your income, you may be bored with the day-to-day routine of your escorting business. If this describes you, then perhaps we can find a way for you to branch out. You can make money and have fun at the same time.

### Being Kept

For some people, the idea of having a primary or exclusive arrangement with a single client is an unappealing idea.

They hold their personal freedom in high value and want to live life on their own terms. Others find the idea of a "sugar daddy" to be highly attractive. Whatever your thoughts, being kept is certainly an option that is offered to some escorts.

The specifics of such an arrangement vary widely, but in general they require sex, affection, and friendship on the part of the boy. Sometimes they involve chores as well, such as in the case of "houseboys." In return, the younger party is offered financial support and often a place to live. The offer is usually made in hope that the arrangement will turn into a true romantic relationship.

If you choose to enter into such an arrangement, be careful to watch out for your long-term interests. Living in another person's house without a formal lease provides you with few rights under the law. Should something ever happen to your lover or your relationship, you may find yourself suddenly bankrupt with nowhere to live. This may be the case even if you have spent years together. If you plan on being kept, always insist on a written arrangement that involves building up financial assets in your name.

## Dancing / Stripping

One of the most common ways escorts bring in extra income is through stripping. Many work as dancers for one bar, club, or theater. Others tour the country performing at a variety of locations. Dancers may work as an individual act or as part of a troupe. They may also perform for women as well as men, although many dancers prefer working for men because they are said to tip better.

How well dancers are paid depends mostly on their fame, looks, and skill. A big-name porn performer will do better than a starting dancer. Over the long-term, personality and persistence can level this out to a surprising extent. Certainly there is a huge demand to see a famous star performing, but if he is rude and arrogant to the customers, his income will drop significantly.

If you are interested in dancing, you should talk to strippers in your area. Find out how they began in the business, and what you need to do to start. Many bars and theaters have amateur nights, some of which offer cash prizes. These are an excellent opportunity to gain experience performing in front of an audience. How you proceed from there is up to you. There are many directions you can take your career.

Incomes from stripping vary widely. Big-name performers are sometimes contracted to dance in exclusive engagements around the country. These can pay hundreds or thousands of dollars for a single evening, plus whatever else he makes in tips. On the other extreme, some local bars require the dancers to actually pay to work there. On a slow night the dancers may actually lose money after working a shift. Most dancers are somewhere in the middle, earning about $100-$300 per evening.

**Weight Training**

One method of making extra money that has gained in popularity over time is for more muscular escorts to work as physical trainers. Such an escort might run advertisements in print publications that show pictures of his body. The pay (typically $30-$70/hr) is not as high as escorting, but it is a legal career that an escort can retire into as his interests change.

If you are considering becoming a trainer, keep in mind that it takes more than just a working knowledge of the local gym. The human body is more complex than any machine, and giving the wrong advice to someone can cause them significant harm. To learn the right way to train, you need to spend a considerable amount of time learning the academics of exercise physiology. Numerous organizations offer certification courses, including the International Sports

Sciences Association (http://www.fitnesseducation.com). You should know that not all trainer certification programs are the same, and many gyms will require you to have specific certifications. Contact your local gym for more information about becoming a certified trainer.

**Adult Videos**

Making and selling porn is a multi-billion dollar business annually. Considering the heavy demand for adult videos, it is not surprising there are many professional escorts working in this field.

By far the simplest way to go about this is to appear in front of the camera. The qualifications to become a porn actor are simple. You need to be reasonably attractive, relatively in shape, and have at least a 5 or 6" dick. These are the minimums, of course. The more you surpass these basic standards, the more successful you can become.

*Amateur Videos* - Amateur porn videos are those that are produced with home video cameras and are primarily sold on the Internet or in the back of magazines. Amateur videos are almost never sold in stores, despite the claim of many low-budget videos to be "amateur."

Amateur videos have an amazing amount of diversity, and cover almost every fetish imaginable. Typically they will be directed, produced, and filmed by the same person, although sometimes two people may work together on a project. Typically a producer will focus on a single style of tape, such as military or twink. They recruit their models locally, as the videos rarely have enough of a budget to fly models in to be filmed.

Amateur videos typically pay models anywhere from $50 to $250. Appearing in an amateur video does not "tarnish" ones image in porn, as the distribution of these videos is so small as to escape notice by most of the industry. Filming an amateur video is more like real sex than in any other type of porn, as amateur video producers focus more on making sex hot than making it appear polished on the screen.

The central clearinghouse for amateur video sales and information on the Internet is the Amateur Models Video Connection (http://www.amvc.com).

*Low-budget and Pro-Am Videos* – Halfway between amateur and professional is a range of videos referred to as low-budget. These are videos that are made to sell in stores, but whose production values are so low that enjoyment of the video is significantly decreased. Typically low-budget movies are sold only in stores, although they can be found on the Internet to some extent.

In low-budget porn, there is likely to be one-to-three crew. Usually the director doubling as a cameraman, with one or two people assisting him with the lighting. They edit their films more heavily than amateur videos, so they need longer to film to collect that footage. Low-budget and pro-am videos tend to pay $500 or less.

As far as finding low-budget video work, it is not hard to do. Low-budget companies are constantly searching for models. Often they recruit models from escort agencies. They also tend to advertise in local gay newspapers.

If you do want to be in porn, you will need to decide whether you want to make it to the top. If you do want to reach the higher levels of the industry, you will want to be wary about doing low-budget porn. Once you have done more than one or two low-budget movies, many professional directors will refuse to work with you. You will also want to be careful for another reason. Low-budget videos are routinely repackaged and re-released on the discount racks of adult bookstores. You may do one low-budget scene, only to find that several years later it has been released on several different tapes.

One offshoot of low-budget videos is a style called Pro-am (short for professional-amateur). These are videos that claim to be amateur, although they are more low-budget in nature. All Worlds Video has heavily pushed several of these lines of tapes, resulting in them developing highly loyal viewing audiences. The Dirk Yates Private Collection is one example of this. The First Time Tryers Series is another. Unlike most low-budget movies, appearing in one of these is actually a good way to launch a porn career. Many actors who have appeared in them have gone on to do numerous professional videos in the industry.

*Professional Videos* – Another option is the route of professional videos. People who live near Los Angeles, San Diego, and San Francisco are set when it comes to finding work, although professional videos are also directed in Amsterdam, Berlin, Paris, and Prague. If you live in one of these cities, you can probably find video work by responding to ads in the local gay papers. Video companies have an insatiable hunger for new models, and are always looking for fresh faces. Just pick up the local gay newspaper in one of these places and look at the help-wanted ads in the back.

If you live outside of these places, you may have a more difficult time getting into professional videos. By far the easiest way to solve this is to move to California, or at least visit there for an extended period of time. Unfortunately doing so is expensive. California has such an overpopulation of escorts that their rates have fallen well below those found in many other areas of the country. You may make a few thousand dollars doing porn, but you will lose a lot more in revenue from your escorting services.

If you live outside the "California Porn Belt," the best way to pursue professional video work may be to aggressively market your image. Pick up a copy of the latest edition of the *Adam Gay Video Directory*, an annual trade publication about the gay porn industry. Look through the guide for models that look similar to you, then determine the companies they work for. Put together a few pictures of yourself and send them along with a letter of interest.

Chances are you will hear nothing back from these companies, or if you do it will be a form rejection letter.

Don't be discouraged. Every month send the companies a new set of pictures. If you are working out, show them the progress you are making. If you have ever posed in front of the camera before, mention your experience. If you have done embarrassing low-budget videos however, you may not want to mention them to the top companies in the industry.

If you ever find yourself on vacation near a porn company's office, call them in advance and ask to meet with one of their directors to introduce yourself. Most of the time the companies will be friendly about your request, although they may not be responsive because of the number of flakes that contact them. Even if they do not set-up an appointment, drop into the company offices to introduce yourself and deliver another set of pictures. Seeing you in person will give them a much better idea of who you are.

Sooner or later a company may respond by calling you. If the representative tells you he is placing you in the casting book, thank him for his assistance and continue to send pictures every month or two. It is extremely easy to be forgotten otherwise. If he is calling to offer you a role in one of their videos, then congratulations! You have just taken a big step into the world of porn.

Of course you may not have to pursue porn at all. Offers may come to you as companies stumble across your website or your ads. Be suspicious about any offers from new companies. Never accept an offer for a percentage of the profits instead of immediate cash. No reputable company has any interest in making that offer except to perhaps a few of the top stars. Chances are that you will not see a dime if you accept.

You should also be wary about accepting vast praise as reality if established talent in the industry discovers you. Many directors will promise to make you a star, but they will almost certainly lose interest as soon as a newer and prettier face comes along. It is easy to be taken in by directors because most people want to believe they will make it to the top. That does not mean you should not accept their offers. It only means you should watch out for yourself. Reputable companies to work for include Falcon, Studio 2000, Bel Ami, Kristen Bjorn, Catalina, All Worlds Video, and Odyssey Men. Any others are either low-budget, or are being independently produced and distributed.

When you are finally offered your first role, do not expect to become rich and famous right away. For one thing, it often takes more than six months or more for a video to be edited and released. This means that anything you film today will not be available for half a year, and probably will not be covered in the magazines for a few months after that. Then there is the matter of pay. Professional porn does pay better than low budget videos, but it is still not very much money. Starting pay is $600-$1,000 for a full sex scene, with jack-off scenes paying about half that. This may be good for a day's pay, but remember that porn is not a steady source of income. Only a handful of performers can even make a basic living from their videos.

If you want to be a porn actor, always remember that filming movies is definitely work and not play. It can be fun at times, but do not expect making porn to be like your fantasies. You are often required to film in adverse conditions (cold weather, for example), and unless you are at the top of the industry you will have no choice who your partners will be. Often you will dislike your co-stars, or at the very least not find them to be particularly friendly. Because of the "unnaturalness" of doing porn, it can be extremely difficult to become erect on the set, even if you never have a problem doing so in your escort work. You will have long days on the set, sometimes 8, 12, or 16-hour days. This is why studios make Viagra commonly available. Expect to have anywhere from five-to-ten crew members on the set in addition to the other actors.

Keep in mind that when you perform in adult videos, you are required to sign away all of your rights to the footage and promotional photos. You may be surprised where and how often your image will crop up. You may be in video advertisements, magazine covers, in books, and phone sex ads. Your pictures will also wind up all over the Internet. Such is the price of fame.

*Producing Porn* – Many people have the idea that producing porn is an instant moneymaker, and is as hot as being on camera. Nothing is farther from the truth. Producing or directing an adult movie is a stressful experience with many headaches and few rewards. You have to love the work to do it. If that is what you want to do, I congratulate you on your patience.

If you want to produce professional porn, you will almost certainly have to move to California. Find a job in the video industry in whatever nonsexual (or sexual) role you can, and learn the industry inside and out. Becoming a director is just like any other career ambition, and requires considerable time and effort.

If you want more immediate results, you may want to consider becoming an amateur director. It requires less than a $2,000 initial investment. About half of that amount will be spent on a video camcorder. The rest is used to hire models for the tape. In amateur porn, you can have them do whatever you want – sex, jacking off, enjoying fetishes, or whatever.

If you produce an amateur movie, always make sure the models are at least 18 years of age. You will need to make a copy of their ID and have them sign model releases. As well You can find a workable model release in most legal guides for photographers. Just modify text to suit your needs. Once you are done making the tape, you can sell it on the Internet through sites like the Amateur Models Video Connection (http://www.amvc.com).

As a side note, if you have grand visions of becoming a scriptwriter for porn, you should save yourself the embarrassment of mentioning it to anyone in the industry. There is no market for selling scripts in porn.

## Nude Magazines

Not everyone with good looks wants to do porn. Some find it demeaning, and others have no patience with the work. Posing nude for magazines may be a fun alternative for these people. Besides bringing in a small amount of money, nude modeling also has the advantage of drawing attention to the model and his escort work.

To begin posing for magazines, visit an adult bookstore and buy a few magazines that have models similar to yourself. This may have to do with your look, body type, ethnicity, or your endowment. Begin sending the magazines pictures of yourself, much as you would if you were trying to enter the video industry. Keep sending pictures every month until you hear back from them. Unlike professional video companies, nude magazines do not fly models across the country to meet with photographers. So expect to travel at your own expense to meet with the photographer.

Taking a different approach, you may want to find a photographer first and worry about the magazine later. The photographer will typically take a few test shots and show them to various companies to pique their interest. If they are interested, they will ask the photographer to shoot several rolls of pictures of you. This method is what led me to *Freshmen* and *Inches*.

There are a few other ways people pose for magazines. Often when a new actor begins performing in adult videos, a professional company will have a photographer shoot the model. The actor is typically paid by the video company for this. The video company then trades the pictures to a magazine in exchange for free advertising space.

Alternately, you may want to have a friend or amateur photographer take several rolls of pictures of you. If you do it this way, you should start submitting them to lower-budget and newer publications. The better publications tend to want more professional looking pictures, whereas the low-budget ones are more flexible with the quality of the photographs. Ask the magazine in advance if they prefer slides or negatives and prints.

However you finally enter into magazines, your shoot will typically take one-to-three hours. Do not expect the shoot to be like it is in your fantasies. With each shot you have to get an erection, let the photographer put you into position, and then wait 30 seconds to a minute while the photographer measures the light and snaps the photo. This process will usually be repeated for several rolls. Some photographers will help "fluff" (play with) you to help you become hard. For the most part though you will either need to play with yourself, or will have to rely on Viagra.

Regarding payment for posing for magazines, expect to make $200 to $300. The money is typically payable on publication, not when the photos are taken. You may have to wait several months to a year or more before the photos finally run. If they run, that is. Magazines are not required to buy photo sets that they request that photographers shoot. Although posing for magazines in conjunction with an adult video may pay slightly less, it has the advantage of paying at the time of the shoot.

As with porn videos, your image is likely to wind up all over the Internet and occasionally in print advertisements. When I posed for *Freshmen*, the photos were scanned and posted on the Internet newsgroups before the magazine even hit the stands. Several years later, I still find the pictures being used by various websites. On occasion people even send my pictures in chat rooms claiming it is a photo of them!

**Running an Online Store**

Those people who are more technologically inclined may be interested in running an online store on their website. Although a store can theoretically sell anything you want, in this case I mean selling adult-oriented products, usually those that are related to you. For example, if you have appeared in porn movies or posed for magazines, sell those items on your site. You may also want to sell more fetish-oriented items, such as your used sex toys or cum-stained underwear. There is a surprisingly high demand for all of these items.

Before you open a store, rent a post office box for your business. This allows you to advertise a mail order address while protecting your privacy from stalkers and online strange people. You may also want to consider contracting with a company on the Web to assist your site in taking credit cards. In exchange for processing credit cards for your stores, they receive approximately 8% of the fees. This is far more than the 2-4% the credit card companies normally take, but will more than pay for itself through additional sales.

Once your site grosses about $6,000 per year, you may want to look into establishing a merchandising account so you can accept credit cards. This will give an immediate boost to your business, and will make handling money considerably easier. Accepting credit cards for your online store also allows you to accept credit cards for your escorting business as well. The initial investment will be easily paid back through additional sales and escorting revenue. The process of establishing a merchandising account is explained in depth in chapter nineteen.

As your business grows, you may eventually want to consider adding other items to your store, such as amateur videos from other producers, books, sex toys, and more. Be careful about your store becoming too general in nature, because it is difficult to compete with the larger adult stores on the Web. The secret to your success may be to personalize your site to the needs of your customers, but keeping it focused on yourself.

If you sell adult-oriented videos on your site, avoid placing X-rated pictures from the movies behind age verification services such as Adultcheck and Mancheck. You will gain a small amount of income from people who are willing to pay to access them, but will lose a lot more in lost sales. You are better off providing the pictures for free and using them for advertising purposes.

**Sexual Surrogacy**

If you have been escorting for long, chances are that you will be able to name at least one time when you helped a client overcome a minor personal difficulty relating to his sexuality. Often this has to do with his self-confidence or his body image. You may have found the experience rewarding, and began thinking of yourself as a sex therapist of sorts.

Commonly known as sexual surrogates, people who provide counseling through the use of sex prefer to call themselves surrogate partners. There is some resemblance to what we do, but surrogate partners actually provide a different service than escorts. As escorts, it is our job to meet the physical needs of our clients as best we can, with emotional needs being met whenever possible. Surrogate partners are the exact opposite. They meet the emotional needs first, providing physical gratification only where necessary to establish the counseling relationship, teach new skills, or provide new perspectives.

Surrogate partners are also professionally trained, subscribe to a written code of ethics, have continuing education opportunities, and almost always work in conjunction with a licensed sex therapist. Escorts have none of those. Furthermore, an escort is chosen by the client based on his looks and personality. A surrogate partner is chosen based on his or her skills, and the sex therapist's recommendation. Finally, escorts and surrogate partners often have completely different legal statuses. In many areas where escorting is illegal, the practices of surrogate partners are allowed by law.

As an escort, you should not advertise yourself or offer services as a surrogate partner. However, you may want to consider eventually becoming certified or someday retiring into this unique career. The International Professional Surrogates Association is always looking for qualified people interested in their certification process. For more information on training and supervised internships, contact the IPSA (http://hometown.aol.com/ipsa1/home.html).

However you branch out your business, keep in mind that escorting will almost certainly pay better than any other opportunity you are likely to encounter. Maintaining a balance between your day-to-day work and other fun projects is important for long-term success. In the next chapter, we will examine a few final issues that you may face as your escorting career passes through the years.

## Chapter Twenty-one
## A Few Other Issues

*Several years ago, I grew tired of being asked for discounts. People were asking me if I offered discounts for first-time customers, and others asked me if I charge a lower rate for repeat visits. Some asked if I charged less for younger customers because they were younger and better looking, and others requested a discount because they were older and hotter. People even wanted lower fees because they were both virginal or experienced lovers.*

*The requests continued. People asked for discounts because they were students or senior citizens, wanted to be friends or did not want any strings attached, and wanted a long-term arrangement or were just in town for business. Some asked for discounts because it was either during the week or on a weekend, during the day or in the evening, and for both short and long appointments. Others asked for lesser fees because they were willing to take me to dinner or were staying in a nice hotel. Finally, people wanted to know if I had sales, gave out coupons, or offered frequent-flyer miles.*

*Sick of being asked for discounts, I decided there was only one thing a sane escort could do – I raised my rates!*

As the years go by and you find yourself continuing to work in the business, you will notice a few challenges and transitions cropping up again and again. Some of these transitions, such as changing your rates, are not unexpected and are a natural part of the evolution of your business. Other changes in your life, such as a growing sense of pride in your work, may actually surprise you when you realize they are occurring.

Regardless of the issues, always remember that you are not the first to face them. Many escorts have experienced them before you. Writing or talking to other escorts can give you a great deal of insight into these matter. Conversely, there will be times when younger and less experienced escorts approach you to assist them with their business and personal growth. It can be tempting to ignore them, especially if you are a busy escort who receives many of these requests. I urge you not to ignore them, and pick their brains and learn from them instead. For example, newer escorts often discover surprisingly creative and effective ways of advertising themselves, ways you may be missing because of your already-established business routine. Trading knowledge and building friendships with other escorts is a great way to increase your knowledge of the industry.

**Chance Meetings**

There will come a day when you are at the mall, on the subway, or at the grocery store when by chance you will run into one of your clients. On these rare occasions, you will need to take care to preserve the client's privacy. Depending on the situation, it may be entirely appropriate to say hello. At other times it may not. As a general rule, if the client is with anyone else, it is a good idea to keep your distance. The more adventurous among you may want to give your client a discreet wink.

Of course, respecting privacy does not always work in reverse. Ideally clients will never approach you when you are in public with friends or family, but sometimes they do anyway. In that case all you can do is handle the situation as best you can, and hope the client does not say anything too inappropriate.

## Changing Your Rates

From time-to-time you may need to raise your rates. This is most often done when you become too busy to handle all of the people who want to hire you. It may also be necessary if you just want to cut back on the number of clients you see. Although it is frequently awkward and uncomfortable to tell your clients that you will be charging them more in the future, the benefit is that you will make more money. At the very least, you will earn the same income while doing less work.

The opposite holds true as well. Some of you may occasionally find yourselves in the position of needing to lower your rates. You may have overpriced yourself when you first entered the business, or may want to lower rates as a way to attract more business. A few other escorts even lower their rates to extend their escorting careers as they grow older.

If you are considering lowering your rates, you should first think carefully about doing so. You may find that re-evaluating your advertising campaign and more aggressively promoting yourself will solve your problems for you. Adding your site to search engines, building a better website, and changing the picture in your print ads are all ways of accomplishing this. There is almost always more you can do to promote your business at little or no cost.

If you decide to lower your rates, no one will complain. You need only to decide whether you are going to lower rates for your current clientele. If you elect not to do so, be careful they do not find out what you are doing.

Of course, raising your rates is not nearly so simple as lowering them. Raising prices for new clients may only require that you inform potential clients when they inquire about your services, but raising rates for existing clients is much more difficult. No client likes to pay more. Some escorts find it easy to raise their rates for the people they see, particularly those clients who are particularly difficult or irritating. Others find it unpleasant to raise rates for any client.

When it comes to handling rate increases, the least controversial method is a no-tier system of pricing. Under this method, people are expected to pay the rate you charged when they first became your client. So if you raise your rates five times, you will have clients paying five different rates. Over time the natural turnover of clients will replace the lower-rate clients with better paying ones. The advantage of this system is that you never need to raise a client's rates. The disadvantages are that it is difficult to remember who is paying what rate, and you may sometimes turn down higher-paying clients because you have appointments scheduled with lower-paying ones.

Another popular system is the exact opposite. In the one-tier method of pricing yourself, all clients are expected to pay the same rate regardless of how long they have been hiring you. Unfortunately, this means you will sometimes irritate clients because you do not offer them a lower rate for hiring you on an ongoing basis. You may also need to raise your rates several times as your business increases. This system is not a good way of keeping your clients happy. On the other hand, it is extremely simple when it comes to billing your clients, as they are all expected to pay the same rate.

My favorite method is a compromise between the two. In the two-tier system, you have two different rates for your clients. One is your current rate for new clients, and the other is your previous rate for most others. For example, suppose you are raising your rate from $150 to $200. Under this system, you would keep most of your clients at $150. You would charge $200 only for new clients as well as for those who have irritated you. If you ever raise your rates to $250, new and difficult clients would then be expected to pay $250. All others would be raised to $200. This system has the advantage of making it relatively simple to remember rates, as well as making established clients feel they are at least getting some discount.

John Preston proposed in his book, *Hustling*, that an escort offer a "frequent-flyer program" of sorts. Under this system, the escort would see the client for a certain number of sessions, after which he would give the client an extra visit for free. I do not necessarily encourage escorts to adopt this system for all of their clients, because it opens itself up to too many possible arguments between the escort and the client. For example, what would happen if you wanted to stop seeing a client as he nears the free visit? It also requires you keep a more detailed record system of your clients. If you do adopt this strategy, make sure your prices are sufficiently high to pay for the free visits. Alternately, you can surprise regular clients with the occasional free session.

Preston's system is also an excellent one to adopt when lowering your rates. Instead of reducing your existing clients from $200 to $150, offer to give them free sessions on occasion. You will save a great deal of revenue that you may otherwise lose.

Regardless of what you finally set as your rate system, you will almost certainly face the issue of informing your clients that their rates are increasing at some point. Many escorts hate this part of the business and often put it off because it can be so awkward. Fortunately there are several steps you can take to minimize the awkwardness of the situation.

- Change all existing advertising to reflect your new rates. Many clients will notice the new rate and will voluntarily begin paying it without being asked.
- Inform your clients by e-mail to avoid awkward conversations. Consider offering to honor the previous rate during their next visit.
- When a client calls to arrange an appointment, politely inform him of your rate change before agreeing to meet. You may wish to use the previous rate for that visit.

- If you use the two-tier system, refer to the lower rate as a preferred or VIP rate. Let the client believe he is one of only a few exclusive people receiving the lower rate.
- Inform clients of the new rate for future meetings after they pay you for a session they have just completed.

When raising your rates, on occasion a client may begin whining and making a nuisance of himself. In a case like this, do not agree to a lower price to shut him up. Doing so will only encourage him to be annoying. When it comes to escorting (and indeed, life in general), approximately 5% of your business will cause you 95% of your stress. Always remember this rule when dealing with irritating clients. You are not doing yourself a favor by continuing to see them.

Do not be surprised as well if your tips go down as your rates go up. Still, when tips are offered, they will tend to be much larger.

It is never fun raising your rates, but with a bit of careful planning you can survive the process without too much stress. Always keep in mind that whenever you raise rates, you will lose a few clients. It is sad when you lose people who you enjoy seeing, but it is part of growing your business. Consider referring these clients to other escorts. It is a great opportunity to do a favor for friends in the business.

**Relationships**

One of the more annoying disadvantages of being an escort is that it can be hard to keep a romantic relationship alive. Issues of jealousy and emotional security are always problematic in relationships; a career in the sex industry only adds to these problems. As a result, escorts often find themselves faced with a choice between an insecure boyfriend and their career. It is unfortunate when this happens, because the escort loses no matter what he decides; he has already lost before any decision is made.

What I have seen and heard suggests that you may experience three primary "trouble times" as you build a new relationship. The first is when you begin dating someone new. It can be difficult to decide when to inform your potential boyfriend that you work in the sex industry. It is usually a good idea to discuss the subject as soon as things progress beyond a brief fling and into a romantic relationship. Unfortunately you may lose a potential lover over the issue. It is still a good idea to tell him quickly, because it can prevent many more strongly hurt feelings later down the line.

The second trouble time begins several months later as the initial sexual intensity of the relationship begins to fade. During this time period, you may find your boyfriend becoming insecure and threatened by your work. He may not view your escorting as cheating, but at the same time he is left home alone while you are out "having fun." Open relationships may provide a temporary solution to the problem, but the underlying causes still remain. Only with time, patience, and communication will he learn that your work is a job like any other, rather than a wild sex party to which he has not been invited. As he begins feeling less threatened by your clients and learns your heart still belongs with him, he will slowly accept your work and its place in your life. Sadly, most "escort-civilian" relationships that I have seen do not survive through this stage.

The third issue usually only affects the busier escorts. It seems to affect most couples as soon as the escort begins intensively working in his field. During this time the escort becomes "sexed-out" from working so often, and loses interest in having sex in his personal life. Alternatively, he may not orgasm at home to save his sexual energy for his work. This in turn upsets his partner, who is feeling as horny as always. Fortunately this problem has a number of obvious solutions. Taking periodic vacations from your work can do wonders for your relationship. Consider raising your rates to lower your number of clients while maintaining your income level. Develop your "sleight-of-hand" techniques as discussed in chapter thirteen to avoid having to orgasm so often. Finally, consider a bit of couple's counseling. The problem may not be a lack of sex at all, but rather a completely separate issue within the relationship.

Whatever happens, remember that relationships are always hard work; escorting does not make them any easier. If you are financially successful in your work, consider taking some of that hard-earned cash and buying your significant-other romantic gifts from time-to-time. A bit of quality time together also goes a long way towards reducing the problems.

Escorts that are already in a prior relationship when they begin escorting will face these same problems. Only in the first case the issue will be obtaining permission from your lover to begin escorting in the first place. Do not expect him to be overjoyed to hear of your new career decision, although you never know how accepting he may be until you bring it up.

If your lover has Internet access, you may want to refer him to the PAPE (Partners of Adult Performers and Entertainers) listserv on eGroups (http://www.egroups.com). It varies from month-to-month how active the discussion is, but it is one of the few resources specifically designed to meet your partner's needs.

## Escorting As a Way of Life

For many escorts, their job is just a job. It does not have any special significance in their lives, except that it is good money for relatively little work. For others, escorting is a way of life. They take pride in their work and feel rewarded when they educate the public about the true nature of professional sex workers. Considering this, it is not surprising that you may find yourself experiencing an increased political awareness about prostitution-related issues.

By no means am I saying you are going to start protesting in the streets and organizing a union for working escorts. Most escorts in Western countries do not choose to become involved in this way. Rather, you can become political by keeping others informed about what is going on. If someone sends you a letter about prostitution-related arrests in your area, send it to every escort you know. Better yet, pick up a copy of your local gay publication and start calling other escorts. You will make some great contacts in the process, many of whom will call you back the next time they hear something first.

Consider doing public education as well. Approach gay and lesbian groups in your area and offer to speak to them about your experiences. Many of them will find it fascinating to speak to a real-life escort. Gay college groups are also great audiences. Not only are they a more open-minded group in general, but also they are always in need of topics for their meetings. You will feel good for speaking to them, and you will open up a few minds in the process.

You may also want to consider coming out to your friends as an escort. You may be surprised how supportive they can be. Over time you may even want to consider telling your family. It is difficult for many people at first, but with time and patience they can become surprisingly accepting. Be prepared for the opposite reaction though. You never know how a person will react until you tell them.

## The Future of Escorting

In the past ten years, technology has radically changed the face of escorting. No longer do escorts have to place their print ads and wait for the phone to ring. Now escorts can work the streets of the information superhighway, finding clients at all hours of the day and night. The impact of the Internet on prostitution was inconceivable ten years ago, and even five years ago most escorts could not have imagined the advertising opportunities available today.

As the next decade rolls by, technology will continue to evolve and to develop. The information revolution will continue to increase speed and access to information. For career escorts, this will provide a unique set of challenges. More computer-savvy people will enter the sex industry every year, establishing newer and better ways of doing business. The increasing speed of information transfer will make it more feasible for escorts to use video-streaming technology. This means not only will clients be able to read about your services, but they will be able to hear and see you talk about your services.

Increased reliance on the Internet instead of traditional print media will bring about the downfall of many of the print publications in which escorts advertise. As the Internet revolution expands into other countries, escorts will flock to the Internet in them as well. The increased ease-of-access to buy and sell escort services may increasingly put financial pressure on the agency and brothel systems as well. The greater effectiveness of escort advertisements will bring about other changes as well, such as recruiting many new people into both client and escort roles in the industry.

The ongoing process of state police agencies becoming active on the Internet will result in an eventual backlash against online escorts. It will be virtually impossible for police departments to end Internet-based prostitution, but numerous escorts will be caught up in the process.

These and many other changes will dramatically affect how the business of escorting is conducted. To strike it rich escorting in the $21^{st}$ century, you will want to be at the forefront of these trends.

In the meantime, there is plenty you can do for your business right now. The next and final chapter will offer you a bit of practical advice from the real experts in the escorting industry – those already working in the field.

## Chapter Twenty-two
## **Professional Advice**

For the final chapter of this book, I asked a number of professional escorts from around the country to contribute their advice and opinions. Their responses follow below and reveal a wide variety of insights and approaches to the escorting industry. I think you will find much wisdom in what they have to say.

--------------------

Don't be afraid to kiss if you're comfortable with that. Don't be afraid to give the client a hug at the end of the date. Don't forget light touch.

Listen to your intuition, it may serve to protect you from potentially bad situations. Be observant of everything from the type of cologne your date prefers to the nearest exit (just in case).

Take extra contact lenses with you on travel dates if you wear them. Above all else, be a good listener to your client, sometimes all he needs is a good ear (not sex).

*Will, Escort/Companion*
*Salt Lake City, Utah*

--------------------

Don't sell yourself short. What you are offering is a very valuable commodity. You as a person are worth more than money can buy. So keep your prices up to make it worth your while. This is a business, your business, don't be haggled down on your fee.

Like any free enterprise, it is up to you. But why make $60 bucks for an hour when the rest of us are getting $300? Work less and charge more.

*Sam Dixon, Porn Star*
*Los Angeles, California*

--------------------

I have been in the business for six years now. From my experience, I'd say there are three important things for anyone thinking about escorting to keep in mind. First, you have to have a strong, well-grounded sense of self. Although the notion that someone is paying you money just to be with you can be an ego boost, it is a temporary high. What most people don't expect is the way escorting can chip away at your sense of self-love and self-worth. Like a roller coaster ride, the highs also bring lows. It does so slowly, and most people don't notice it until they're mired in self-doubt and low self-esteem. Always remember that your worth as a person is NOT tied to the money you make. It is tied to how well you treat others.

Second, always remember that the client is a person with feelings. Sure, many of them are not guys you'd normally want to pick up if you weren't being paid for your time. On the surface, they may also seem like they just want to use you to get off. And yes, some will even treat you like you're "just a whore." But underneath, many are yearning to feel wanted and attractive. If you try honestly and earnestly to find something good in each person you meet, they will notice that you are sincere, and will reward you with praise and repeat calls. Ultimately you will feel better about yourself because you will be providing a service of real value. Whether anyone is willing to admit it or not, at the core escorting is really sex therapy!

Finally, don't spread yourself too "thin" by only doing numerous superficial connections. Remember to find meaningful and deep relationships in your life - either with friends or lovers - to maintain the depth of feeling that will round out your life. You will be a better person for it. Good luck!

*Jake Walker, Escort*
*San Francisco, California*

---

I think a lot of escorts go into the business thinking that it is going to be glamorous, non-stop sex with other hot-looking guys. It isn't. It takes a person with a nice personality and good acting skills to survive in the business. A nice body and a cute face are secondary when it comes to longevity.

Find out upfront what your client wants. If you don't feel comfortable with his requests, don't take the call. If you do, you will only burn yourself out and will disappoint the client. Remember that the client is putting out a lot of money for HIS enjoyment, not yours. The escort is there to satisfy the client, period. If you can satisfy your client and enjoy the activity with him, then you will possibly have a repeat customer. Better to turn one down if you are not comfortable with what he wants, and wait for the ones that will give you some degree of pleasure as well.

*Tod Morgan, Escort*
*Chicago, Illinois*

---

I am frequently asked, "How can you have sex with just anyone? I have to be turned on before I can have sex!" I always answer that I am turned on when I have sex with strangers. Everyone has *something* that is erotic about them. It may take you a while to find it, but it is there. Once you find it, focus on it. Make love to that erotic part of the stranger before you. Perhaps it's his beautiful eyes, or the wonderful smell of his armpit. Maybe he has the greatest foreskin you've ever seen, or he has the warmest, most endearing laugh you've ever encountered. There's always something to find in each man. Once you discover it, you can overlook the fact that he's overweight, that his roots are showing, or that he leers at you a little too much. The best part is he'll know you're actually turned on and that you're making love. He'll have a great experience... and so will you!

*Brian, Escort and Webmaster*
*Los Angeles, California*

--------------------

Don't talk about clients' private lives. Do not forget to ask for clients' phone numbers. Do not give any attitude after you are done with your client (even if it was the most boring session of the millennium). Above all, keep smiling.

*Tim, Masseur and Escort*
*Los Angeles, California*

--------------------

Like any career you choose, to be successful you have to like your job and enjoy what you do. If you don't, it will show and you will send a negative energy that is unattractive. Nothing will turn a client off faster than a bad attitude.

Good looks and a good physique alone will not be enough to survive in this business. Considering this is a service oriented business, you need to provide physical, emotional, and intellectual stimulation. In my personal experience, this is not at all just about sex nine times out of ten. More than anything, escorting is about human contact, the need for romance and affection, and the desire to feel wanted, loved, and belonging (even if it is just for a brief moment). It is often unsaid and understated, but when it gets right down to it, that is how clients want you to make them feel. So be aware of the understated and unsaid expectations, and give the best time you can.

*Geoffrey, Escort, Model, and Dancer*
*Tampa, Florida*

---

If you're not happy with what you're doing, move on or change your strategy.

*Justin Powers, Escort and Porn Star*
*New York City, New York*

---

When I first started I was a little baffled as what to charge for my rates. That was due to the fact I did not take the time to research my market. I find most of the guys who escort to be pretty friendly, and as I got to know them I learned more about the local scene. If I had gotten more information, I would have started with higher rates and certainly would have made more money. If I had to do that again, I would have contacted some of the guys to learn what they are up to, as well as check out the Internet and see what is being offered in my area.

Secondly, remember you are a professional in this job and therefore have certain responsibilities. I find that I have to educate my clients quite a bit when it comes to sex and safer sex practices. Not that this is my mission, but you definitely need to be able to be a role model for this stuff. Don't bareback because some guy asks you to. This is important when you get married men or guys that for whatever reason are not educated. I know this opens up all sorts of controversial issues, but I believe it's important that we do help people sexually.

Thirdly, if you are working on your own, work with a friend. Leave an address and phone with him so that if anything happens, you are traceable. I often get the friend to call when I am there after the hour to check on me. At least for the first time - I ease up when I get to know the guy.

*Mike C., Escort*
*Toronto, Canada*

--------------------

The best advice I could offer someone new to this business is to stay strong and be true to yourself. Know what you want to get out of escorting, and what your boundaries and limits are. Always follow your gut instincts and do what feels right to you. For example, if you don't get a good feeling about a client over the phone or the Internet, don't be afraid to say no. If a client wants you to bareback and will offer you more money, don't do it if it makes you uncomfortable. Know yourself and follow your heart and your instincts, and you'll do just fine.

*Alek, Escort*
*San Francisco, California*

--------------------

Probably the most important thing is to keep a high level of confidentiality and discretion regarding your clients. An escort holds a lot more power then he realizes, and a few ill-spoken words can spoil your reputation.

Take a few moments to get into a good mood, and review your overall appearance before you meet a client. You never know who has the potential to be a great regular client. Always try to be low-key in the way you dress and conduct yourself when you escort. I have never heard a client complain that I was too polite or kind to him, or that I was not flashy enough to make him happy.

Keep an eye out for crabs! They can really wreck your client-escort relationship and give you a bad name.

*Dave, Escort*
*Chicago, Illinois*

---

My advice for escorts is a simple phrase, "to thy own self be true." If you don't feel comfortable with a possible client, then proceed no further no matter what. There are things more important than money. Self-respect is one of them.

Another piece of advice I have is that in this marvelous world of e-commerce, escorts should have clients prepay for services to be rendered (remember, you are charging for companionship, NOT SEX)! This ensures the legitimacy of the appointment and guarantees that professional escorts won't be wasting their time.

One last bit of advice: There is someone out there for everyone. There is a great diversity of clients, so it is therefore natural to assume that the same would exist for escorts. People will pay to be with you, so be the best "you" that you can be, and stop trying to be someone else's clone.

*Dax Michaels, Escort and Erotic Massage Professional*
*Philadelphia, Pennsylvania*

---

Love yourself enough to realize you always have choices in every aspect of this business, as well as in your life. You don't "have" to do anything, not even be an escort, let alone certain sexual acts. So don't lie to yourself by saying you do. You're not a victim here, but a valuable part of our human community.

Learn to understand and appreciate the Universe and its karmic consequences. Approach every client with a level of respect and honor in whatever station of life they are in / don't waste your precious energy on bad experiences and evil people. Let it go, FAST! Speaking of karma, what you GIVE comes back to you a hundredfold! Donate to charities.

Keep a network of supportive friends who know what you do. Talk to them, laugh with them, be angry with them, and learn to cry with them.

Be alert. Take a deep breath, and listen.

*James, Sacred Intimate Erotic Masseur*
*New York City, New York*

---

Never underestimate what people will do for sex when in need, and never let anyone tell you having sex isn't a true profession. It takes talent and human understanding to do what we do for a profession. After all, it IS the oldest profession in the book.

*Steve, Escort*
*Denville, New Jersey*

---

The escort field is a very lucrative one, especially nowadays with Internet technology. What we are beginning to see is amazing! No more middlemen, etc.

However, you must be careful. While the money is good, remember you are selling your body. You must be mentally and physically ready. Always get to know your client before you set off to make your fortune. I advise a pocket beeper and a cellular phone, unless of course you have your own residence and are completely open. Always play safe and get the money before you begin. It's a whole new world thanks to the technology, so go out and make some money!

*Kelly Stevens, Escort*
*Hermosa Beach, California*

--------------------

The only suggestion that I have is for those of us who keep records on our computers: To be sure to install and use a good encryption program for security. A very good free one, F-secure Desktop, is available from DataFellows (http://www.datafellows.com).

*Anonymous, Escort*
*San Jose, California*

--------------------

I find in my work as a masseur and escort that it is a lot less sexual than I had expected it to be. I find, in many cases, that the client wants intimacy and affection more than "raw" sex. I have been amazed at how deeply affected some men have been from our time together when I thought I really hadn't done anything.

Society in general does not support our profession as it does more traditional corporate drones, so it is necessary for escorts to realize what an important and specialized role we have in the scheme of things. We must also support ourselves and others in maintaining our integrity and efficacy.

*Curt Knudson, Masseur/Travel Escort*
*Minneapolis, Minnesota*

--------------------

To anyone anticipating entry into the escort business, I would advise that one should examine his reasons for getting into the business. There are countless valid reasons, but if one enters the business out of financial desperation or as an attempt to escape something in life, it probably is not a good idea. Examine motives and establish some goals for what you wish to accomplish via the business.

It is a very good idea to find someone else that is in or has been in the business in your community who can offer some advice and help you understand the particular market you are entering. Advice from someone who has been there can save a lot of anguish, and can potentially help keep you out of harm's way. Start slowly. Get the feel for the business gradually then work up to more calls per week. Discuss your experiences with someone with more experience and ask for guidance in handling situations.

Make a list (yes, an ink-on-paper list) of what you will and will not do. Keep the list by the phone and be honest in your communications. Determine your compatibility with a client by matching his activities with yours. If he wants X, and X is on your "I would rather die than do that" list, tell him you don't do that. If he has to have that, it is best for him to find someone else than for you to go through with a call and have an awkward time explaining why you won't do X after the client felt you would.

Check your comfort level. Not every client will look like your ideal guy. Don't be swayed by the beauty of the good-looking ones, and always look for something good and positive in those clients to whom you are not so attracted. The average-looking guys usually have a lot going for them in other areas.

Develop a tough skin. As with any business, there will be customer satisfaction situations that cannot be resolved. On occasion, some mean things will be said to you. Stay professional and honest. Don't strike back with the same verbal abuse and don't take a bad situation personally. Be able to put the work in a box at the end of the day and walk away from it. On the other hand, don't let a great call go to your head. You're there to offer a service, not to fall in love. Stay professional at all times.

Know when to quit. For some, escorting can be a decades-long primary or secondary occupation. Some can balance this work with other jobs and have a good second income. Others will need to look beyond this business and towards other goals and growth needs. As this is a business about taking care of the needs of others, be aware of your own needs for security and personal growth, and use them as a springboard to move into other areas when the time feels right for you.

Most importantly, take vacations from the business. Go on a real date, take a trip, sit around the house, or read a book. Refresh and relax. When you go back to work, you'll do a better job and you will enjoy it more (as will your clients).

*Mike, Retired Escort (1978-1989)*
*Scottsdale, Arizona*

---

Working as an "escort" in a brothel is quite different than working through the Internet, advertising in gay magazines, or on the street. In a brothel, the client has an opportunity to observe your behavior, dress, and appearance <u>before</u> making contact. Therefore, it is important to understand the type of clients that visit the brothel as well as what the brothel expects of you.

You will need to understand what the brothel will provide for you and what they expect of you. A first class brothel will provide clean rooms for you to entertain your client, an adequate supply of condoms and lubricants as well as massage oil, a nice place to meet your clients, and most importantly, free regular medical checks to ensure that you are free of any sexually transmitted diseases. As part of the medical program, the brothel should provide an orientation for new escorts to help them to determine if a client has a medical problem before any type of sexual activity has begun. All brothels should demand that condoms be used for anal sex, and they should recommend that you use condoms for oral sex as well. Remember that you will be engaged in sexual activities many times in a day or week, greatly increasing your exposure to STDs over the average person's.

The type of clients that frequent a brothel will determine how you should act and dress. In most cases, an escort should be clean, shaved and neatly dressed. The use of overpowering colognes is generally frowned on. Nice light cologne is generally preferred and should have a masculine aroma. Cleanliness is very important; you should smell clean and fresh.

Hairstyle is also very important. You should keep your hair clean, fresh smelling, and cut to style. Shaved heads (skinheads) do not do well in a brothel. Long hair beyond shoulder length should be tied back and kept neat and clean. Many customers will view long hair as feminine.

Behavior is very important, and your personality/character will determine how you behave. No potential client wants a loud mouth braggart, no matter how well you are endowed or perform in bed. The most successful escorts in a brothel keep a low profile, act professionally, and always approach the client in a positive manner. Most successful brothels will have a list of guidelines to help you be successful as well as rules to maintain the brothel atmosphere.

*Cal, Owner of the Blue Boy Club & Brothel*
*Amsterdam, The Netherlands*

--------------------

Don't trust anyone online that is younger than 25 because they are always messing with you. You get a sixth sense for fakes and liars after a while. Most of the time if someone wants to hook up, you need to grasp at the chance right then and there. They are horny at that moment, and you might never hear from them again.

Charge more if you go to a hotel, because you might have to pay for hotel parking (and that can be a bitch).

*Matt, Escort*
*Long Beach, California*

--------------------

An aspiring escort needs to delve into him or herself and figure out what it is that makes him or her special. It could be a variety of things (huge dick, muscles, tight ass, multi-lingual, super-sweet, or whatever) and really play that up. It's not just about marketing and identifying differentiation from other escorts; it's important in defining one's role as an escort. In all of my endeavors, I am inspired daily by the words of Edith Piaf, "Use your faults, use your defects. Then you're going to be a star." Get into yourself, find your strengths, and present yourself with confidence!

*Jasen Rhodes, Escort*
*New York City, New York*

--------------------

When beginning an escorting career, understand all the ramifications that can come of it. You could be arrested. You could be found out. Any possible outcome could obliterate your life as you know it. On the other hand, life is always a risk (as is any worthwhile endeavor). Think intelligently and your life as an escort will do more than suffice.

*Eric Magyar, Escort*
*Cherry Hill, New Jersey*

--------------------

As a professional escort, and after being in this profession for four years, I have to offer one word of knowledge that will get you far: LISTEN. That's right, be a good listener and let a client know you are there for him and to listen to what he says. Most of my clients communicate with me like this. Sometimes I feel like I am more a counselor than an escort, and I'm sure other escorts agree. Be true to yourself and it will show to others (my motto).

*JR, Escort*
*Atlanta, Georgia*

---

Have an open mind, a sense of adventure, and a sense of humor. Becoming an escort constitutes embarking upon an adventurous journey of discovery, and if you maintain an inquisitive, open attitude about the biz, you will learn more than you ever expected about yourself, sexuality and human nature in general. Be willing to forgive yourself for any mistakes or errors in judgment you make along the way.

Smile at least once in a while. Even if you have the breathtaking physique of a Greek statue, for most clients your attractiveness will disappear permanently if you scowl your way through an appointment. Unless you intend to work as a sulky "bad boy," realize that grumpiness, grimness and gloom are a turn-off. Indeed, there are some escorts who are NOT blessed with any type of extraordinary physical comeliness but who, because of their inner qualities of intelligence and warmth, develop a coterie of clients who remain loyal to them for years.

Be willing to honor your agreements with clients, and if, for any reason, you doubt whether you can honor an agreement, don't make it in the first place. If a client is looking for a dark-eyed, hairy-chested Greek "bottom-man" and you're a blue-eyed, smooth Irishman comfortable only as a "top," don't agree to do the gig, pretending over the phone that you're going to be able to fit the bill. Most clients resent duplicity and cherish honesty in an escort, and I've even had prospective clients call me back after I've had to say "no" to them for one reason or other and ask for an appointment anyway.

Stick to your agreements about the duration of appointments. If you've agreed to get together for an hour, that means you should be ready and willing to spend 60 minutes with your client. It's fine if he doesn't want the whole time, but do not delude yourself into thinking that you will hear from him again if you "get him off" quickly and hustle him out the door in 30 minutes.

Create a support system for yourself, and if possible, include a colleague or two in it. Although the escorting profession seems to attract more than its fair share of malcontents and ne'er-do-wells, I must say that some of the most wonderful human beings I've ever met have been escorts. I recommend seeking out a few of these gems to have as friends.

Be alert to the possibility of a chemical substance abuse problem playing a role in your career as an escort. Sometimes people suffering from alcoholism or other types of chemical substance dependencies become escorts as a way either to finance their habits or as a way to avoid the difficulty they have in handling the rigors of a regular 9-to-5 job. If this applies to you, take my word for it that escorting is 100% guaranteed NOT to provide a long-lasting, satisfactory answer to your problem. Instead of hoping for unreasonable results from a career in escorting, get help. It's free and easy to come by. Call Alcoholics Anonymous (the number is in your phone book). Occasionally a client himself may turn out to have a chemical substance dependency, and if he starts to exhibit its accompanying insane behavior during an appointment, realize that you are not required to tolerate the intolerable. Just leave, or if he came to you, shove him out the door by whatever means strike you as most appropriate.

Take good care of yourself. Get plenty of sleep, eat regular meals, take time off to go out with friends, and pamper yourself once in awhile in whatever way will make you feel refreshed, whether it's getting a massage, treating yourself to a weekend away, or just spending an evening reading a book by a favorite author.

*Pete, Escort*
*New York City, New York*

---

The most important thing is to treat your client as if he is not a client at all. They don't want to feel as if they are paying for your service, and don't want to feel abused. Don't take advantage of them by asking them for things, either. Forget the business side, and consider them as a person. It will get you far more in the long run.

*Arnaud, Brothel Escort*
*Amsterdam, The Netherlands*

---

If you're going to escort seriously and in a professional manner, then you should always try to keep a positive, upbeat attitude about it. You should not feel that escorting is morally wrong, bad, or degrading. It should be something that you enjoy doing, and be proud of when you are able to help someone else feel better about himself. Know that it won't last forever (although it can last a long time), and plan ahead. Most of all, enjoy life as much as you can!

*Emmett Andrews, Escort*
*Cleveland, Ohio*

---

My best advice is to be as honest with yourself as you should be with your clients. Don't allow yourself to be talked into something you don't want to do, and be completely honest and let your clients know how you feel.

If you're not really looking for sexual adventure and are not open to try new experiences, try looking for another line of work. The happiest people are the ones who can make a career of their vice, so try anything once and enjoy it!

*Ted Matthews, Escort and Porn Star*
*Los Angeles, California*

---

My only advice for those people who want to get into escorting is that you have to be yourself. Doing so helps build a client's trust in you, and if he finds you trustworthy, he will always come back for more. A good attitude is also important. Even if you are not handsome or good looking, a good attitude will make a client see you as beautiful. Lastly, love your job (escorting). Don't take it for granted, and always remember to give your best no matter what.

*Carl, Masseur*
*San Francisco, California*

## Afterword

...And so this book comes to an end.

It took me two-and-a-half months to write the rough draft of this book, and another four months longer to edit it. During this process my own knowledge of the field of escorting has increased considerably. The dozens of people I questioned for this book have educated me about many facets of escorting I had taken for granted. After four years in the business, I thought I knew most of what there was to know about escorting. Now I realize that my education is just beginning.

When I first read John Preston's *Hustling* back in 1997, I remember being somewhat disappointed because the author's strong personal biases about urban escorting colored all that he wrote. Now I realize that I unfairly criticized Mr. Preston. His book was based primarily on his own experiences, much as this book is heavily influenced by my own. If my perceptions of the profession clash with your reality, I hope you will accept my apologies in advance.

Whatever flaws this book may have, I must say I am pleased with the result. There is a noticeable shortage of books about male prostitution, especially ones that provide helpful insights and advice into avoiding the various pitfalls of the profession. My intention from the start was to write *the* how-to book on male prostitution, so that working escorts everywhere would be able to avoid these dangers. I certainly hope it helps you avoid a few.

As a matter of fact, I hope this book helps you do a lot more than just avoid the pitfalls. I strongly believe that the escorting industry is a perfectly legitimate career option for any enterprising person who has his life together. It may take a single-minded dedication to your career for years-on-end, but in the end you may be able to earn millions. People often ask me what I plan to do when I become too old to escort. I usually laugh at the question. By the time I become too old to escort, I plan to retire. You can do the same if you put your mind (and body) to the task.

If reading the book convinced you that the sex industry is not the career for you, I hope you were still able to gain some unique insights into the world of the male escort. Whatever you decided, I hope you will drop by my website at http://www.aaronlawrence.com, and send me a note saying hello. I always enjoy hearing from my readers to know what they think of my books.

Besides, we may need to meet for dinner. You do remember our little agreement in the preface, right?

Aaron Lawrence

Appendix One
## Online Advertising Opportunities

Escort websites come-and-go on a regular basis. Although every attempt has been made to verify the accuracy of this information, some of these links are bound to be invalid by the time you try them.

### Listservs
http://www.egroups.com
- A variety of escort-related listservs are offered through this website, including "Escortmale" for escorts, "Escorts4us" for clients, and "PAPE" (Partners of Adult Performers and Entertainers) for partners of sex workers. There are also many other escort listservs here for specific geographical areas and types of escorts.

### Escort-Review Websites
http://www.male4malescort.com

### Escort-Referral Websites
http://www.escorts4you.com
- Escorts4you is one of the longest-running and best escort-referral sites on the Web.

http://www.ozgay.com
- Ozgay is primarily a site for Australian escorts.

http://www.escorts.net
http://www.executivemaleescorts.com

http://hardjocks.com/escortsmain.htm
http://www.rentboy.com
- *Rentboy is one of the best escort-referral sites on the Web. Charges for advertising. Primary sponsor of the Hustlerball circuit party.*

http://www.m4m4sex.com
- *Also known as Mastervu. M4m4sex is a well-established escort-referral site.*

http://www.perfectmen.com
- *A good escort-referral site.*

http://www.maleescorts.com
http://men-for-rent.com
http://www.gayescort.org
http://www.asgardescorts.co.uk
- *Asgard Escorts is primarily UK-based but has escorts in other countries as well. An excellent place to advertise transsexual and transvestite escort services.*

http://www.guyzclub.com/escorts
http://americanmale.net
http://www.boyzusa.com
http://www.boys-next-door-live.com
http://books.dreambook.com/wellbelove/escorts.html

## Link Sites
http://www.manquest.com/gayscape/escortsandmodels.html
http://gay.sexhound.net/gayzone
http://www.bglad.com
http://musclevideos.com/MV-links-Escorts.html
http://www.pridesites.com/gogay
http://www.menonthenet.com
http://www.tuxxxedo.com

## Gay Publications
http://www.nextmagazine.net   (New York)
http://www.frontiersweb.com   (California)

http://www.ebar.com/barclas.htm   (Bay Area, California)

**Webrings**
http://www.maleescort.org/webring.html
http://www.escorts4you.com/webring/
http://members.aol.com/ftplogic/Web_Ring/index.htm
http://www.webring.org/cgi-bin/webring?ring=prostright;list
- *This webring is focused on prostitutes' rights and is more political than business in nature.*

## Appendix Two
## **Resources for Escorts**

Many of these organizations have a specific focus; however do not let that keep you from calling. These groups are usually happy to hear from people in the business when they require advice or assistance. Give them a call whether you are searching for a doctor or lawyer, want to become politically involved, or simply want to expand your network of other sex workers. Many of these organizations have years of experience and contacts throughout the community. If one is in your area, you may even want to give them a call to introduce yourself and ask about their organization. They tend to be small and personable operations, so do not be afraid to say "hello."

If you are one of the many escorts who do not see any resources near you, you may still want to give the closest organization a call and see if they can offer any referrals. If you do not see an organization listed for your country, try giving a few of these groups a call. Many maintain networks of active organizations around the world and may be able to refer you to one in your own area.

*On the Internet*

International Sex Worker Foundation for Art, Culture, and Education
- http://www.iswface.org

Sex Work Cyber Resource & Support Center
- http://www.sexwork.com

Hook Magazine
- http://www.hookonline.org

*Australia*

**Scarlet Alliance**
P.O. Box 76
Red Hill, ACT 2603
Tel: (02) 6239 6098
Fax: (02) 6239 7871
E-mail: scarlet@dynamite.com.au

**South Australian Sex Industry Network**
*Street Address:*
64 Fullarton Road
Norwood, SA 5065
*Mailing Address:*
P.O. Box 7072 Hutt Street,
Adelaide SA 5000
Tel: (08) 8362 5775
Fax: (08) 8363 1046

**Workers in Sex Employment (WISE)**
*Street Address:*
29 Lonsdale Street
Upstairs
Braddon, ACT
*Mailing Address:*
P.O. Box 67
Braddon, ACT 2601
Tel: (02) 6247 3443
Fax: (02) 6247 3446
http://www.bayswan.org/wise.HTML
E-mail: sera@spirit.com.au

*Canada*

**Sex Workers Alliance of Vancouver**
Box 3075
Vancouver, BC V6B 3X6
http://www.walnet.org/swav
E-mail: swav@walnet.org

*United States*

**Blackstockings**
1122 East Pike Street
PMB 884
Seattle, WA 98122
Tel: (206) 722-2665
http://www.blackstockings-seattle.com
E-mail: blackstockings@blackstockings-seattle.com

**BaySwan (Bay Area Sex Worker Advocacy Network), Coalition on Prostitution, and The Prostitute's Education Network**
P.O. Box 210256
San Francisco, CA 94121
Tel: (415) 751-1659
http://www.bayswan.org

**Call Off Your Tired Old Ethics (COYOTE)**
**COYOTE - San Francisco**
2269 Chestnut St #452
San Francisco, CA 94123-2607
Tel: (415) 435-7950

**COYOTE – Los Angeles**
1626 Wilcox Ave #580
Los Angeles CA 90028-6273

**Cyprian Guild**
P.O. Box 423145
San Francisco, CA 91412
Tel: (415) 292-3342

**Prostitutes of New York (PONY)**
P.O. Box 174
Cooper Station
New York, NY 10276-0174
Tel: (212) 713-5678
E-mail: pony@panix.com

**St. James Infirmary Occupational Health and Safety Clinic for Sex Workers**
c/o San Francisco City Clinic
356 7$^{th}$ Street
San Francisco, CA 94103
Tel: (415) 487-5573

Appendix Three
**Related Reading**

Adams, Matt. Hustlers, Escorts, and Porn Stars: The Insider's Guide to Male Prostitution in America. Self-Published: Las Vegas, 1999.
 *An overview of the male prostitution industry in the United States. The book is an excellent resource for all serious escorts.*

Aggleton, Peter (ed). Men Who Sell Sex. Philadelphia: Temple University Press, 1999.
 *A collection of articles about male sex workers in countries around the world. I cannot vouch for the accuracy of most of the material, but the chapter on the United States is incorrect, offensive, and degrading to those of us who work in the profession.*

Edmonson, Roger. Boy In the Sand: Casey Donovan, All-American Sex Star. Los Angeles: Alyson Publications, 1998.
 *A biography of Casey Donovan, the first gay porn superstar. He later became an escort, and actively worked until his death in 1987. It is a well-written book, and perfect for those interested in the history of contemporary male prostitution and pornography.*

Gibson, Barbara. Male Order: Life Stories from Boys Who Sell Sex. New York: Cassell, 1995.
 *Case studies of four boys and two transgendered youth who prostituted themselves on the streets of London. There is considerable depth to their stories, which will interest*

*anyone curious to learn more about what brings a person to the streets.*

Goldstone, Stephen E. The Ins and Outs of Gay Sex: A Medical Handbook for Men. New York: Dell Publishing, 1999.
  *An excellent book written by an openly gay doctor about the medical side to gay sexuality. It covers STDs, the physiology of sex, anal/genital medical problems, and common sexual dysfunctions. Although not specifically written for escorts, it is an extremely handy resource to have available.*

Isherwood, Charles. Wonder Bread and Ecstasy: The Life and Death of Joey Stefano. Los Angeles: Alyson Publications, 1996.
  *An extremely well-written biography of Joey Stefano: a porn superstar, escort, and veteran of the dance circuit who died of a drug overdose in 1994.*

Itiel, Joseph. A Consumer's Guide to Male Hustlers. Binghamton, New York: Harrington Park Press, 1998.
  *Tips and stories from the author about picking up hustlers around the world.*

Lawrence, Aaron. Suburban Hustler: Stories of a Hi-Tech Callboy. New Jersey: Late Night Press, 1999.
  *A collection of 24 short stories about how the author entered the field of hi-tech prostitution and became a successful callboy.*

Nagle, Jill. (ed). Whores and Other Feminists. New York: Routledge, 1997.
  *A book of essays written by pro-sex work feminists. This book contains an excellent essay comparing the dynamics of male and female prostitution.*

Preston, John. Hustling: A Gentleman's Guide to the Fine Art of Homosexual Prostitution. New York: Masquerade Books, 1994.

    *An excellent if somewhat outdated how-to book on male prostitution. The book was written before the Internet began, and focuses primarily on escorting in urban environments. A must-read for all serious escorts.*

Saxon, Grant Tracy. The Happy Hustler. New York: Warner Paperback, 1975.

    *An extremely well-written autobiography written by a bisexual hustler-turned-escort agency owner. Although the book was later revealed to be a hoax, the author clearly knew too much about the sex industry to be a complete outsider. This book is out-of-print and can be difficult to find. An excellent read with a great deal of useful insights into escorting.*

Steward, Samuel M. Understanding the Male Hustler. Binghamton, New York: The Haworth Press, 1991.

    *A collection of mock interviews between the author and a fictitious hustler. The author attempts to generalize his "findings" to all male hustlers, as if his research were factually based.*

Sycamore, Matt Bernstein (ed). Tricks and Treats: Sex Workers Write About Their Clients. Binghamton, New York: Harrington Park Press, 2000.

    *A collection of essays from male and female sex workers writing about their clients and their experiences. Although it has an emphasis on the downscale, it does entertain and provide some well-developed insights into others in the industry.*

West, Donald J. Male Prostitution. Binghamton, New York: Harrington Park Press, 1993.

    *An extremely dry sociological study of male prostitution in London, primarily focusing on homeless and run-*

*away youth recruited through the Streetwise Youth Program. Filled with facts and figures, this book is of interest only to researchers and those building a complete library of books about escorting.*

Whitaker, Rick. Assuming the Position: A Memoir of Male Hustling. New York: Four Walls Eight Windows, 1999.

*A poorly written memoir about a cocaine addict who prostitutes himself to support his habit and then wonders why he is not enjoying life. Whitaker's hustler-like approach towards his clients is as thoroughly unimpressive as are his negative conclusions on the entire field of prostitution.*

Appendix Four
**Checking Your Client for STDs**

It is extremely important to know what to look for when checking your client for STDs. The list below is not an exhaustive list of symptoms, nor is it meant to provide a formal diagnosis. This is simply a list of warning signs.

If you have any concerns that your partner may have an STD, you should politely recommend he see his physician and excuse yourself from the situation. Before you leave, you should thoroughly wash your hands and any part of your body that came into contact with your client.

**What to Worry About:**

*Sores and Ulcers*
- A red open sore on the shaft of his penis near the head. There may be more than one. (Possibly syphilis)
- A cluster of small, pink sores that may be crusted-over on the head or shaft of his penis, under his foreskin, or near his anus. (Possibly herpes)
- One or more small (pimple to pea-sized) sores filled with a white slime on his thighs, anus, dick, balls, or stomach. Occasionally on his arms, back, or face. (Possibly molluscum contagiosum)

*Discharge*
- A green or yellow discharge from his penis. (Possibly gonorrhea)
- A reddish streak in the seat of his underwear from anal discharge. (Possibly syphilis, gonorrhea, or herpes)

- A faint stain on the front of his underwear. (Possibly urethritis)
- A yellow-green steak on the inside front of his underwear from penile discharge. (Possibly gonorrhea)
- Excessive amounts of a clear or white fluid that emerges before the client has an erection. It may appear similar to precum. (Possibly urethritis)

*Warts, Blisters, and Other Marks*
- One or more small warts on his dick, anus, balls, thighs, or butt. They may look like tiny cauliflowers, or like dark skin blemishes. (Possibly genital warts)
- A cluster of small, clear blisters on the shaft or head of his penis, under his foreskin, or near his anus. (Possibly herpes)
- Dark purple blotches found anywhere on his body. (Possibly Kaposi's sarcoma from HIV infection)

*Other Symptoms*
- Small brownish-red dots at the base of his pubic hair. (Possibly crab lice)
- Abnormal lines on his hands, especially between his fingers. Also found on arms, stomach, and genitals. (Possibly scabies)
- A yellowish color to his eyes. (Possibly hepatitis)

**What Not to Worry About:**

- A clear substance emerging from his penis after he becomes aroused. (Probably precum)
- Small, fleshy, half-inch "tags" near his anus. (Probably skin tags or hemorrhoids)
- Tiny red bumps at the base of his pubic hair where he has shaved. (Probably folliculitus, a minor skin irritation from shaving)